Oracle E-Business Suite R12 Integration and OA Framework Development and Extension Cookbook

A practical step-by-step guide to develop end-to-end extensions to Oracle E-Business Suite Release 12, with detailed illustrations and explanations

Andy Penver

BIRMINGHAM - MUMBAI

Oracle E-Business Suite R12 Integration and OA Framework Development and Extension Cookbook

First published: March 2013

Production Reference: 1200313

Published by Packt Publishing Ltd.
Livery Place
35 Livery Street
Birmingham B3 2PB, UK.

ISBN 978-1-84968-712-6

www.packtpub.com

Cover Image by Neha Rajappan (neha.rajappan1@gmail.com)

Credits

Author
Andy Penver

Reviewers
Parvez Achhwa

Brian Badenhorst

Stephen Phillips

Acquisition Editor
Rukhsana Khambatta

Lead Technical Editors
Suchi Singhal

Sruthi Kutty

Technical Editors
Prasad Dalvi

Amit Ramadas

Project Coordinator
Anish Ramchandani

Proofreaders
Aaron Nash

Linda Morris

Indexer
Hemangini Bari

Production Coordinator
Conidon Miranda

Cover Work
Conidon Miranda

About the Author

Andy Penver currently lives and works in the U.K. as a solution architect for a large public sector client. He studied at Christ Church (University of Kent). He has over 18 years of experience in working with Oracle E-Business Suite. He has worked in both the private and public sectors, and has a strong technical background. He has led and managed teams of consultants through the full project lifecycles on some very large programs throughout the U.K. and Europe. Andy has been heavily involved in two large-scale, award-winning implementations of a shared service centre.

Andy is currently the Managing Director of his own consultancy, NU-TEKK Limited.

Andy has previously authored and published a book called *Oracle E-Business Suite R12 Core Development and Extension Cookbook*.

I would like to thank my parents, my wife and three children, SJ, James, and Jack for their understanding and support while I spent many hours and late nights on the book. I would also like to thank my colleagues for their help in reviewing and commenting on the material in the book. In particular, I would like to thank Brian Badenhorst, Steve Phillips, and Parvez who all have helped me in some way to produce this book.

About the Reviewers

Parvez Achhwa has more than 22 years of experience in information systems technologies, with the last 17 years in Oracle Apps 11*i*/12*i* (CRM and Financials) implementation, BI, Business Process Automation, and management of large-scale projects. He is a rare breed to possess both functional and technical skills at various landscapes. In recent years, he has also developed Siebel implementation skills.

Presently, he is working with DAMAC Holding as Oracle ERP Manager.

> I would like to thank Andy for giving me the opportunity to review this book.

Brian Badenhorst works as an Oracle E-Business Consultant and has over 10 years of experience in designing and developing robust solutions for a range of clients in both the UK private and public sectors. Backed by an engineering background, he has the ability to put forward strategic solutions and he has significant experience in fulfilling bespoke requirements.

Brian works as a freelance consultant and is the Managing Director of his own business.

This is the first book that Brian has been involved in.

Stephen Phillips was born in London in 1959 and moved to Australia in 1969 when his family emigrated. He studied Computer Science at the University of Melbourne and has worked in IT in both Australia and the U.K. for over 30 years. He began his career at the Government Computing Service (GCS) in Melbourne, Australia in 1981, working on Burroughs mainframes. Since that time he has worked in all scales of equipment and on projects ranging from large-scale implementations of Oracle HRMS to small PC-based systems for a single client.

Stephen has worked extensively with Oracle software since 1989 and moved back to London in 1994 in order to broaden his experience.

Since his return to the U.K. he has worked for a number of prestigious clients, including Oracle UK, Reuters, Lloyds TSB, Walkers Snack Foods, The John Lewis Partnership, and the Ministry of Justice. Stephen has worked on Data Migration projects with a number of these clients, as part of their implementation of Oracle HRMS/Payroll.

In 2003, Stephen completed the MSc degree with the Open University. The major area of his dissertation was artificial intelligence, as applied to the compiling of public transport timetables.

www.PacktPub.com

Support files, eBooks, discount offers and more

You might want to visit www.PacktPub.com for support files and downloads related to your book.

Did you know that Packt offers eBook versions of every book published, with PDF and ePub files available? You can upgrade to the eBook version at www.PacktPub.com and as a print book customer, you are entitled to a discount on the eBook copy. Get in touch with us at service@packtpub.com for more details.

At www.PacktPub.com, you can also read a collection of free technical articles, sign up for a range of free newsletters and receive exclusive discounts and offers on Packt books and eBooks.

http://PacktLib.PacktPub.com

Do you need instant solutions to your IT questions? PacktLib is Packt's online digital book library. Here, you can access, read and search across Packt's entire library of books.

Why Subscribe?

- ▶ Fully searchable across every book published by Packt
- ▶ Copy and paste, print and bookmark content
- ▶ On demand and accessible via web browser

Free Access for Packt account holders

If you have an account with Packt at www.PacktPub.com, you can use this to access PacktLib today and view nine entirely free books. Simply use your login credentials for immediate access.

Instant Updates on New Packt Books

Get notified! Find out when new books are published by following @PacktEnterprise on Twitter, or the *Packt Enterprise* Facebook page.

Table of Contents

Preface

Extending Oracle E-Business Suite

This book is about the ways in which we can extend Oracle E-Business Suite (EBS) and focuses on more recent tools and technology. Its primary focus is to show how we can integrate with EBS, personalize and develop OA Framework pages with EBS, and to show how we can use BI Publisher to create and mail merge documents within EBS. The book has many detailed examples to work through with tips and explanations about how various components can be configured and how we can extend standard functionality and the various ways in which we can do it. It complements my first book, *Oracle E-Business Suite R12 Core Development and Extension Cookbook*, which focuses on writing concurrent programs, the personalization and development of professional forms, creating workflows, and using common utilities and scripts within EBS.

This book is aimed at developers who are new to E-Business Suite, or those who are strong in one particular area and need to expand their knowledge in other areas. Experienced developers may also use the book to brush up on their skills, or to pick up tips that may help them. The book focuses on the newer technologies being used in the more recent releases of EBS. There are plenty of detailed screenshots throughout each chapter giving clear instructions. This helps to provide a clear and full understanding of what we are doing and why. Each topic will develop a solution to a scenario, and will show how we need to set up our development tools right through to deploying it within EBS.

At the end of each chapter, the reader should have developed a good understanding of the topic and will be able to take away the knowledge gained and start using it in practice. The book also comes with complete, fully-tested code and scripts that can be downloaded. The examples have been developed using a Vision instance of Oracle E-Business Suite Release 12 (12.1.1). It would be helpful to know some SQL, PL/SQL, XML, and Java, but it is not essential, as the code is already written and fully documented. We will be going through each chapter example step-by-step, so you will not be expected to write any code that is not detailed in the book.

If you are new to Oracle EBS or a consultant who has worked with Oracle E-Business Suite before, you will be aware that there are many technical components to consider; there are many features using a range of different tools and the footprint seems to be expanding all the time. One of the key features of EBS is its flexibility. Not all organizations are the same and there are many ways you can configure EBS to make it specific to an organization's needs. Whenever possible, an organization should always attempt to use standard functionality to meet their requirements. However, there are occasions where business requirements cannot be met using the standard Oracle-provided functionality, and this can be anything from renaming a label on a screen, to automating a process that would take many hours for someone to process manually.

There are various ways in which you can change behavior in Oracle EBS. The simplest way to change behavior is through configuration. For example, extending Oracle through profile options, value sets, descriptive flexfields are ways to extend applications through configuration. In addition, Oracle also gives us the ability to change Oracle OA Framework pages through personalization. It is a powerful feature that allows us to change behavior without needing to change any standard objects. These are mechanisms provided by Oracle to change how the application looks, or how the application behaves. On the other hand, there are some extensions that require writing code, creating new objects, or even extending or replacing existing objects. These types of extensions are in addition to the code or objects that Oracle delivers.

A powerful feature of Oracle is the ability to extend EBS, but when doing this, there is a strict set of development standards that must be adhered to. There are two primary ways to modify Oracle EBS; the first is customization by extension, as we have just described, and the second is customization by modification. Customization by modification is where standard objects are changed, meaning that the change needs to be reapplied when a newer version of the object is released by Oracle.

Customizations by modification are not supported by Oracle and should always be avoided. There are rarely occasions where there is a real business justification for a customization by modification. There are often alternatives, such as exploring other solutions or looking at ways to change the requirements or processes. It is important to understand the difference between customization by extension and customization by modification, as the two terms are often used loosely. When we extend Oracle EBS by supported methods, the standard functionality is still supported by Oracle as it has not been amended by the extension, whereas customization by modifying a standard object means the standard object also becomes unsupported by them.

A worthwhile feature of Oracle EBS is that it uses a common toolset and also has a vast amount of documentation written about the supported ways in which you can extend the product. The first place to start would be the Oracle Release 12 Documentation Library. This provides many documents, all relating to Oracle EBS. Another essential resource is Oracle Support (previously known as Metalink), which is a portal provided by Oracle for support, documentation, white papers, and patches among many other things related to EBS. To access the portal, you need to register and you also need to provide a support identifier, which is only provided when there is a support contract with Oracle Support. So, if you are new to EBS or if you have been around for a while, you can nearly always find examples or documentation relating to your specific requirement. There are nearly always numerous business processes and solutions available to satisfy it. The best way to provide a solution is to have an understanding of what options are available. Having knowledge of the various ways in which we can extend EBS will give us a much better chance of coming up with better solutions. This book will provide recipes that will cover some simple and some more complex solutions. It will utilize a majority of the Oracle toolset and will, hopefully, broaden your knowledge. Expanding our knowledge of the toolset will allow us to provide a more varied set of solutions, resulting in having a better chance of providing a better, more robust solution for a given problem.

Understanding the EBS architecture

Before we really get into the book it is important to understand the E-Business Suite architecture in Release 12. We need to understand where the files are kept and how it is installed. If you are a beginner, you will need this information to understand some key concepts and pick up some terminology that is often used when we discuss Oracle EBS.

In Release 12, there has been a significant change in the file system when it is installed. The change quite simply is used to segregate code, data, and configuration. This makes maintenance much easier. There will be a number of terms that you will encounter regularly when we discuss EBS. A server is a term for a number of processes that provide specific functionality on a single machine. A tier is a term used to describe a logical group of services, which can be on one or more physical machine. A machine is used to describe a computer or group of computers. A node is a group of computers that work closely together as a cluster.

Essentially, there are three tiers per instance of EBS. The Database Tier (DB Tier), the Application Tier (APPS Tier), and the Desktop Tier. The desktop tier is the client interface where users will connect to Oracle EBS through a web browser. When Oracle is first used, the browser will install a J2SE plugin which will use Oracle's own Java Virtual Machine (JVM) rather than the browser's own JVM. The application tier (also known as the middle tier) processes all of the business logic. It comprises of three servers or service groups. These are Web Services which process requests from the desktop client. Then there are the Forms services which manage all of the listening and secure requests for Oracle forms. Then there is the concurrent processing server, which processes concurrent requests that are submitted.

When Oracle EBS is installed on all variants of UNIX, the install is performed by the root user. However, as part of the installation process there will be two OS users. One that will own the application node file system (the applmgr user) and the other will own the database node file system (the oracle user). When installed on Windows, there is one OS user that owns the file system. The following diagram shows the basic architecture:

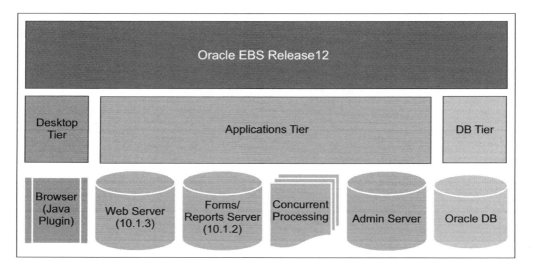

The directory structure of the Application Tier and Database Tier will help to understand where the files are stored. The following directory structure should help to understand where various files are stored within EBS:

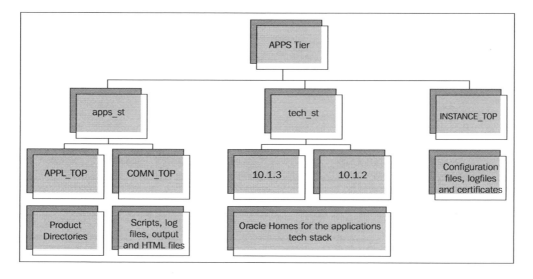

The following shows the directory structures of some core directories on the Applications Tier:

Profile	Directory	Description
APPL_TOP	/apps_st/appl	This directory is the base directory where all of the product tops are stored.
AU_TOP/forms/US	/apps_st/appl/au/12.0.0/forms/US	This directory is where all forms are stored.
AU_TOP/resource	/apps_st/appl/au/12.0.0/resource	This directory is where all libraries are stored.
COMMON_TOP	/apps/apps_st/comn	This is the base directory for scripts, log files, output files, and HTML files.
ORACLE_HOME	/apps_st/10.1.2	This is the directory structure for the forms' server files.
iAS_ORACLE_HOME	/apps_st/10.1.3	This is the directory structure for the web server files.
INSTANCE_TOP	/inst/apps/<CONTEXT_NAME>	This is the top directory for the configuration files.
ADMIN_SCRIPTS_HOME	/inst/apps/<CONTEXT>/admin/scripts	This is where admin scripts are stored to start and stop services.

The following table describes where the files are stored on the Database Tier:

Profile	Directory	Description
ORACLE_HOME	/db/tech_st/10.2.0	This directory is the base directory where all of the database files are stored.
Data Files	/db/apps_st/data	This directory is the base directory where all of the data files are stored.

Within EBS, each product has its own database user within Oracle. The user will own the objects that store data, such as tables. This is in the form of an abbreviation of the product (AP for Account Payables and HR for Human Resources for example) and is referred to as a schema. The passwords are, by default, the same as the schema name, but this is nearly always changed after install. On the file system on the APPS tier, each product has its own file system. The file system has the same root directory as the product \ user name in Oracle. For example, there will be a directory structure for Payables (AP) that has a root directory of AP_TOP. There is one very important schema called the APPS schema. The apps schema owns all of the code, such as packages, triggers, views, java classes. Each product user has grants providing access to the APPS schema for all of its objects. Therefore, the APPS schema has access to all of the objects, that is the code and the objects owned by the product schemas. It is important that as a developer, you can access the APPS database schema. All objects that you will require access to are accessible from this schema. When we create custom objects, we need to create a custom schema and all of the data storing objects will reside in this schema. Usually, an on-site DBA will perform this task, but we will go through this in one of the recipes we have.

If you would like to understand more relating to the core concepts of EBS, you can get more detailed information from the Oracle Applications Concepts Release 12 from the Release12 Documentation Library. You can get the documentation from Oracle by following this link `http://docs.oracle.com/cd/B53825_08/current/html/docset.html`.

Before we start

One final word before we get into the recipes. Hopefully, you will find the book extremely useful. There are thousands of pages written about how to extend and customize Oracle E-Business Suite. This book is not going to cover every solution to every problem. In fact, it will not even come close. The recipes are designed to take us through the different features of the tools and extensions that you may need to utilize in your own solutions. Use the book to get a feel for how each tool and product can be used. It will provide a core understanding of how things can be done and the standards that we need to adhere to. You will need to expand on what you learn here and apply the knowledge you gain to design a solution or solutions to your own scenarios. I personally am a great believer of learning through practice. Expanding your knowledge by understanding the fundamentals is essential to providing the best solutions. Oracle uses many tools and technologies in its suite of applications, of which there is too much to cover in this book.

What this book covers

Chapter 1, Personalizing OA Framework Pages, looks at some recipes that will implement personalizations to an OA framework page. We will look at a number of different types of personalization and the levels at which we can create personalizations. At the end of the chapter, readers will have an understanding of how we can personalize OA framework pages in EBS. Readers will understand which responsibilities are used to administer personalizations and which profile options need to be changed to view the personalization links. Throughout the chapter, we will be creating a variety of different examples that will give a broad understanding of what we can achieve through personalizing OA framework pages.

Chapter 2, Getting Started with OA Framework Pages, deals with the creation of OA Framework pages. We start off by looking at the architecture of OA Framework pages as it is important to understand this before we start any development. Further, we will go through the process of setting up our development environment and what we will need to do to get up and running. Towards the end of the chapter readers will have an understanding of the components required to develop and test an OA Framework page.

Chapter 3, Creating a Master Detail Page in OA Framework, will explain the process of creating a master detail page in the OA Framework. Readers will have an understanding of how we can create master detail pages in the OA framework. Finally, we will go through the process of deploying our page in Oracle E-Business Suite (EBS) and running it through the application.

Chapter 4, Adding a Creation Page and LOV Region in OA Framework, explains how to make changes to the OA Framework pages we have created. This chapter gives the readers an understanding of how they can create pages that interact with the database. We will also know how to use the debugger that is provided in JDeveloper.

Chapter 5, Advanced OA Framework, helps in learning some more advanced features of OA Framework pages which includes a lot more coding. The chapter will continue to develop the pages we have worked on so far.

Chapter 6, BI Publisher, looks at recipes that will explain how BI Publisher integrates with E-Business Suite to allow us to generate formatted data with a very feature rich output. We will look at how it integrates with commonly used desktop applications, such as Microsoft Word and Excel. At the end of the chapter, readers will understand how to set up our development environments. We will learn to create our report templates, and how to generate the XML data that the template requires to produce a report output in a number of different formats. We will look at how the report mail merges the data with Word documents, and how we can use a feature called Bursting to send formatted documents out by e-mail.

Chapter 7, Desktop Integration, looks at how we can integrate with E-Business Suite using the desktop integrator. Oracle E-Business Suite provides a framework that allows us to integrate with Microsoft Office-based tools. It is called Web ADI (Application Desktop Integrator). Users tend to be in favor of using the tools, as it integrates with the Microsoft Office tools we are all used to working with. At the end of this chapter readers will learn how we can use Excel-based spreadsheets to view and upload data to EBS. We will understand how data can be validated, and how we can include structured data entry methods, such as lists of values and drop down lists to spreadsheets. We will understand how we can create a new integrator to upload data and how to assign an integrator to a responsibility.

Chapter 8, Utilities, looks at a number of utilities that you will find extremely useful. We will show how to create a custom schema and how to configure it on EBS. We will also look at ways to use common utilities, which will reduce risk and save enormous amounts of time. Usually, the biggest reason for problems when migrating extensions or configuration is when there are human tasks. We will also look at how to start and stop an environment.

What you need for this book

Oracle uses many great tools to develop extensions. The tools we will mostly focus on in this book are the following:

- ▶ Oracle JDeveloper with OA Extension
- ▶ SQL Developer
- ▶ BI Publisher
- ▶ Microsoft Excel

Microsoft Word

Other utility programs we will be using are:

- ▶ WinSCP — a windows based FTP frontend
- ▶ PuTTY — a UNIX command line window
- ▶ JAD - a Java decompiler

Developing code in EBS

There are a number of languages used for programming and writing scripts that Oracle supports. We are going to primarily focus on the following in this book:

- ▶ PL/SQL
- ▶ Java
- ▶ SQL
- ▶ XML

UNIX shell scripting

Other languages are also less commonly used within EBS and fall outside the scope of this book.

Who this book is for

This book is written for individuals who want to learn how to develop extensions in Oracle E-Business Suite. If you are involved in development or supporting an E-Business Suite implementation, you should find this book very useful. The book gives detailed explanations, so minimal technical expertise is required. It is suitable for beginners who have little experience, or developers who may want to use the book to brush up on their skills.

Conventions

In this book, you will find a number of styles of text that distinguish between different kinds of information. Here are some examples of these styles, and an explanation of their meaning.

Code words in text are shown as follows: "You may also notice that there is also a ZIP file called oafch2.zip provided in the code bundle."

A block of code is set as follows:

```
SELECT flv.lookup_code,
       flv.meaning
  FROM fnd_lookup_values flv
 WHERE flv.lookup_type = 'XXHR_SOCIETY_LOV'
```

Any command-line input or output is written as follows:

```
$JAVA_TOP/<customFolder>/oracle/apps/<ApplicationShortName>/<moduleName>/
<subModuleName>/webui
```

New terms and **important words** are shown in bold. Words that you see on the screen, in menus or dialog boxes for example, appear in the text like this: "Obtain the version of EBS you are on. To do this, log on to EBS and click on the **About this Page** link.".

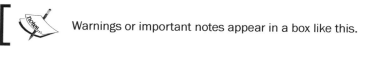

Warnings or important notes appear in a box like this.

Tips and tricks appear like this.

Reader feedback

Feedback from our readers is always welcome. Let us know what you think about this book—what you liked or may have disliked. Reader feedback is important for us to develop titles that you really get the most out of.

To send us general feedback, simply send an e-mail to feedback@packtpub.com, and mention the book title via the subject of your message.

If there is a topic that you have expertise in and you are interested in either writing or contributing to a book, see our author guide on www.packtpub.com/authors.

Customer support

Now that you are the proud owner of a Packt book, we have a number of things to help you to get the most from your purchase.

Downloading the example code

You can download the example code files for all Packt books you have purchased from your account at http://www.packtpub.com. If you purchased this book elsewhere, you can visit http://www.packtpub.com/support and register to have the files e-mailed directly to you.

Errata

Although we have taken every care to ensure the accuracy of our content, mistakes do happen. If you find a mistake in one of our books—maybe a mistake in the text or the code—we would be grateful if you would report this to us. By doing so, you can save other readers from frustration and help us improve subsequent versions of this book. If you find any errata, please report them by visiting http://www.packtpub.com/submit-errata, selecting your book, clicking on the **errata submission form** link, and entering the details of your errata. Once your errata are verified, your submission will be accepted and the errata will be uploaded on our website, or added to any list of existing errata, under the Errata section of that title. Any existing errata can be viewed by selecting your title from http://www.packtpub.com/support.

Piracy

Piracy of copyright material on the Internet is an ongoing problem across all media. At Packt, we take the protection of our copyright and licenses very seriously. If you come across any illegal copies of our works, in any form, on the Internet, please provide us with the location address or website name immediately so that we can pursue a remedy.

Please contact us at copyright@packtpub.com with a link to the suspected pirated material.

We appreciate your help in protecting our authors, and our ability to bring you valuable content.

Questions

You can contact us at questions@packtpub.com if you are having a problem with any aspect of the book, and we will do our best to address it.

1
Personalizing OA Framework Pages

In this chapter we will cover:

- ▶ Getting started with personalizations
- ▶ Setting the personalization profile options
- ▶ Discovering information about a page
- ▶ Clearing the cache
- ▶ Creating a user-level personalization
- ▶ Adding tool tips
- ▶ Creating an item
- ▶ Re-ordering items on a page
- ▶ Adding a button to a page
- ▶ Hiding a button on a page
- ▶ Making a field required
- ▶ Adding a flexfield to a page
- ▶ Using SPEL to trigger personalizations
- ▶ Deactivating personalizations
- ▶ Deleting personalizations

Introduction

OA Framework pages have been implemented using an object-oriented design approach that allows us to be pretty flexible when it comes to making changes to the user interface. The objects that we see on each page are made up of smaller objects that are stored independently in a repository called Meta Data Service (MDS).

In this chapter, we will discuss how to make changes to the user interface through personalization. When we personalize a page, we are altering the declaration of a page's interface. At runtime, objects are loaded from the repository and are rendered in a browser. What we see is determined by the metadata definition, which specifies how objects are displayed on the page. We can create a personalization at multiple levels such as site, function, organization, or responsibility. The good thing is that they can be configured directly from the UI page and are likely to survive an upgrade, as opposed to extensions. One thing you cannot modify with personalizations is the business logic.

At the end of this chapter, readers will have an understanding of how we can personalize OA Framework pages in EBS. Readers will understand which responsibilities are used to administer personalizations and which profile options need to be changed to view the personalization links. Throughout this chapter, we will be creating a variety of different examples that will give a broad understanding of what we can achieve through personalizing OA Framework pages.

Getting started with personalizations

It is important that we understand some common terminology and gain an understanding of how an OA Framework page is constructed before we get started. Let's start off by understanding that OA Framework has been developed by Oracle and is based upon a **Model View Controller** (**MVC**) architecture developed using Java 2 Platform, Enterprise Edition (J2EE).

- **Model**: A model can be thought of as the data and is implemented using **Oracle Business Components for Java** (**BC4J**). This comprises three layers, which are the **entity object** (**EO**), **view object** (**VO**), and **application module** (**AM**).
  - **Entity object**: This is based upon a database table and all of the database transactions will go through the EO.
  - **View object**: This is based upon any number of entity objects or it can be an SQL statement, if the page is read only.
  - **Application module**: This is a container for the view object and it manages transactions that occur. Each page has a root AM to maintain the transaction context.
- **View**: A view defines a user interface that is rendered as an HTML page. This is implemented with **user interface XML** (**UIX**).

► **Controller**: A controller is java code that handles events when they occur at runtime. There are two methods that are called when the page runs.

In this recipe, we are going to set up some records that we will use throughout the chapter. We are going to demonstrate our personalizations in the manager self-service screens. We will need to perform the following tasks before we get started with personalizing OA Framework pages:

► Creating a custom responsibility

► Creating a new user

► Creating an employee record

► Assigning a manager

► Attaching an employee to a user record

Creating a custom responsibility

Now to create our new responsibility that we will use to access core HR screens, we will create a test employee record and ensure that the employee is a manager of other employees. This will be used to access some of the self-service screens where we will create some personalizations in the upcoming recipes.

How to do it...

Perform the following steps to create a new responsibility called XX Test HRMS Manager:

1. Log in to Oracle E-Business with the **System Administrator** responsibility.

2. Navigate to **Security | Responsibility | Define** and the **Responsibilities** window will open.

3. Enter the required data as given in the following table:

Item name	Item value
Responsibility Name	XX Test HRMS Manager
Application	Human Resources
Responsibility Key	XXTESTHRMSMGR
Description	XX Test HRMS Manager
Data Group	
Name	Standard
Application	Human Resources
Menu	GLB HRMS Navigator
Request Group	
Name	HR Reports and Processes

4. Click on the **Save** button in the toolbar (or press *Ctrl + S*) to save the record.

5. The **Responsibilities** screen should now appear as shown in the following screenshot:

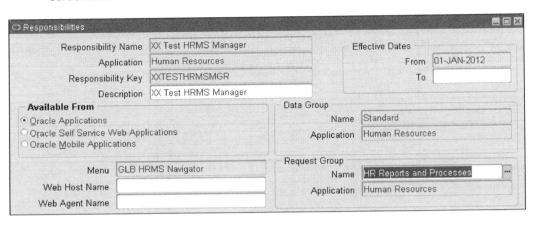

6. Now create a test manager self-service responsibility.

7. Click on the new record icon.

8. Enter the required data as given in the following table:

Item name	Item value
Responsibility Name	XX Test Manager Self-Service
Application	Human Resources
Responsibility Key	XXTESTMGRSS
Description	XX Test Manager Self-Service
Data Group	
Name	Standard
Application	Human Resources
Menu	Manager Self Service
Request Group	
Name	

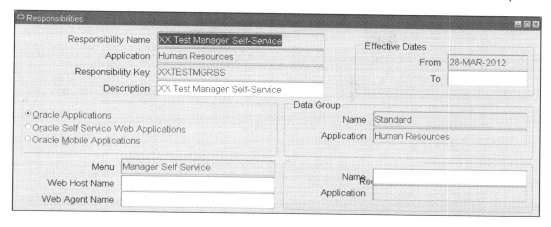

9. Click on the **Save** button in the toolbar (or press *Ctrl + S*) to save the record.

10. Exit the form.

How it works...

We have now created a new responsibility where we can access the HRMS screens.

Creating a new user

We are going to create a user called XXUSER that we will use throughout the chapter for our personalizations. We will add the responsibilities, that we will use throughout the chapter. Also, the user will be assigned an employee record so that when we access the manager self-service screens, there is relevant data available for our personalizations that we are going to create.

How to do it...

To create the user, perform the following steps:

1. Log in to Oracle and select the **System Administrator** responsibility.

2. Navigate to **Security | User | Define**.

3. Enter XXUSER in the **User Name** field.

4. Enter a password in the **Password** field and press the *Tab* key.

5. Enter the password again and press the *Tab* key.

6. Set **Password Expiration** to **None**.

7. Navigate to the **Direct Responsibilities** tab.

8. Add the following responsibilities:

   ❑ Application Developer

   ❑ Functional Administrator

   ❑ Manager Self-Service

   ❑ System Administrator

   ❑ XX Test HRMS Manager

   ❑ XX Test Manager Self-Service

The **Users** screen should now appear as shown in the following screenshot:

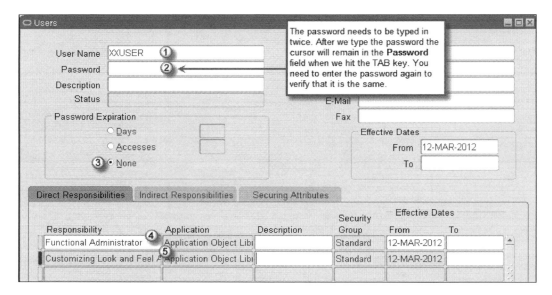

9. Save the form.

How it works...

We have now created our user called XXUSER. The user has access to the responsibilities, which we are going to need throughout the chapter.

Creating an employee record

Now we are going to create an employee called **Employee Manager**, which we will use throughout the chapter for our personalizations. As suggested by the name, this employee will be the manager of other employees.

How to do it...

To create the employee, perform the following steps:

1. Log in to Oracle with the XX Test HRMS Manager responsibility.
2. Navigate to **People | Enter and Maintain**.
3. When the **Find Person** screen opens, click on the **New** button.
4. Enter the required data as given in the following table:

Item name	Item value
Last	Manager
First	Employee
Gender	**Male** (or **Female**)
Action	**Create Employment**
Person Type	Employee
Social Security	123123123
Date of Birth	28-MAR-1970

5. Update the **Latest Start Date** field to 01-JAN-1990.
6. Save the record, and when prompted, click on the **Correction** button.
7. Click on **OK**, when prompted with the message **The original hire date will be updated to be the same as the start date**.
8. Make a note of the employee number that has been automatically generated.

 If the employee number has not been automatically generated, type one manually and save the record as a **Correction**.

The data entered should look similar to the following screenshot:

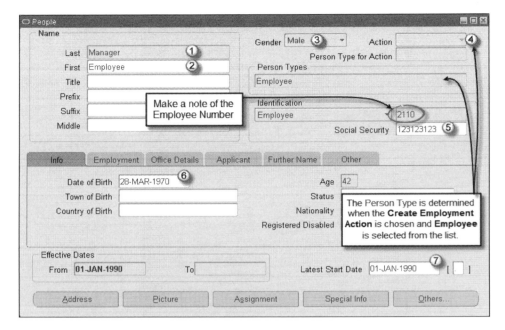

How it works...

We have now created an employee record that we will configure as the manager of other employees. We need to do this so that the self-service screens we are going to personalize will have some data returned in them and we can complete some of the upcoming recipes.

Assigning a manager

We are now going to update the assignment record of an existing employee so that the employee we have just created is the manager of an existing hierarchy and when we perform some personalizations, there is some data returned in the forms we are going to personalize.

How to do it...

To assign a manger, perform the following steps:

1. In the **Enter and Maintain person** screen, click on the **Find Person** (torch) icon in the toolbar.

2. Enter 1197 for the employee number.

3. Click on the **Assignment** button.

4. Click on the **Supervisor** tab.

5. Enter our employee number in the **Worker Number** field. (The employee number is 2110 for the employee that was created in the preceding recipe. It may be a different number on the environment you are using.)

6. Tab out of the field and select the **Correction** button, if prompted.

7. The **Name** fields will automatically populate to **Manager, Employee,** and so on (our test employee), when we tab out of the **Worker Number** field.

8. Save the form and close it.

How it works...

We have assigned our employee as a manager of another employee. This means that we will then inherit the hierarchy of the employee we became the manager of and hence we will have data in the self-service screens that we are going to personalize.

Attaching an employee to a user record

We are going to associate the employee we have just created to our user called XXUSER. When we log in as the XXUSER responsibility, the self-service screen will display data on the screens appropriate to the employee record that we have associated with our user. As we have assigned our employee record as the manager of other employees, we will see the data of the employees in the screens we are going to access in manager self-service.

How to do it...

To create the user, perform the following steps:

1. Select the **System Administrator** responsibility.

2. Navigate to **Security | User | Define**.

3. Press the *F11* key to enter a query.

4. Enter XXUSER in the **User Name** field and press *Ctrl + F11* to execute the query.

5. In the **Person** field enter Manager and Employee, and press the *Tab* button.

6. Save the form.

How it works...

We have now associated our employee with our user. Therefore, when we log in as our user XXUSER, we will be able to access the self-service screens as a manager of other employees.

Setting the personalization profile options

There are three profile options that allow us to personalize self-service screens. The three profile options are as follows:

▶ **Personalize Self-Service Defn**: When set to **Yes**, a **Personalize Page** link will appear at the top of each self-service page

▶ **FND: Personalization Region Link Enabled**: When set to **Yes**, a **Personalize Region** link will appear on each region of a self-service page

▶ **FND: Diagnostics**: When set to **Yes**, an **About this Page** link will appear at the bottom of each self-service page

How to do it...

To set the three profile options, perform the following steps:

1. Log in to Oracle with XXUSER and select the **Functional Administrator** responsibility.
2. Navigate to **Core Services | Profiles**.
3. In the **Name** field of the **Search** screen, type Personalize%.
4. Click on the **Go** button.

You will see that the **Personalize Self-Service Defn** profile option value is set to **No** at site level, as shown in the following screenshot (circled):

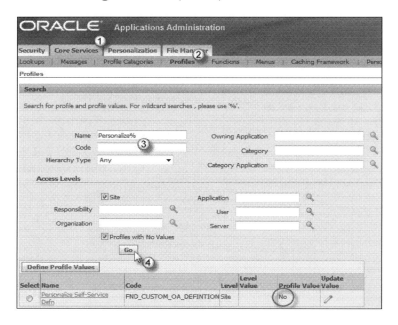

We are now going to update the profile option to **Yes** at user level for the XXUSER user:

1. Click on the **Update Value** (pencil) icon.
2. Click on the **User** tab and click on the **Add Another Row** button:

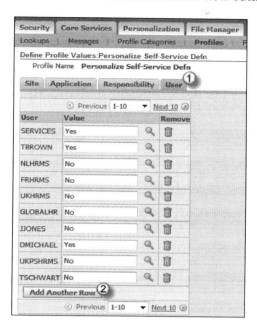

3. In the **User** field, enter the name of our user, XXUSER.
4. Navigate to the **Value** field and click on the list icon.
5. Click on the **Go** button.
6. Click on the **Quick Select** icon for the **Yes** value as shown in the following screenshot:

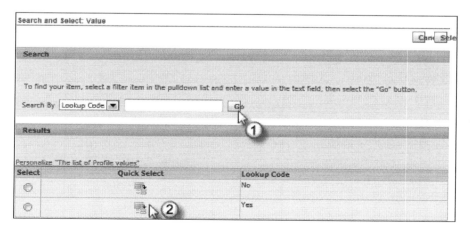

7. When you are returned to the **Profiles** screen, click on the **Update** button and wait for the confirmation that the record has been saved.

8. Now navigate to **Core Services | Profiles** to return to the profiles screen.

We will now check to see if the value has been set. To do this, perform the following steps:

1. In the **Name** field of the **Search** screen, type `Personalize%`.

2. In the **Access Levels** region, enter `XXUSER` in the **User** field.

3. Click on the **Go** button.

The value we set for our user will be displayed as shown in the following screenshot. We can see that there is a **Personalize Page** link that has now appeared as a result of setting the profile option to **Yes**.

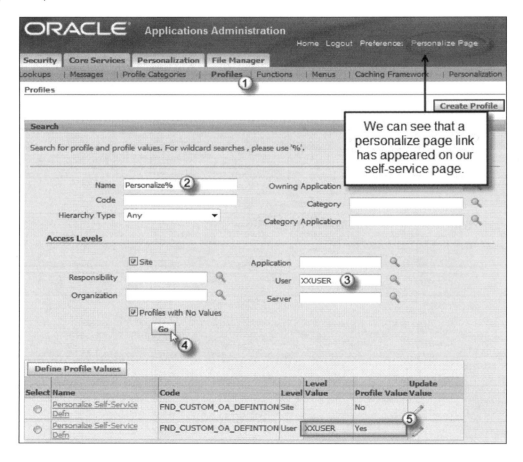

We are now going to set the values for the other two profiles options at user level in the same way.

Repeat these steps but this time set the **FND: Personalization Region Link Enable** profile option to **Yes**.

We can now see that the personalize region links are now displayed in the self-service page, as shown in the following screenshot:

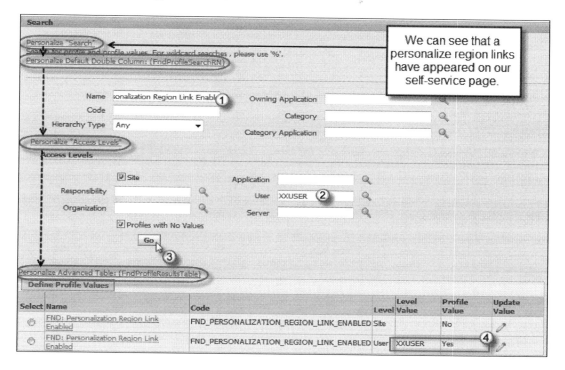

We are now going to set the value of the FND: Diagnostics profile option at site level in the same way:

1. In the **Name** field of the **Search** region, enter FND: Diagnostics.

2. Click on the **Go** button.

3. Click on the **Update Value** (pencil) icon.

4. Under the **Site** tab, set the **Site Value** field to **Yes**.

5. Click the **Update** button and wait for the confirmation that the record has been saved.

6. Now navigate to **Core Services | Profiles** to return to the **Profiles** screen.

7. In the **Name** field of the **Search** screen, type FND: Diagnostics.

8. Click on the **Go** button.

We can now see that the **About this Page** link is now displayed in the self-service page, as shown in the following screenshot:

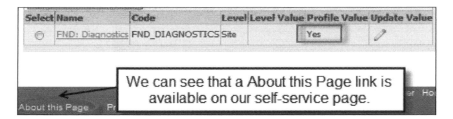

How it works...

We have set the profile options that enable links on self-service pages. This will provide access to the required links on the screen so that we can create our personalizations.

Discovering information about a page

The **About this Page** link is used to find key information about the objects and the structure of the page. It is essential when we want to create personalizations and also if we need to extend a page.

How to do it...

To look at the information available on the **About this Page** link, perform the following steps:

1. Log in to Oracle with the XXUSER and select the **Functional Administrator** responsibility.

2. Navigate to **Core Services | Profiles**.

3. Scroll to the bottom of the page and select the **About this Page** link.

   If we look at the page, we can identify some key information as shown in the following screenshot:

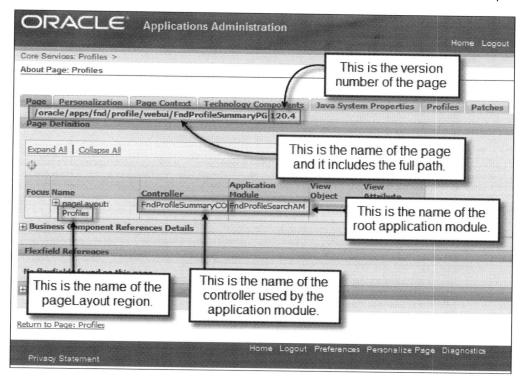

4. Click on the **Expand All** link and scroll down the page.

We can see the objects that are displayed on the page such as items and buttons. We can also see the view object used for the table, as shown in the following screenshot:

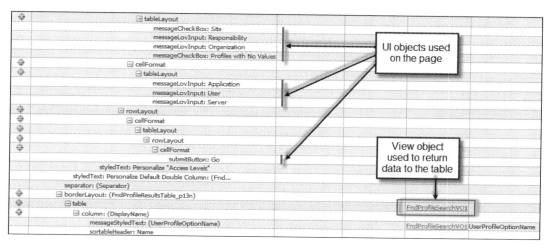

Now if we click on the FndProfileSearchVO link, we can see the following query behind the view object, as shown in the following screenshot:

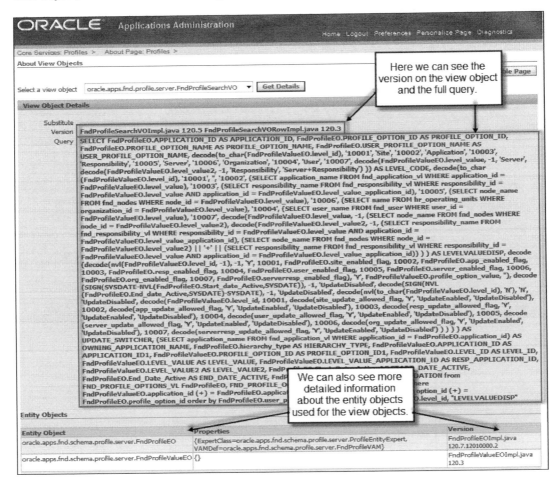

How it works...

We used the **About this Page** link to discover information about a self-service page. This will be a very common feature that will be used when we personalize pages.

Clearing the cache

When we make changes to a screen in self-service, the page is often stored in the cache. We might therefore not see the changes that we make on the screen. When this occurs, we will need to clear the cached page so that we will see the changes we have made to a page through personalization. We will need to clear the cache when we add some of the personalizations in the recipes in this chapter. When we are required to clear the cache, we can perform the following tasks.

How to do it...

To clear the cache, perform the following steps:

1. Log in to Oracle with XXUSER and select the **Functional Administrator** responsibility.
2. Navigate to **Core Services | Caching Framework**.
3. Click on the **Global Configuration** link from the left-hand side navigation pane.
4. In the **Global Cache Configuration** screen, click on the **Clear All Cache** button as shown in the following screenshot:

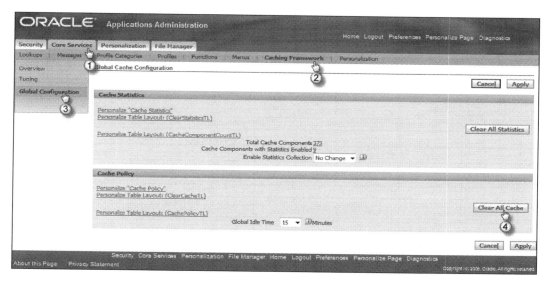

5. When prompted with the warning shown in the following screenshot, click on the **Yes** button:

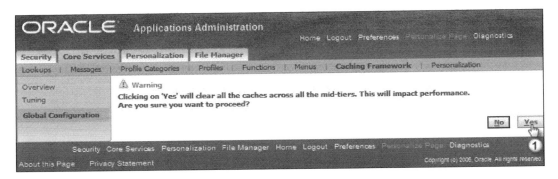

How it works...

We have now cleared the cache so that changes we have made will now become visible as the page is re-cached when we access the page we have personalized. Remember that the entire cache is cleared out when we do this for all of the self-service pages.

Creating a user-level personalization

We will now create a user-level personalization. This feature allows end users to save a search they commonly use. However, not all search pages have this feature.

How to do it...

To create a user-level personalization, perform the following steps:

1. Log in to Oracle with XXUSER and select the **XX Test Manager Self-Service** responsibility.

2. Navigate to **Absence Management**.

3. Click on the **Advanced Search** link as shown in the following screenshot:

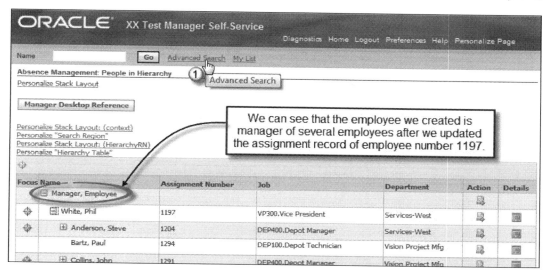

4. In the Advanced Search screen, select the **Show table data when any condition is met** radio button.

5. From the **Add Another** drop-down list, select **Department**.

6. Click on the **Add** button.

7. Enter Services-West in the **Department** condition as shown in the following screenshot:

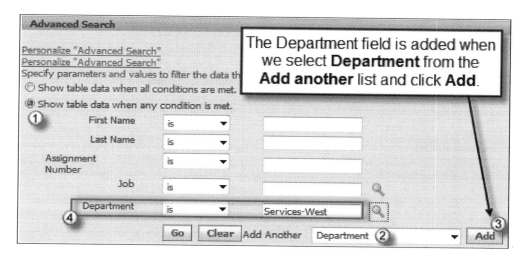

8. Click on the **Save Search** button.

9. In the **View Name** field shown in the following screenshot, enter XXX Services-West Report:

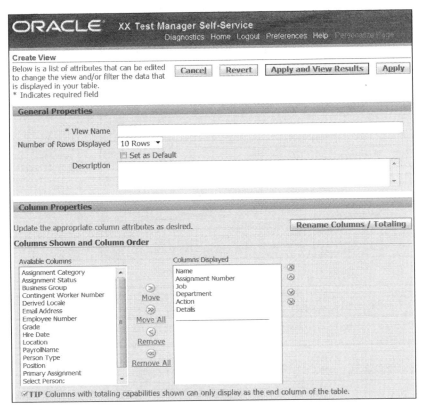

10. In the **Column Properties** region, shift the **Employee Number** and **Location** columns to the **Columns Displayed** list.

11. Shift **Employee Number** up in the list so that it is just after the **Name** field.

12. In the **Sort Settings** region, set the **First Sort** column to **Name**.

13. Set **Sort Order** to **ascending**.

The steps performed here are summarized in the following screenshot:

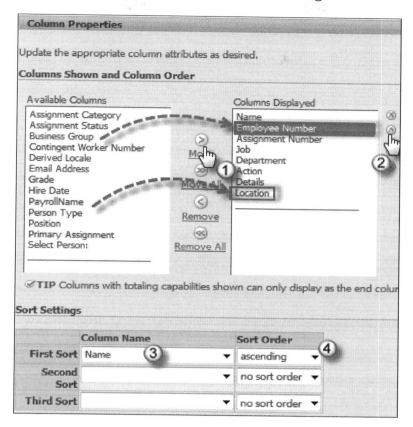

14. Click on the **Apply** button.

    We will now see the view, which we created in the list of personalized views, in the following screenshot:

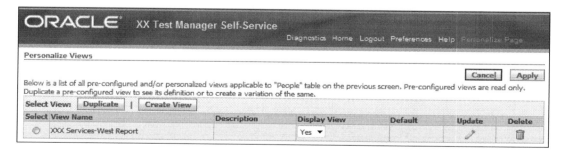

15. Click on the **Apply** button and we will return to the **Advanced Search** region.

16. Click on the **View** button.

17. Select **XXX Services-West Report** and click on the **Go** button.

We can see that the view we created returns the records we would expect, given the restrictions we made.

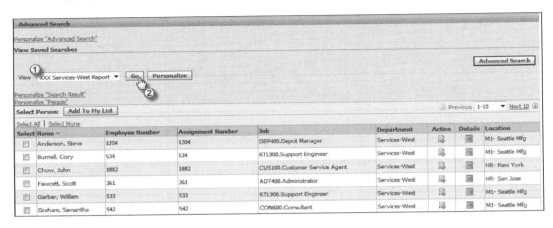

How it works...

XXUSER can now select this view whenever he/she logs in and navigates to **Advanced Search | Views** and selects the user view that we have created.

Adding tool tips

A tool tip is used to add text to a screen to provide information about a region or item. In this recipe, we are going to add some tips to the screen. We will be adding a simple tool tip to a page and we will also add text that we retrieve from a message stored in the message repository. We will also show the difference between a short tip type and a long tip type. We will perform the following tasks in this recipe:

► Adding a tool tip to a page
► Creating new messages
► Adding a short tip type
► Adding a long message tip type

Adding a tool tip to a page

We are now going to add a tool tip to a page. It could relate to anything and really does depend on what we are trying to achieve. Common uses for tool tips are providing information about a region and instructions about an item on a page.

How to do it...

To add a tooltip, perform the following steps:

1. Log in to Oracle with XXUSER and select the **XX Test Manager Self-Service** responsibility.
2. Navigate to **Absence Management**.
3. Click on the **Action** icon.
4. Click on the **Personalize Page** link at the top-right corner of the page.
5. Click on the **Complete View** radio button.
6. Click on the **Expand All** link.
7. On the top line of the page (**Page Layout: Oracle Self Service Human Resources: Absence Management**), select the **Create Item** icon as shown in the following screenshot:

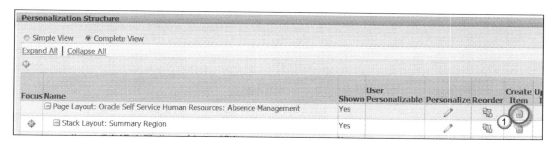

8. From the **Level** drop-down list, select **Site**.
9. From the **Item Style** drop-down list, select **Tip**.

10. Complete the properties of the item as per the following table:

Property	Value
ID	XX_ABS_TIP
Text	XX Absence Management region tip

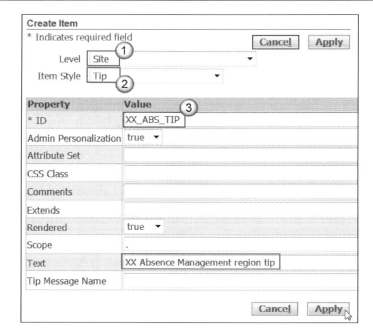

11. Click on the **Apply** button.
12. Scroll down to the bottom of the application and click on the **Return to Application** link.

How it works...

We have just added a tip to a page and can see the results in the following screenshot:

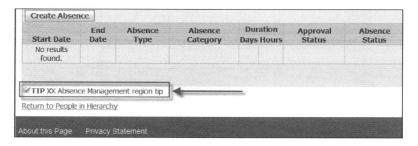

Creating new messages

We can also use the message dictionary to use as a tip. This will allow us to modify the screen tip or merge data into the message, if required. We will now define two messages in Oracle EBS, which we will use to create a short tip and a long tip on a page. Each message, by default, displays this text before each message: **APP:<application short name>-<Number> unless the number field is null or 0**.

How to do it...

To create a message, perform the following steps:

1. Log in to Oracle with the **Application Developer** responsibility.
2. Navigate to **Application | Messages** and the **Messages** window will open.
3. Create a new message with the following data:

Item name	Item value
Name	XX_ABS_TYPE_ST
Language	US
Application	Application Object Library
Number	0
Current Message Text	Absence Type Short Tip

4. Save the form.
5. Create the second message with the following data:

Item name	Item value
Name	XX_ABS_TYPE_LT
Language	US
Application	Application Object Library
Number	0
Current Message Text	This is a longer tip that may span multiple lines.

6. Save and exit the form.

The form should appear as shown in the following screenshot (the image has been amended to remove blank lines):

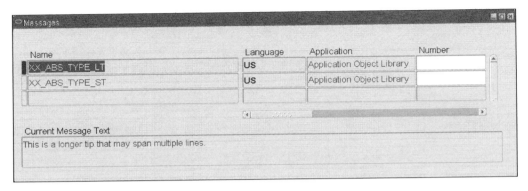

How it works...

We have now configured our message that we will use to create our short and long tip personalizations.

Adding a short tip type

We are now going to create a personalization that will add a short tip to a self-service screen. The short tip called XX_ABS_TYPE_ST will reference the message that we have just created.

How to do it...

To add a short tooltip on an item, perform the following steps:

1. Log in to Oracle with XXUSER and select the **XX Test Manager Self-Service** responsibility.
2. Navigate to **Absence Management**.
3. Click on the **Action** item.
4. Under the **Absence Summary** tab, click on the **Personalize Search** link in the **Search** region.
5. Click on the **Personalize** icon for the **Message Choice: Absence Type** item.
6. Click on the **Choose Levels Displayed** button.
7. Shift all of the items other than **Site** and **Responsibility** back to the **Available Levels** side as summarized in the following screenshot:

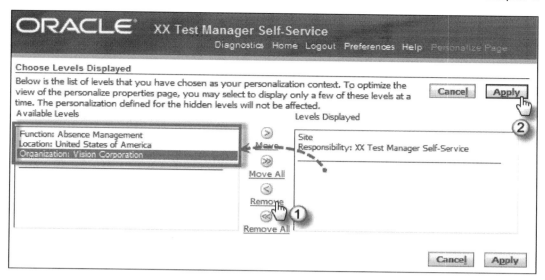

8. Click on the **Apply** button.

9. Set **Tip Message Name** at responsibility level of **XX_ABS_TYPE_ST**.

10. Set **Tip Type** at the **Responsibility** level to **shortTip** as shown in the following screenshot:

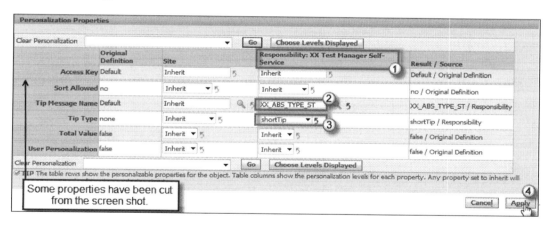

11. Click on the **Apply** button.

12. Click on the **Return to Application** link.

How it works...

We can see that the message is displayed as a tip underneath the **Absence Type** field as shown in the following screenshot:

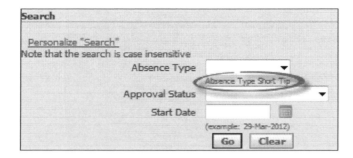

Adding a long message tip type

We are now going to create a personalization that will add a long tip to a self-service screen. The short tip will reference the message we have just created called XX_ABS_TYPE_LT. We will see the difference between the tips we have created and how they are displayed on the screen.

How to do it...

To add a long tool tip on an item, perform the following steps:

1. Log in to Oracle with XXUSER and select the **XX Test Manager Self-Service** responsibility.

2. Navigate to **Home | Absence Management**.

3. Click on the **Action** icon for an employee record.

4. Under the **Absence Summary** tab, click on the **Personalize "Search"** link in the **Search** region.

5. Click on the **Personalize** icon for the **Message Choice: Absence Type** item.

6. Click on the **Choose Levels Displayed** button.

7. Shift all of the items other than **Site** and **Responsibility** back to the **Available Levels** side.

8. Click on the **Apply** button.

9. Set **Tip Message Name** to the responsibility level **XX_ABS_TYPE_LT**.

10. Set **Tip Type** to the responsibility level **longMessage,** as shown in the following screenshot:

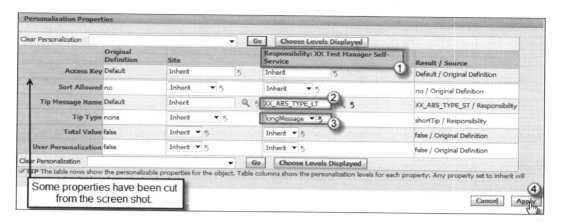

11. Click on the **Apply** button.

12. Click on the **Return to Application** link.

How it works...

We can see an icon next to the **Absence Type** field and when clicked, it opens a new window with the message text from the XX_ABS_TYPE_LT message we created earlier, as shown in the following screenshot:

Creating an item

Okay, in this recipe we are going to add an item to a screen. We can add an item to a screen without extending a page as long as the field exists in the view object of the region we are extending. A view object will nearly always contain many more data items than are visible on the screen. To find out the items that are in the view object, we need to do a little bit of investigation into the view object. Once we have checked the available items, we can personalize the page to make the items visible on the screen. We can also order the items in the region we are displaying them.

How to do it...

To add an item to a page, perform the following steps:

1. Log in to Oracle with XXUSER and select the **XX Test Manager Self-Service** responsibility.

2. Navigate to **Home | Personal Information**.

3. Click on the **Action** icon for an employee record.

   We are going to add a new item to the **Basic Details** region. This item will specify the employee original start date after the **Full Name** field.

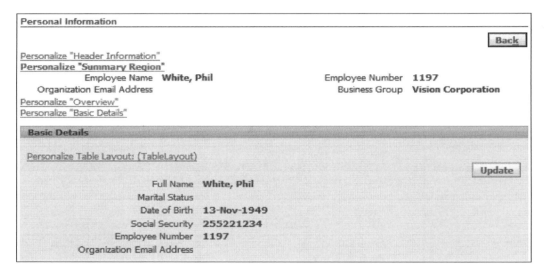

However, before we add the item, we need to find out some information about the page as we need to know the view object that is used by the **Basic Details** region and the name of the attribute for the original start date item.

4. Scroll down to the bottom of the page and click on the **About this Page** link.

5. Then, click on the **Expand All** link.

6. Scroll down until you see the details for the **Basic Details** region.

   We can see that the view object for this region is **BasicDetailsCurrentVO**.

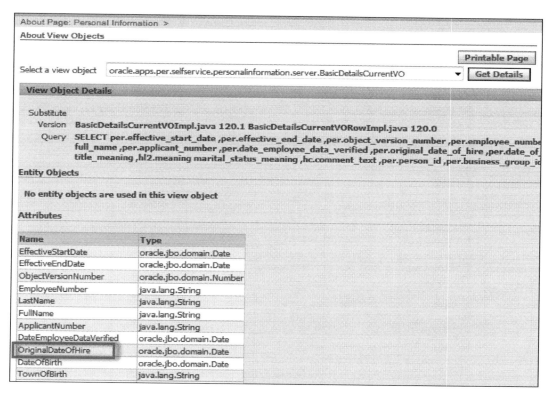

	cellFormat				
		tableLayout			
		messageStyledText: Full Name		BasicDetailsCurrentVO	FullName
		messageStyledText: Marital Status		BasicDetailsCurrentVO	MaritalStatusMeaning
		messageStyledText: Date of Birth		BasicDetailsCurrentVO	DateOfBirth
		messageStyledText: Social Security		BasicDetailsCurrentVO	NationalIdentifier
		messageStyledText: Employee Number		BasicDetailsCurrentVO	EmployeeNumber
		messageStyledText: Contingent Worker Number		BasicDetailsCurrentVO	NpwNumber
		messageStyledText: Organization Email Address		BasicDetailsCurrentVO	EmailAddress
	styledText: Personalize "Basic Details"				

7. Scroll down and expand the **Business Component References Details** section.

8. Click on **oracle.apps.per.selfservice.personalinformation.server. BasicDetailsCurrentVO** for the basic details view object.

9. If we look at the attributes returned by the view object, we will notice that the original start date field is called **OriginalDateOfHire**:

About Page: Personal Information >

About View Objects

Printable Page

Select a view object oracle.apps.per.selfservice.personalinformation.server.BasicDetailsCurrentVO ▾ Get Details

View Object Details

Substitute

Version **BasicDetailsCurrentVOImpl.java 120.1 BasicDetailsCurrentVORowImpl.java 120.0**

Query SELECT per.effective_start_date ,per.effective_end_date ,per.object_version_number ,per.employee_numbe full_name ,per.applicant_number ,per.date_employee_data_verified ,per.original_date_of_hire ,per.date_of title_meaning ,hl2.meaning marital_status_meaning ,hc.comment_text ,per.person_id ,per.business_group_id

Entity Objects

No entity objects are used in this view object

Attributes

Name	Type
EffectiveStartDate	oracle.jbo.domain.Date
EffectiveEndDate	oracle.jbo.domain.Date
ObjectVersionNumber	oracle.jbo.domain.Number
EmployeeNumber	java.lang.String
LastName	java.lang.String
FullName	java.lang.String
ApplicantNumber	java.lang.String
DateEmployeeDataVerified	oracle.jbo.domain.Date
OriginalDateOfHire	oracle.jbo.domain.Date
DateOfBirth	oracle.jbo.domain.Date
TownOfBirth	java.lang.String

Now that we have the information about the item we want to add, we can create the item through personalization:

1. Scroll to the bottom of the page and click on the **Return to About Page** link.

2. Scroll down to the bottom of the next page and click on the **Return to Page: Personal Information** link.

3. In the **Personal Information** page, click on the **Personalize "Basic Details"** link.

4. In the **Personalize Region: Basic Details** screen, click on the **Create Item** icon for the **Default Single Column: Basic Details** object as shown in the following screenshot:

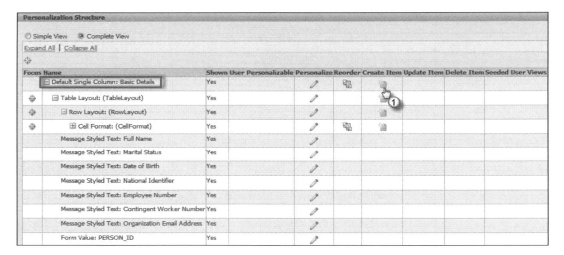

5. From the **Item Style** list, select **MessageStyledText** to add a display only field.

6. Set the values of the following properties:

Property	Value
ID	XXOrigHireDate
Prompt	Orig. Hire Date
View Attribute	OriginalDateOfHire
View Instance	BasicDetailsCurrentVO

7. Click on the **Apply** button.

How it works...

We have now added the item, but note that we need to move the item just next to the **Full Name** field and also the font for the item's data is not the same as the other data. We are going to reorder the item in the region in the next recipe.

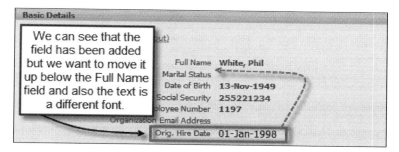

Re-ordering items on a page

We will now re-order the items in the region and we will also set the CSS Class property of the item so that the font matches the other items in the region.

How to do it...

To re-order items in a region, perform the following steps:

1. Navigate to **Home | XX Test Manager Self-Service | Personal Information**.
2. Click on the **Action** icon.
3. Click on the **Personalize "Basic Details"** link.
4. Click on the **Complete View** radio button.
5. Click on the **Expand All** link.
6. For the **Default Single Column: Basic Details** object, click on the **Reorder** icon, as shown in the following screenshot:

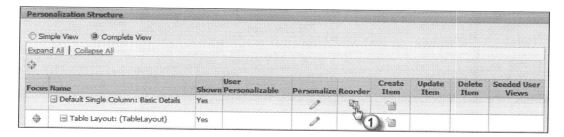

7. In the **Function** table, click on the up arrow icon until the **Orig. Hire Date** field is in the desired location, as shown in the following screenshot:

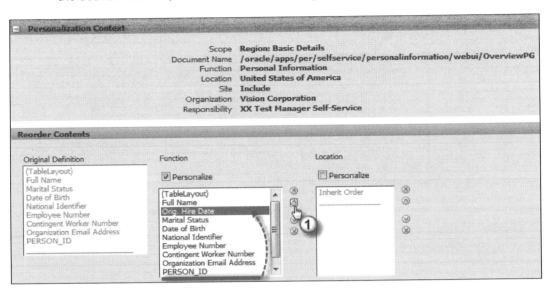

8. Click on the **Apply** button.

9. Click on the **Update Item** icon for the **Message Styled Text: Orig. Hire Date** field, as shown in the following screenshot:

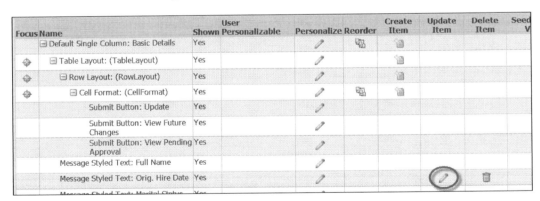

10. Set the CSS Class property to **OraDataText**.

11. Click on the **Apply** button.

12. Click on the **Return to Application** link.

How it works...

We have now moved the item so that it is just below the **Full Name** field and we have set the property to use the Oracle CSS Class so that the font for the data is the same as the other data items.

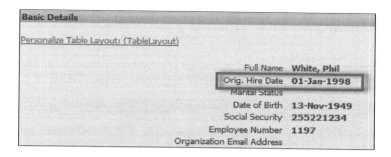

Adding a button to a page

We are now going to add a button to a page that is going to link to a website when the button is clicked. The link will go to the Google Search page, but this link could easily be a link to a new page that we have created.

How to do it...

To add a button to the **Basic Details** page, perform the following steps:

1. Log in to Oracle with XXUSER and select the **XX Test Manager Self-Service** responsibility.

2. Navigate to **Home | Personal Information**.

3. Click on the **Action** icon.

4. Click on the **Personalize "Basic Details"** link.

5. Click on the **Complete View** radio button.

6. Click on the **Expand All** link.

7. In the **Personalize Region: Basic Details** screen, click on the **Create Item** icon for **Default Single Column: Basic Details** as shown in the following screenshot:

Focus	Name	Shown	User Personalizable	Personalize	Reorder	Create Item
	⊟ Default Single Column: Basic Details	Yes		✎	⬚	🗑
◈	⊟ Table Layout: (TableLayout)	Yes		✎		🗑 ①

8. In the **Create Item** page, select **Button** from the **Item Style** drop-down list.

9. Complete the details of the following property items as per the table:

Property	Value
ID	XX_BasicDetails_Btn
Destination URI	http://google.com
Prompt	Google

10. Click on the **Apply** button.

11. Click on the **Return to Application** link.

How it works...

We have now created a button in the **Basic Details** region. The button will open the URL that we have entered in the **Destination URI** property. We can see this in the following screenshot:

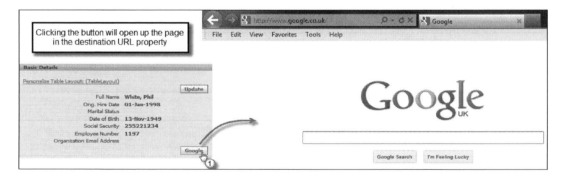

There's more...

Okay, well what if we want to go to another OA Framework page? We can do this too. We will now update the button to call another OA Framework page, but first we must gather some information to get the URL of the page we want to navigate to. Let's get the information for the **My Employee Information** page:

1. Navigate to **Home | My Employee Information**.

2. Click on the **About this Page** link.

3. Click on the **Page Context** tab.

4. Click on the **Expand All** link.

5. Scroll down to the **(JSP) My Employee Information** line.

You will notice that the page has lots of information on it. Now that we have clicked on the **Expand All** link, a quick way to find the information we require would be to bring up the browser search page facility and search for the name of the page we want the information for as shown in the following screenshot. To activate the search facility in a browser window, press *Ctrl + F*. We can then type in the characters we want to search for. We can use this to help speed up our fact finding as often there is a lot of information on a page we need to sift through. In this example, we can see that the **My Employee Information** page has a function of HR_MGR_VIEWS_SS and a destination URL of OA.jsp?page=/oracle/apps/per/selfservice/mgrviews/webui/ManagerViewsPG&OAFunc=HR_MGR_VIEWS_SS.

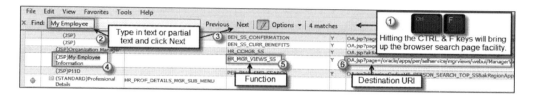

6. Navigate back to **Home | Personal Information**.

7. Click on the **Action** icon.

8. Click on the **Personalize "Basic Details"** link.

9. Click on the **Complete View** radio button.

10. Click on the **Expand All** link.

11. In the **Personalize Region: Basic Details** screen, click on the **Update Item** icon for the **Button: Google** item we created earlier, as shown in the following screenshot:

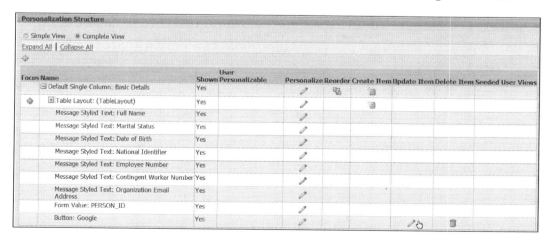

12. Update the details of the following property items as per the table:

Property	Value
Destination Function	`HR_MGR_VIEWS_SS`
Destination URI	`OA.jsp?page=/oracle/apps/per/selfservice/mgrviews/` `webui/ManagerViewsPG&OAFunc=HR_MGR_VIEWS_SS`
Prompt	`My Employee Info`

13. Click on the **Apply** button.

14. Click on the **Return to Application** link.

15. Now click on the **My Employee Info** button.

You should now have opened the **My Employee Information** page as shown in the following screenshot:

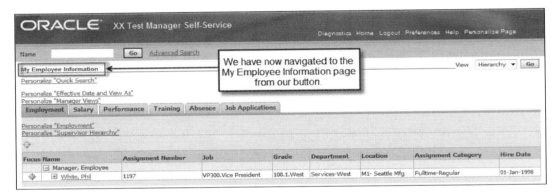

Hiding a button on a page

To perform this recipe, we will use the button created in the *Adding a button to a page* recipe.

Getting ready

Now, we are going to show how we can hide a button. We are going to show the button on the page for our custom responsibility, but hide it for other users. We can do this by setting the **Rendered** property of the button to **False** at the **Site** level and set it to **True** at the **Responsibility** level for our custom responsibility.

How to do it...

To hide a button on a page, perform the following steps:

1. Log in to Oracle with XXUSER and select the **XX Test Manager Self-Service** responsibility.

2. Navigate to **Home | Personal Information**.

3. Click on the **Action** icon.

4. Click on the **Personalize "Basic Details"** link.

5. Click on the **Complete View** radio button.

6. Click on the **Expand All** link.

7. Click on the **Personalize** icon for the **Button: My Personal Info** object.

8. Click on the **Choose Levels Displayed** button.

9. Shift all levels other than the **Site** and **Responsibility** levels to the left-hand side as shown in the following screenshot:

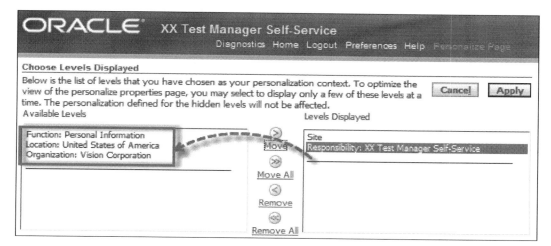

10. Click on the **Apply** button.

11. Set the **Rendered** property at the **Site** level to **False**.

12. Set the **Rendered** property at the **Responsibility** level to **True**:

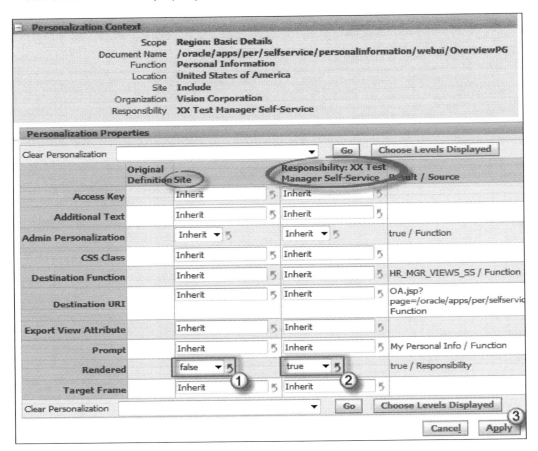

13. Click on the **Apply** button.

14. Click on the **Return to Application** link.

You will see that in the **Personal Information** page, the **My Personal Info** button is still available.

15. Navigate to the **Home** page.

16. Change the responsibility to **Manager Self-Service**.

17. Navigate to the **Personal Information** page.

18. Click on the **Action** icon.

How it works...

We can now see that the button is no longer displayed for other responsibilities. We can set the **Rendered** property to **False**, when we do not want an item to be displayed.

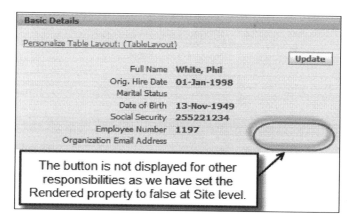

Making a field required

We can also change the **Required** property of an item to make users enter data. At this stage, you should be getting the idea about changing properties of items and getting a feel for what can be achieved. To gain a better understanding, it would be a good idea to investigate what properties can be changed and what effect it has on the item. Next, we will make a field required.

How to do it...

To make a field required on a page, perform the following steps:

1. Log in to Oracle with XXUSER and select the **XX Test Manager Self-Service** responsibility.
2. Navigate to **Home | Personal Information**.
3. Click on the **Action** icon.
4. In the **Basic Details** region, click on the **Update** button.
5. Select the **Correct or complete the current details** radio box and click on **Next**.
6. Click on the **Personalize "Basic Details"** link.
7. Click on the **Complete View** radio button.
8. Click on the **Expand All** link.

9. Press *Ctrl + F* to bring up the search facility on the browser.

10. Type in `First` and scroll down to **Message Text Input: First Name** (which will be highlighted from the find).

11. Click on the **Personalize** icon for the **First Name** field.

12. Click on the **Choose Levels Displayed** button.

13. Shift all levels other than the **Site** and **Responsibility** levels to the left-hand side.

14. Click on the **Apply** button.

15. Set the **Required** property at the **Responsibility** level to **true** as shown in the following screenshot:

Prompt				Definition
Read Only false	Inherit ▼ 5	Inherit ▼ 5		false / Original Definition
Rendered true	Inherit ▼ 5	Inherit ▼ 5		true / Original Definition
Required no	Inherit ▼ 5	yes ▼ 5		yes / Responsibility
Search Allowed false	Inherit ▼ 5	Inherit ▼ 5		false / Original Definition

16. Click on **Apply**.

17. Click on the **Return to Application** link.

How it works...

In this recipe, we have set the **Required** property of an item so that it has become mandatory for the user to enter data. We can now see that the **First Name** field is now required as it has * next to the prompt:

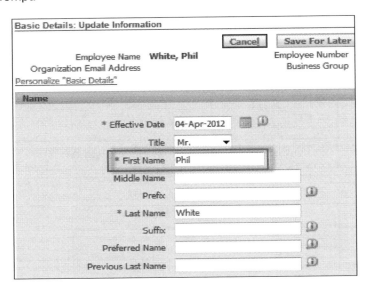

Adding a flexfield to a page

In this recipe, we are going to show how we can create a descriptive flexfield (DFF) and then display the flexfield on the screen. Again, we need to gather some information about the page and find out if a flexfield is available for a particular region. We will then configure a segment on the DFF and show how we can display it on the screen.

How to do it...

To add a flexfield to a page, perform the following steps:

1. Log in to Oracle with XXUSER and select the **XX Test Manager Self-Service** responsibility.

2. Navigate to the **Absence Management** page.

3. Click on the **Action** icon for an employee record.

4. Click on the **Create Absence** button and the **Enter Absence Details** screen will open as shown in the following screenshot:

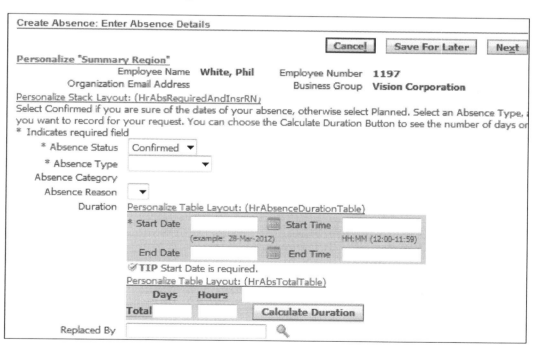

5. Scroll down to the bottom of the page and click on the **About this Page** link.

6. Click on the **Expand All** link.

7. Scroll down to the **Flexfield References** section and we will see what flexfields are available on this screen.

The following screenshot shows us that the **PER_ABSENCE_ATTENDANCES** flexfield is available:

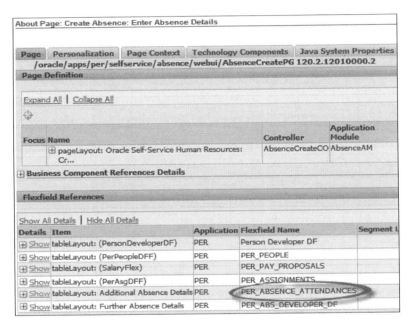

Getting the title of a descriptive flexfield

Now, we have the flexfield name and we can add a descriptive flexfield segment to the flexfield. First, we will get the title of the **Additional Absence Information DFF**. To do this, perform the following steps:

1. Log in to Oracle with the **Application Developer** responsibility.

2. Navigate to **Flexfield | Descriptive | Register** and the **Descriptive Flexfields** window will open.

3. Press the *F11* key to enter a query and enter PER_ABSENCE_ATTENDANCES in the **Name** field.

4. Press *Ctrl + F11* to execute the query and the following record should be returned.

   We can see that the **PER_ABSENCE_ATTENDANCES** flexfield is returned from the query. Make a note of the flexfield title **Additional Absence Details**.

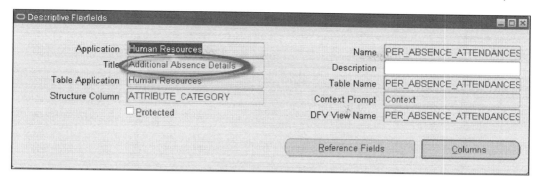

5. Exit the **Descriptive Flexfields** screen and navigate to **Flexfield | Descriptive | Segments** and the **Descriptive Flexfields Segments** window will open.

6. Press *F11* to enter a query.

7. When in **ENTER-QUERY** mode, type `Additional Absence Details` in the **Title** field and press *Ctrl + F11* to execute the query.

8. If the **Freeze Flexfield Definition** checkbox is checked, uncheck it.

9. Click on **OK** when the warning message appears.

10. Click on the **Segments** button for the **Global Data Elements** record.

The steps taken are summarized in the following screenshot:

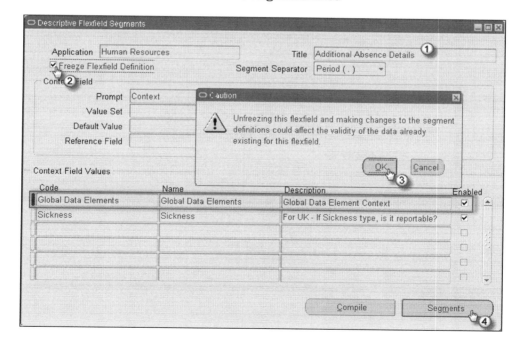

Adding a DFF segment

Now, we can create a new DFF segment for the **Global Data Elements** context as performed in the following steps:

1. Enter the following data in the **Segments Summary** screen:

Property	Value
Number	45
Name	Test DFF
Window Prompt	Test DFF
Column	ATTRIBUTE20
Value Set	
Displayed	checked
Required	checked

2. Click on the **Open** button.

3. Enter the following data:

Property	Value
Name	Test DFF
Description	Test DFF
Enabled	checked
Displayed	checked
Required	unchecked
Display Size	10
Description Size	10
Concatenated Description Size	25
List of Values	Test DFF
Window	Test DFF

4. When you change the **Display Size** field, click on **OK** when the warning appears.

5. Click on **Save**.

6. Close the **Segments** screen.

7. Close the **Segments Summary** screen.

8. Check the **Freeze Flexfield Definition** checkbox to recompile the flexfield definition.

9. Click on **OK** when the warning appears.

10. Click on **Save** and **OK** when a note message appears.

11. Exit the form.

Enabling a flexfield on a self-service page

Now that we have created a DFF segment, we are going to show the flexfield in the **Create Absence** screen. To do this, perform the following steps:

1. Change responsibility to the **XX Test Manager Self-Service** responsibility.
2. Navigate to the **Absence Management** page.
3. Click the **Action** icon for an employee record.
4. Click on the **Create Absence** button.
5. Click on the **Personalize Page** link.
6. Click on the **Complete View** radio button.
7. Click on the **Expand All** link.
8. Press *Ctrl + F* to bring up the search facility on the browser.
9. Type in `Additional` and scroll down to the **Flex: Additional Absence Details** record (which will be highlighted from the find).
10. Click on the **Personalize** icon for the **Flex: Additional Absence Details** field.

    The steps are summarized in the following screenshot:

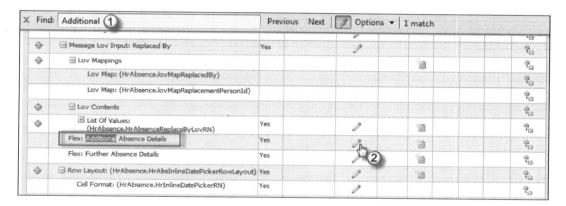

11. Click on the **Choose Levels Displayed** button.
12. Shift all of the items other than **Site** back to the **Available Levels** side.
13. Click on the **Apply** button.
14. Set the **Rendered at Site** level to **true**.
15. Click on the **Apply** button.
16. Scroll to the bottom of the page and click on the **Return to Application** link.

How it works...

We have now updated the page so that the flexfield is displayed in the **Enter Absence Details** screen, as shown in the following screenshot:

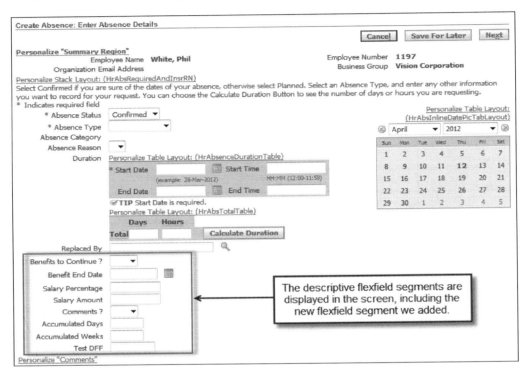

The descriptive flexfield segments are displayed in the screen, including the new flexfield segment we added.

Using SPEL to trigger personalizations

SPEL stands for **Simplest Possible Expression Language**. A SPEL statement will return a Boolean value of either `True` or `False` and can be used for conditionally setting a property of an item on a page.

Adding a SPEL statement

In this recipe, we are going to use SPEL to set the properties of an item. We are going to set the **Read Only** property based on a SPEL statement. If the SPEL statement returns `True`, the item will be made read only to the user.

How to do it...

To set properties using SPEL, perform the following steps:

1. Log in to Oracle with XXUSER and select the **XX Test Manager Self-Service** responsibility.

2. Navigate to the **Absence Management** page.

3. Click on the **Action** icon for an employee record.

4. Click on the **Create Absence** button.

5. Click on the **Personalize Page** link.

6. Click on the **Complete View** radio button.

7. Click on the **Expand All** link.

8. Press *Ctrl + F* to bring up the search facility on the browser.

9. Type in Comments and scroll down to the **Message Text Input: Absence Comments** record (which will be highlighted from the find).

10. Click on the **Personalize** icon.

11. Click on the **Choose Levels Displayed** button.

12. Shift all of the items other than **Site** and **Responsibility** back to the **Available Levels** side.

13. Click on the **Apply** button.

14. Set the **Read Only** property at the **Responsibility** level to **SPEL**.

15. Set the **Responsibility** level for the **SPEL** statement to **${oa.FunctionSecurity. XXABSREADONLY}**, as shown in the following screenshot:

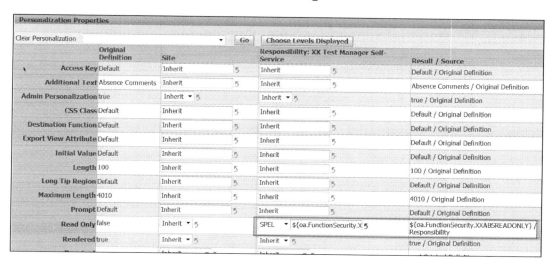

16. Click on the **Apply** button.

17. Scroll down to the bottom of the page and click on the **Return to Application** link.

How it works...

You may notice that the comments item is now not displayed on the screen. This is because we need to create the function and add it to the menu for the SPEL condition to be returned.

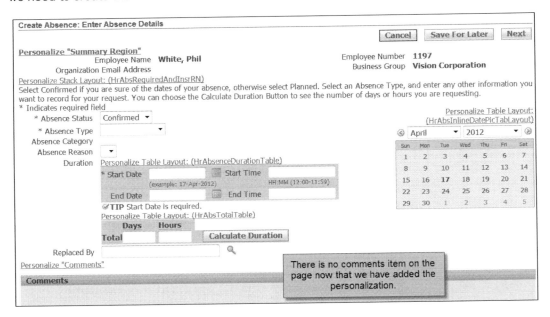

Creating a function

We are now going to create a function that we will add to a menu.

How to do it...

To create a function, perform the following steps:

1. Log in to Oracle with XXUSER and select the **Application Developer** responsibility.

2. Navigate to **Application | Function**.

3. Create a function with the following details:

Item name	Item value
Function	XXABSREADONLY
User Function Name	XX Absence Read Only
Description	XX Absence Read Only
Type	Subfunction

The function will be displayed as shown in the following screenshot:

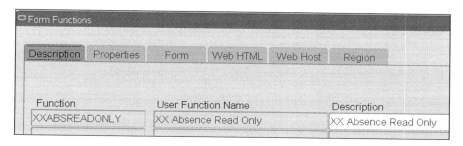

4. Save the record and dismiss the confirmation message.

Adding a function to a menu

We will now add a function to a menu attached to the **XX Test Manager Self Service** responsibility. The function will be present in the menu, which will mean that the SPEL statement will return `True`.

How it works...

To add a function to a menu, perform the following steps:

1. Log in to Oracle with XXUSER and select the **Application Developer** responsibility.
2. Navigate to **Application | Menu**.
3. Query back the **Manager Self Service** menu.
4. Add the function **XXABSREADONLY** to the menu with the following details:

Item name	Item value
Seq	200
Function	XX Absence Read Only

5. Save the menu and dismiss the confirmation message to compile the menu.

We can see that the function has now been added to the menu as shown in the following screenshot:

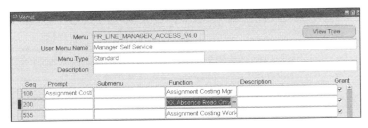

Deactivating personalizations

In this recipe, we will show how we can deactivate personalizations.

How to do it...

1. Log in to Oracle with XXUSER and select the **XX Test Manager Self-Service** responsibility.

2. Navigate to **Absence Management**.

3. Click on the **Action** icon for an employee record.

4. Click on the **Create Absence** button.

   We can see our personalization that adds the flexfield as shown in the following screenshot. But we now want to deactivate this personalization.

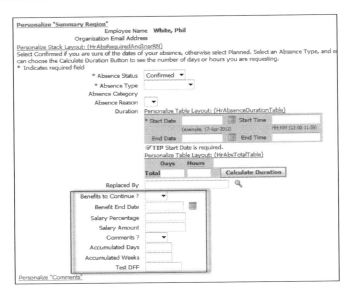

5. Click on the **Personalize Page** link.

6. Click on the **Manage Levels** button, as shown in the following screenshot:

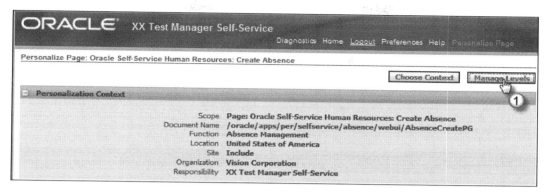

7. In the resulting page, check the **Site level** checkbox.

8. Click on the **Deactivate** button, as shown in the following screenshot:

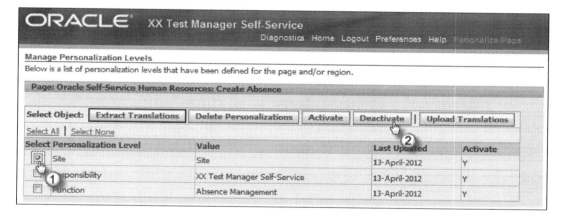

You can see that the personalization has now been deactivated:

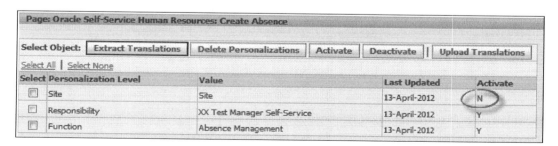

9. Scroll down to the bottom of the page and click on the **Return to Personalization Structure** link.

10. Scroll down to the bottom of the page and click on the **Return to Application** link.

How it works...

We can now see that the personalization we created to display the flexfield has been deactivated. This is because we have deactivated the personalization.

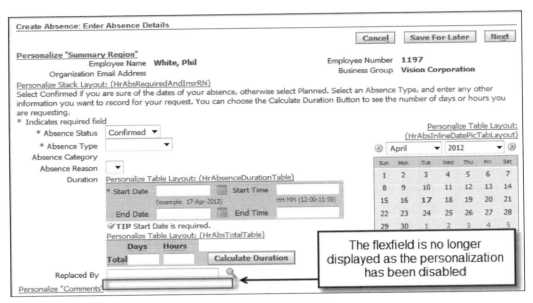

There's more...

If we want to disable all personalizations, we can do that by setting a profile option called **Disable Self-Service Personal** to **Yes**.

Deleting personalizations

In this recipe, we will discover how we can delete personalizations. We have created personalizations in the personal information screen. We are going to show how we can find the regions belonging to the personal information pages and how we can delete them from the **Functional Administrator** responsibility.

How to do it...

To delete personalizations, perform the following steps:

1. Log in to Oracle with XXUSER and select the **Functional Administrator** responsibility.

2. Navigate to **Personalization | Application Catalog**.

   In the **Document Path** field, enter the following path of the personal information page from the *Creating an item* recipe discussed earlier in this chapter.

   ```
   /oracle/apps/per/selfservice/personalinformation/
   ```

    This will restrict the records returned to just the regions or pages used in the personal information pages.

3. Click on the **Manage Personlizations** icon for **OverviewPG**.

   A summary of the steps is shown in the following screenshot:

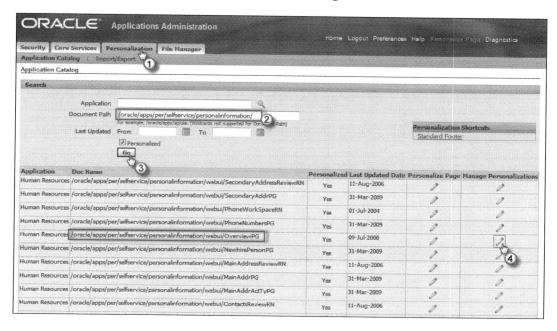

4. Check the **Select** checkboxes of the personalizations we want to delete.

5. Click on the **Delete Personalizations** button as shown in the following screenshot:

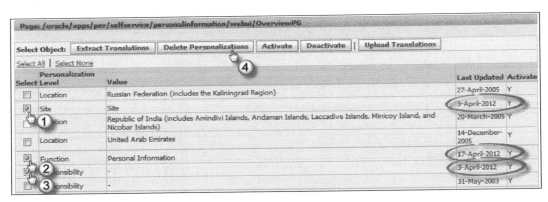

6. Click on the **Yes** button to confirm the deletion as shown in the following screenshot:

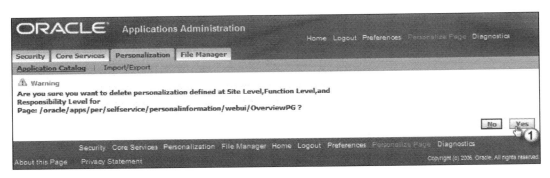

How it works...

This recipe showed how we can delete personalizations. We can do this from a single screen, which makes it easier for us to manage our personalizations. You will see that the personalizations have now been deleted.

2
Getting Started with OA Framework Pages

In this chapter, we will cover the following recipes:

- Getting started with OA Framework
- Installing the database objects
- Setting up our development environment
- Setting the environment variables
- Transferring the DBC file from the application server
- Creating a shortcut to JDeveloper
- Creating an EBS user and assigning responsibilities
- Adding database connections in JDeveloper
- Setting the OC4J settings and project properties
- Running a page
- Creating a new project
- Creating the model layer for a query page
- Creating the view layer for a query page

Introduction

In this chapter, we will be looking at creating OA Framework pages. We will first look at the architecture of OA Framework pages, as this is important to understand before we start any development. Then, we will go through the process of setting up our development environment and what we will need to do to get up and running. We will then create our first page. We will create the components that we need to develop our first page. The working examples will provide a good understanding of how a page is constructed, and we will discuss various points throughout the chapter that are important to gain a sound understanding of the concepts required to start building your own pages.

At the end of the chapter, readers will have an understanding of the components required to develop and test an OA Framework page.

Getting started with OA Framework

Oracle Applications Framework (**OAF**) has been around for a number of years now. It was quite a big shift for Oracle with the core applications in EBS being developed in Oracle Forms. However, with the advent of Java and its utilization in web-based applications, which provided a flexible UI console and a much faster processing speed, Oracle decided to make the move from the popular and stable Oracle Forms to OAF.

Initially, the first module to be completely built using OAF within EBS was Oracle HRMS - Self Service. It was followed by other products and modules, such as iProcurement, iSupport, iStore, iRecruitement, iExpenses, and iSupplier to name a few.

OA Framework was introduced by Oracle's **Applications Technology Group** (**ATG**). They developed a framework called Oracle Applications Framework, which was based on **Java 2 Platform: Enterprise Edition** (**J2EE**) and **Model View Controller** (**MVC**) architecture. To develop OA pages, we require:

- JDeveloper 9i: 11i Applications [11.5.10.3 onwards]
- JDeveloper 10g: R12 Applications

JDeveloper is an **Integrated Development Environment** (**IDE**) that is used to design, develop, and deploy web-based applications. For OAF development, JDeveloper comes with in-built OA components plugged in. JDeveloper with OA extension needs to be downloaded from Oracle Support for the specific version of EBS of the instance pages are to be deployed in.

Looking to the future, JDeveloper 11g is used for Oracle Fusion. The user interface is built using **Applications Development Framework** (**ADF**). This is a different technology to OA Framework and the two are in no way compatible with each other.

OAF Architecture

Let's now gain an understanding of the architecture and methodology of OA Framework pages before we get into building our first page. It is important that we understand this, as it will help us when we get round to developing pages. OA Framework pages are based on a design pattern called the Model View Controller known as MVC. The purpose of the MVC is to separate the data, business logic, and the user interface layers of an application.

Okay, so what are the components of the MVC?

- **Model**: Well, the model is a representation of the data, and contains the logic for accessing and manipulating the data.

- **View**: The View is a representation of the data via a user interface. It will also accept requests from a user and informs the controller.

- **Controller**: The Controller is the business logic, so it determines what to do with requests from the View and also requests from the Model. It is the glue if you like that processes requests from the Model and also from the View. It is the business logic.

The advantages of using an MVC design are:

- Separation of components

- Usage of open industry standards

- Structured code

- Easier to extend and re-use components

- Easy to maintain and test

OA Framework pages are based upon the MVC design pattern. It has the following five layers:

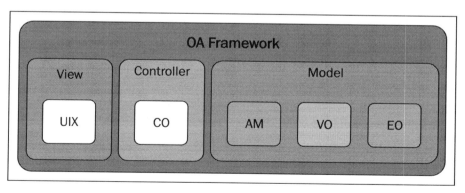

The five layers in OA Framework are:

- **User interface XML (UIX)**
- **OA Controller (CO)**
- **Application module (AM)**
- **View object (VO)**
- **Entity object (EO)**

User interface XML (UIX)

This is the View part of the MVC design pattern. The user interface layer is XML based and an XML file is generated per page. The naming convention is `PageNamePG.xml` or `RegionNameRN.xml`. The development of OAF pages is declarative, that is, there is no drag-and-drop allowed. The objects on a page are visible in the Structure Pane when we select the page in the Application Navigator tab and select the `xxxPG.xml` file. To add components, we right-click objects in the Structure pane and add components via a pop-up menu. We can define the object by specifying the properties of the object via the property inspector. When we modify objects defined for the page, the XML file is automatically updated by JDeveloper. It is not possible to update the XML file from JDeveloper, and although you can edit the file from the file system opened in a text editor, this is definitely not advisable.

When we create a new page, it will be formed of regions. Regions have items (text inputs, buttons, and so on); so, in JDeveloper, we would construct a page by creating a page, adding regions, and then adding items to the regions.

OA Controller (CO)

This is the Controller part of the MVC design pattern. The Controller essentially is the logic of a page and is coded in Java. It has two events. The first event is called the `process request (pr)` event, which controls the logic when a page renders for the first time. The second event is the `process form request (pfr)`, and is an event that is triggered when any interaction occurs on the page, such as a user clicking on a button.

Application module (AM)

This forms a part of the Model of the MVC design pattern. It is an important part of the Model as it is the part which governs the entire session pool, including the state of any transactions. It facilitates activity between the frontend and the database. Each page we create should be attached to an application module.

View object (VO)

This forms a part of the Model of the MVC design pattern. It is a query that is primarily based upon the entity object and returns the data that is displayed to the user through the user interface. View objects can also be linked together via view links.

Entity object (EO)

This forms a part of the Model of the MVC design pattern. It is based upon a database table and encapsulates all of the business rules and logic for that table. It is required on a page whenever the page needs to insert, update, or deleted any data. Entity objects can also be linked together via entity associations.

 The model part of the MVC design pattern in OA Framework is also known as the **Business Components for Java** (BC4J).

File locations

Let's look at where to find standard pages on the application server.

Standard files

If we are looking for standard OA Framework files, we can find them on the application server at the following locations.

UIX and CO

```
$JAVA_TOP/oracle/apps/<ApplicationShortName>/<moduleName>/<subModuleNa
me>/webui
```

VO and AM

```
$JAVA_TOP/oracle/apps/<ApplicationShortName>/<moduleName>/<subModuleNa
me>/server
```

EO

```
$JAVA_TOP/oracle/apps/<ApplicationShortName>/schema/server
```

Custom files

If we are looking for custom pages, we can find them on the application server at the following locations:

UIX and CO

```
$JAVA_TOP/<customFolder>/oracle/apps/<ApplicationShortName>/<moduleName>/
<subModuleName>/webui
```

VO and AM

```
$JAVA_TOP/<customFolder>/oracle/apps/<ApplicationShortName>/<moduleName>/
<subModuleName>/server
```

EO

```
$JAVA_TOP/<customFolder>/oracle/apps/<ApplicationShortName>/schema/server
```

MDS repository

In EBS, we store some of the OAF pages on the file system in the application server, and other components are uploaded into a repository called the **Meta Data Services** (**MDS**). It is a repository of components, such as buttons, fields, or checkboxes that are grouped together when a page is rendered. The relationship between the components and how they are combined is used to define the meaningful structure of a page.

There is a utility to import and export the structure of a page to the MDS, and we never ever directly change the data in the MDS tables (JDR tables).

Bouncing apache

Apache is an HTTP (web) server, which runs on the application server.

On occasions when we make any changes to a page, that is, the Java or XML files, we need to clear the page definition that is cached. We did this in the *Clearing the cache* recipe in the previous chapter, but in certain circumstances, we may need to bounce (stop and start) apache.

Installing the database objects

Create the database objects for this chapter before you start, by using a script provided called `7126_02_01.sh`.

Getting ready

We are going to create a table, view, and synonym for the new block we will create. We will also create a package that will handle all of the database transactions, such as insert, update, and delete. Finally, we will create a sequence that will be used to generate a unique number for new records. The next section provides details of how to run the script.

Create XXHR schema

If you have not done so already, create a new custom schema called XXHR. Please refer to *Chapter 8, Utilities* to create the schema if you have not done so already before running the database installation script given in the next section.

How to do it...

To create the database objects required for this chapter, perform the following tasks:

1. Create a local directory `c:\packt\scripts\ch2`, where the scripts are downloaded and extracted to.

2. Open Putty and connect to the application tier user.

3. Create a new directory on the application tier under `$XXHR_TOP/install`:

```
cd $XXHR_TOP/install
    mkdir ch2
```

> **Downloading the example code**
>
> You can download the example code files for all Packt books you have purchased from your account at `http://www.packtpub.com`. If you purchased this book elsewhere, you can visit `http://www.packtpub.com/support` and register to have the files e-mailed directly to you.

4. Navigate to the new directory:

```
cd ch2
```

5. Open **WinSCP**, and FTP the files from `c:\packt\scripts\ch2` to `$XXHR_TOP/install/ch2` as shown in the following screenshot:

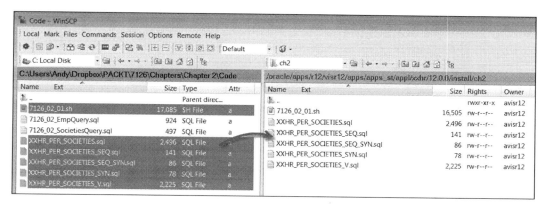

6. In Putty, change the permissions of the script with the following command:

```
chmod 775 7126_02_01.sh
```

7. Run the following script to create all of the objects by issuing the following command:

```
/7126_02_01.sh apps/apps
```

8. The script checks that all of the files are present in your `$XXHR_TOP/install/ch2` directory, and will prompt you to continue if they are all there; so, type `Y` and press **Return**.

9. After the script has completed, check the `XXHR_7126_02_01.log` file for errors. (It will be created in the same directory, `$XXHR_TOP/install/ch2`.)

10. Run the following query to check that all of the objects have been created successfully:

```
SELECT OWNER, OBJECT_NAME, OBJECT_TYPE, STATUS
     FROM ALL_OBJECTS
    WHERE OBJECT_NAME LIKE 'XXHR_PER_SOC%'
ORDER BY 1, 2
```

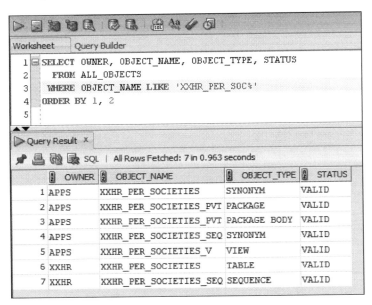

How it works...

We have created a number of objects that we are going to use in the upcoming recipes. The XXHR_PER_SOCIETIES table will store details relating to clubs or societies that the employee belongs to. We have created a **SYNONYM** to the APPS user as all of our objects need to be accessed by the APPS user. The table will store the raw data, and so we have also created a view that has the meanings and descriptions visible to the user as well. The sequence we have created will generate a unique number each time a new record is created.

You may also notice that there is also a ZIP file called oafch2.zip provided in the code bundle. This is a completed version of the examples that we develop throughout this chapter. You will be able to extract files and open them once we have installed JDeveloper in the upcoming recipes.

You will need to follow the first few recipes before you can open this file, as these will show us how to configure our environment.

Setting up our development environment

Now that we understand the basics regarding the architecture of OA Framework, we are going to get started with our development environment. We will be preparing our development environment ready to create our OA Framework pages. We will perform the following tasks to install the correct IDE and connect to an EBS database instance.

Downloading and installing JDeveloper with OA extension

Our first step is to download and install JDeveloper. However, we must ensure that we download the correct version of JDeveloper with OA Extension. To get the correct version, we will first establish the version of **E-Business Suite** (**EBS**) we are on. We will then download JDeveloper from Oracle Support and install it.

How to do it...

To download and install the correct version of JDeveloper, perform the following steps:

1. Obtain the version of EBS you are on. To do this, log on to EBS and click on the **About this Page** link.

 If you remember from the *Setting the personalization profile options* recipe in *Chapter 1, Personalizing OA Framework Pages,* the **About this Page** link is made available by setting the **FND: Diagnostics profile option to** Yes.

2. Click on the **Technology Components** tab and you will see the version of Oracle EBS that you are using, as shown in the following screenshot:

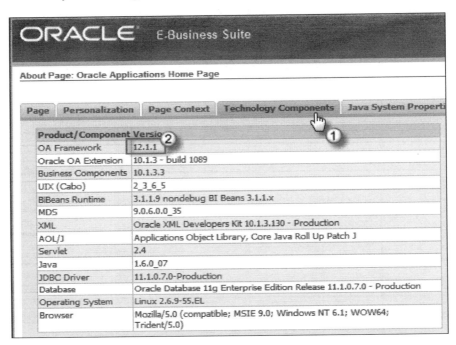

We will now download JDeveloper with OA Extension from Oracle Support.

1. Log in to Oracle Support web portal at https://support.oracle.com.

2. Find the note *How to find the correct version of JDeveloper to use with eBusiness Suite 11i or Release 12.x [ID 416708.1]*. Type 416708.1 in the search box, and click the search icon.

3. Click on the version we require to download as shown in the following screenshot:

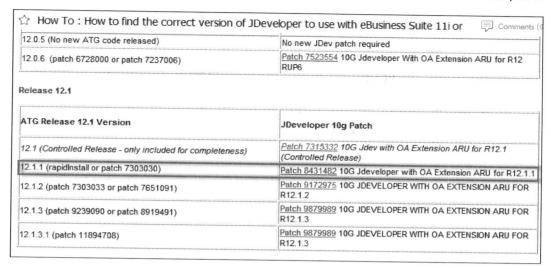

ATG Release 12.1 Version	JDeveloper 10g Patch
12.0.5 (No new ATG code released)	No new JDev patch required
12.0.6 (patch 6728000 or patch 7237006)	Patch 7523554 10G Jdeveloper With OA Extension ARU for R12 RUP6

Release 12.1

ATG Release 12.1 Version	JDeveloper 10g Patch
12.1 (Controlled Release - only included for completeness)	Patch 7315332 10G Jdev with OA Extension ARU for R12.1 (Controlled Release)
12.1.1 (rapidinstall or patch 7303030)	Patch 8431482 10G Jdeveloper with OA Extension ARU for R12.1.1
12.1.2 (patch 7303033 or patch 7651091)	Patch 9172975 10G JDEVELOPER WITH OA EXTENSION ARU FOR R12.1.2
12.1.3 (patch 9239090 or patch 8919491)	Patch 9879989 10G JDEVELOPER WITH OA EXTENSION ARU FOR R12.1.3
12.1.3.1 (patch 11894708)	Patch 9879989 10G JDEVELOPER WITH OA EXTENSION ARU FOR R12.1.3

4. Click on the **Download** button to download the correct version to your PC.

5. Unzip the file into a local directory called `C:\oaf`.

How it works...

We have now downloaded and installed JDeveloper. There is no setup as such with JDeveloper, as we just need to unzip the contents of the downloaded zip file to a directory. In this case, we extracted the files to `C:\oaf`; so, bear this in mind throughout the chapter, especially if you decided to unzip JDeveloper to a different directory. If you have decided to do this, ensure that the zip file is unzipped to a directory path *without* spaces in it.

You will notice that JDeveloper has created the following three directories under the `C:\oaf` directory (or the directory you chose to unzip it in):

`jdevhome`—All pages and code we develop. Also, contains the `.dbc` file to connect to the database instances.

`jdevbin`—All Jars, executables for `Jdev` and `FND` classes.

`jdevdoc`—Contains all of the Oracle OAF tutorials, the Developer Guide (HTML), and an explanation of all the classes, methods, and parameters.

Setting the environment variables

The following environment variables should be set for JDeveloper. `JDEV_USER_HOME` is mandatory and needs to be set before launching JDeveloper.

- `JDEV_USER_HOME` points to the directory which contains my projects.
- `JDEV_JAVA_HOME` points to the Java SDK that is required for development. It is not usually required to set this variable.

How to do it...

To set the `JDEV_USER_HOME` environment variables, perform the following:

On Windows:

1. Right-click on **My Computer** or **Computer**, and select **Properties** from the menu.
2. Click on **Advanced System Settings** to open the **System Properties** window.
3. Click on the **Advanced** tab.
4. Click on the **Environment Variables** button.
5. Select the **New** button for user variables.
6. In the **Variable name** field, enter `JDEV_USER_HOME`.
7. In the **Variable value** field, enter the directory of the `jdevhome\jdev` directory, for example, `C:\oaf\jdevhome\jdev` as shown in the following screenshot:

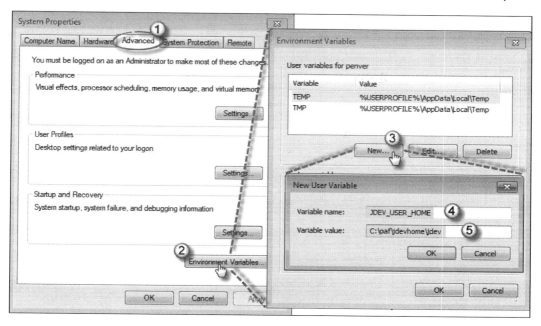

8. Click on the **OK** button.

On Unix, at the command prompt, run the following command:

```
export JDEV_USER_HOME = /oaf/jdevhome/jdev
```

How it works...

We have now set the environment variable required to run JDeveloper. This is so that JDeveloper knows which directory structure to look for and which version of the Java SDK to use. There may well be multiple installations of the Java SDK installed on a computer, which is why we need to define the JDEV_USER_HOME variable.

Transferring the DBC file from the application server

We will now transfer the database connection file (DBC) from the application server of our EBS environment. We will transfer this to our local directory so that we can create database connections for JDeveloper so that we can run our OAF pages locally during development.

How to do it...

To transfer the .dbc file, perform the following tasks:

1. Open **WinSCP** and connect to the application server.

2. FTP the .dbc file to your local PC from the **$INST_TOP/appl/fnd/12.0.0.0/secure** directory on the application server to the **jdevhome\jdev\dbc_files\secure** directory as shown in the following screenshot:

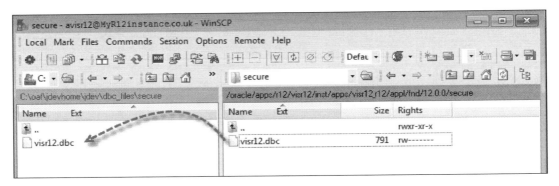

How it works...

We have now transferred the .dbc file that we need to create a database connection to our EBS R12 environment. The file contains the server and port details, and we will reference this file when we open up JDeveloper and create our database connection. We can put multiple .dbc files here if we want to connect to multiple instances on EBS, but the file must be obtained from the application server for each environment we need a connection for.

Creating a shortcut to JDeveloper

We are now going to create a shortcut to the JDeveloper executable and put it on our desktop. For the purposes of the book, it is assumed that we are developing using a Windows operating system and therefore, we will create a shortcut to `jdevw.exe`, as this is the executable we use on Windows. On other operating systems, we would use the `jdev.exe` executable.

How to do it...

To create a shortcut to JDeveloper, perform the following:

1. Navigate to the directory, `C:\oaf\jdevbin\jdev\bin`.
2. Right-click on the `jdevw.exe` and select **Send To | Desktop** (create shortcut).
3. Rename the shortcut on the desktop if desired, for example, `Jdev R12`.

How it works...

We have now created a shortcut to the Windows version of JDeveloper on our desktops. If you are using a Linux-based operating system, you will need to launch the `jdev.exe` instead.

Creating an EBS user and assigning responsibilities

We are now going to log in to EBS and create a user we will be using to develop our OA Framework pages. We will also assign responsibilities to the user so that we can test our connections and access the Oracle tutorials if required.

How to do it...

To create the user, perform the following:

1. Log in to EBS with the `SYSADMIN` user (or a user that has access to the System Administrator responsibility).
2. Select the **System Administrator** responsibility.
3. Navigate to **Security | User | Define**.
4. Enter `OAF_USER` in the **User Name** field.
5. Enter a password `oracle01` in the password field and press the **TAB** key.
6. Enter the password again and press the **TAB** key.

7. Set the **Password Expiration** to **None**.

8. Navigate to the **Direct Responsibilities** tab.

9. Add the following responsibilities:

   ❑ Framework ToolBox Tutorial

   ❑ Framework ToolBox Menu Lab (1)

   ❑ Framework ToolBox Tutorial Labs

   ❑ Framework ToolBox Tutorial Labs (New)

   ❑ OA Framework ToolBox Tutorial

   ❑ OA Framework ToolBox Tutorial Labs

The user's screen should now look similar to the following screenshot:

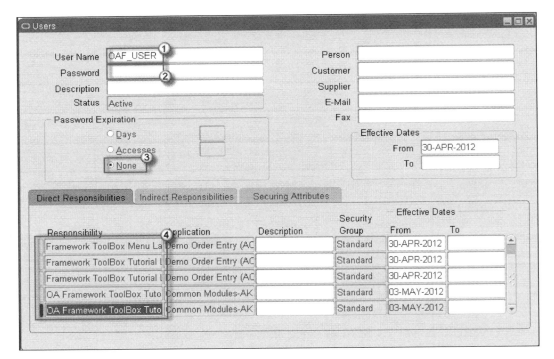

10. Log out of Oracle EBS.

11. Log back in with the OAF_USER user.

12. When logging in to EBS with the OAF_USER, change the password to welcome1 when prompted.

How it works...

We have now created a new user that has access to the toolbox responsibilities for OA Framework tutorials. We will use this to test our connection when we configure JDeveloper for the first time.

Adding database connections in JDeveloper

We are now going to create a database connection to our EBS environment. We always connect using the apps user, so you will need the <apps password> to complete this task.

How to do it...

To add a database connection, perform the following steps:

1. Start **JDeveloper**.
2. Click on the **Connections** tab in **Applications Navigator**.
3. Right-click on the **Database** node, and select **New Database Connection**.

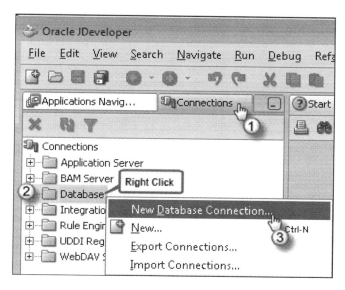

The new database connection wizard will now be displayed.

4. Click on **Next** on the welcome page (and check **Skip this Page Next Time** if desired).

5. In the **Connection Name** field, type `VISR12` (this is just a name for the connection and can be anything relevant), and click on **Next**.

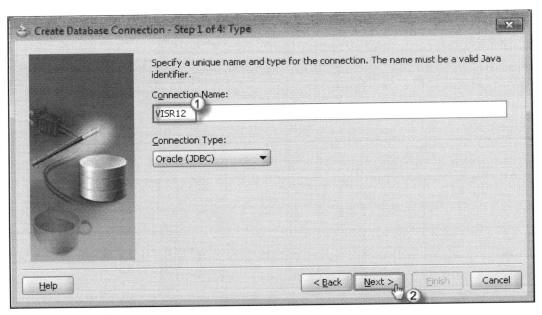

6. When prompted, enter `apps` in the *username* field and the **<apps password>** in the *password* field, that is, `apps/apps` and click on **Next**.

7. Enter the following **connection** details:

> If you are unsure of the connection details for your environment, you can get the details from the `.dbc` file we transferred earlier. Navigate to your `C:\oaf\jdevhome\jdev\dbc_files\secure` directory and open the `.dbc` file in a text editor. The host will be the value after the DB_HOST entry, and the port will be the port defined for the DB_PORT entry.

The following screenshot shows the details of the environment I am using. The host name, port, and SID will be different for the environment you are using.

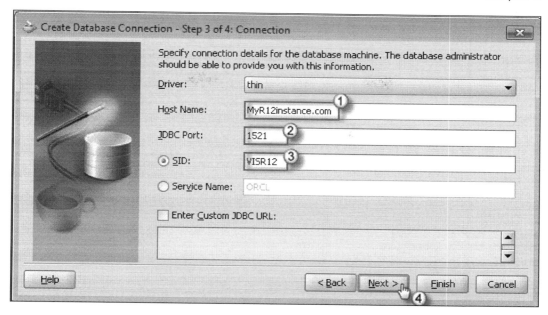

8. Click on the **Next** button.

9. Click the **Test Connection** button and then **Finish** as shown in the following screenshot:

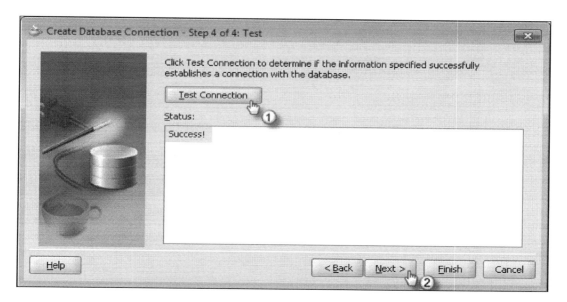

How it works...

We have now created and tested a database connection in JDeveloper. When we get the **Success!** message when testing the connection, we know we have connected successfully to the database of our EBS environment.

Setting the OC4J settings and project properties

OC4J stands for **Oracle AS Containers for Java EE**. It is essentially a lighter version of the Oracle Application Server, and it allows us to run our OAF pages locally on our PC. We will now configure our OC4J settings and set the runtime properties of each of our tutorial projects.

How to do it...

To test our configuration, perform the following:

1. Open **JDeveloper**.
2. Check the OC4J Settings in **Tools | Embedded OC4J Preferences | Global | Startup**.
3. Check if the **Host Name or IP Address Used to Refer to Embedded OC4J** is set to **Default Local IP Address,** as shown in the following screenshot:

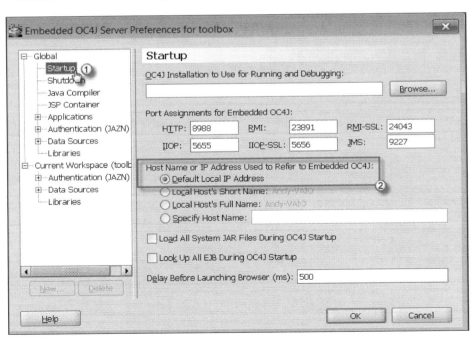

4. Click on **File | Open** from the menu.

5. Open the **toolbox** workspace from `<JDEV_Install>\jdevhome\jdev\myprojects\toolbox.jws`.

6. Set the following project settings for each of the tutorials:

   - ExtendedLabSources
   - LabSolutions
   - SampleLibrary
   - Tutorial

To set the `Tutorial` runtime properties first, perform the following steps:

1. Right-click on **Applications | toolbox | Tutorial**.

2. Click on **Project Properties** from the pop-up menu.

3. Navigate to **Oracle Applications | Runtime Connection.**

4. Set the following fields:

   - **DBC File Name:** `C:\oaf\jdevhome\jdev\dbc_files\secure\VISR12.dbc`
   - **User Name:** OAF_USER
   - **Password:** welcome1

 The **Password** field is the EBS password for the OAF_USER user we have created. If you have set the password to something other than welcome1, set the password value to your password.

   - **Application Short Name**: ICX
   - **Responsibility Key:** FWK_TBX_TUTORIAL

The screen should now look similar to the following screenshot:

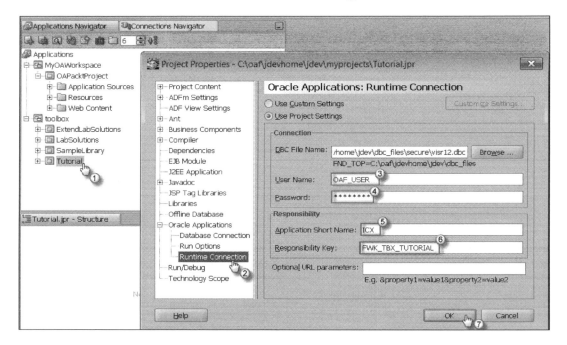

5. Click on **OK**.

6. Repeat steps 7-10 for the **ExetendedLabSources**, **LabSolutions**, and **SampleLibrary** sample projects.

> You may need to check if the **Application Short Name** and **Responsibility Key** are valid combinations. The **LabSolutions** project in the environment I am using has a **Responsibility Key** of FWK_TOOLBOX_TUTORIAL_LABS, which has an **Application Short Name** of DEM.

How it works...

We have now set the runtime properties of the **Tutorial** project. We can check the **Application Short Name** and **Responsibility Key** are valid by looking them up in EBS. To do this, log on and connect to the System Administrator responsibility.

1. Log in to Oracle with the **System Administrator** responsibility.

2. Navigate to **Security | Responsibility | Define**, and the **Responsibilities** window will open.

3. Query back the FWK_TBX_TUTORIAL responsibility key, as shown in the following screenshot:

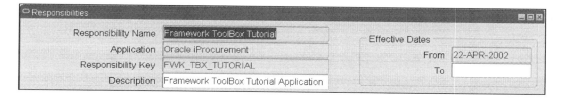

We can see that the Application used with this responsibility is **Oracle iProcurement**. To find **Application Short Name** of **Oracle iProcurement**, perform the following steps:

4. Navigate to **Application | Register**, and the **Applications** window will open.

5. Query back the Oracle iProcurement application as shown in the following screenshot and we can see the **Application Short Name** is **ICX**:

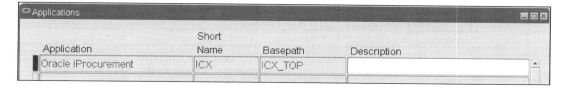

Running a page

We will now test that we can run a tutorial OA Framework page from within JDeveloper.

How to do it...

To run the tutorial web page, perform the following steps:

1. Right-click on `test_fwkturial.jsp` in **Applications | toolbox | Tutorial | Web Content**, and select **Run** from the pop-up menu.

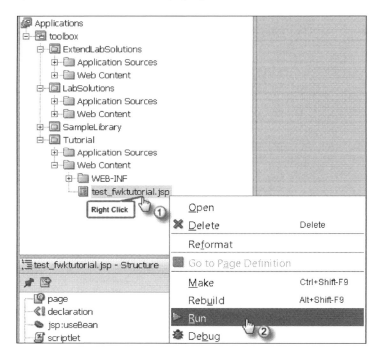

The following `.jsp` page will open. This checks that the OC4J server is running. To check, we can run an OA Framework page click on the **Hello, World!**.

The following tutorial of **Hello, World!** page will open:

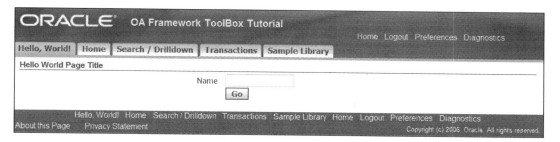

How it works...

We have now tested that the OC4J server runs locally on our machine and that we can run an OA Framework page. Therefore, we have tested our connectivity and can now get down to developing our own OA Framework page.

There can be problems connecting to an EBS environment through a VPN connection and running an OC4J server locally. You may well get a connection refused error message when attempting to run the test page. Ensure that the OC4J Settings in **Tools | Embedded OC4J Preferences | Global | Startup** and the **Host Name or IP Address Used to Refer to Embedded OC4J** are set to **Default Local IP Address** as we did earlier. If the problem persists, please refer to Oracle Support as there are solutions to various problems posted on the forums.

Creating a new project

Okay, now that we have set up our development environment, we are ready to create our first project. We will perform the following tasks to create a project and set up our runtime parameters for the project:

- ▸ Creating a new workspace and project
- ▸ Setting the project runtime parameters

Creating a new workspace and project

We are now ready to get started. We first of all need to create a new workspace and project.

How to do it...

To create a new workspace, proceed with the following steps:

1. In JDeveloper, in the **Applications Navigator** tab, right-click on **Applications** and select **New OA Workspace** from the pop-up menu.

2. In the **New Oracle Applications Workspace** window, enter the following details:

   ❑ **File Name:** MyOAWorkspace.jws

   ❑ **Directory Name:** C\:oaf\jdevhome\jdev\myprojects

3. Check the **Add a New OA Project** checkbox.

4. Click on **OK**.

   A summary of the steps is shown in the following screenshot:

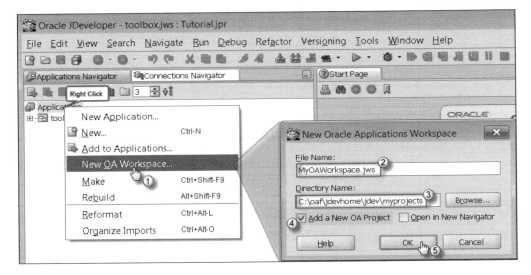

   The new project wizard will now open when **OK** is clicked.

5. When the **Oracle Applications Project Wizard** welcome page opens, click on **Next**. (Check the **Skip this Page Next Time** checkbox so that the welcome page does not appear each time the wizard is invoked).

6. In **Step 1 of 3**, complete the following details:

   ❑ **Project Name:** OAPacktProject

   ❑ **Directory Name:** C:\oaf\jdevhome\myprojects

   ❑ **Default Package:** oracle.apps.xxhr.emp

   The displayed page will look like the following screenshot:

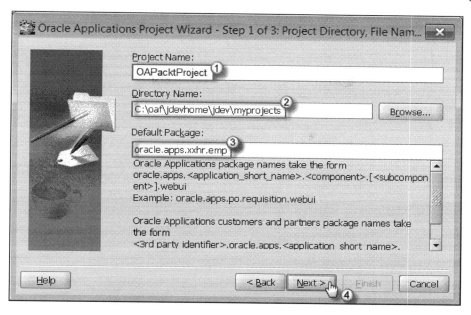

7. Click on the **Next** button.

8. In **Step 2 of 3**, click on the **Next** button.

9. In **Step 3 of 3**, complete the details as follows:

   ☐ **DBC File Name:** C:\oaf\jdevhome\jdev\dbc_files\secure\
   visr12.dbc

> The .dbc file may have a different name for your environment.2 lines.

   ☐ **User Name:** OAF_USER
   ☐ **Password:** welcome1

> This is the OAF_USER password, if it has been changed from
> welcome1.

   ☐ **Application Short Name:** ICX
   ☐ **Responsibility Key:** FWK_TBX_TUTORIAL

10. Click on **Next**.

11. Click on **Finish** to complete the wizard.

12. Click on the **Save All** button from the toolbar.

How it works...

We have now set up our new workspace and project for development of our OA Framework pages. The purpose of a workspace and project is to define the container and parameters for the project where we will create our OAF page.

Setting the project runtime parameters

We are now going to set the project runtime parameters.

How to do it...

To set the runtime parameters, perform the following steps:

1. Double-click the OAPacktProject.jpr to open up the project properties.
2. Navigate to **Oracle Applications | Run Options**.
3. Shift **OA Diagnostics** to the **Selected Options** side.
4. Click on **OK**.
5. Click on the **Save All** button from the toolbar.

How it works...

We have now configured the parameters that JDeveloper uses for our project when we run a page.

Creating the model layer for a query page

In the next couple of recipes, we will be creating a search screen. The search screen will be based upon a view, but we will not create an entity object. If we are not performing database transactions, we do not need to create an entity object, although we will do that later in the chapter. We will be creating our application module to search for employees. Therefore, we need to create an application module and view object, and link them together. We will then test that we can return records from EBS using the Oracle Business Component Browser. We will test the configuration before we start creating the user interface in the next recipe. It is really important for us to check that we have successfully set up our application module before we go on to create the user interface. To do this, we will perform the following tasks:

► Creating the application module (AM)

► Creating a view object (VO)

► Linking the view object to the application module (VO to AM)

► Testing the application module (AM)

Creating the application module (AM)

We are now going to create the application module for the employee search. The application module will be based upon a view (via a view object) that we created in the script we ran at the beginning of the chapter.

How to do it...

To create the application module, perform the following steps:

1. Right-click the **OAPacktProject** project in the navigator and select **New** from the pop-up menu.
2. Navigate to **Business Tier | ADF Components** and select **Application Module**.
3. Click on **OK**.

   The steps are summarized in the following screenshot:

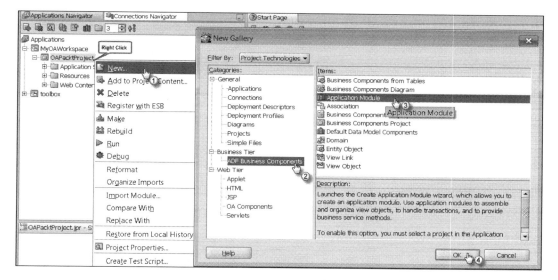

4. When the **Create Application Module** welcome page opens, click on **Next**. (Check the **Skip this Page Next Time** checkbox so that the welcome page does not appear each time the wizard is invoked).
5. In **Step 1 of 4**, enter the following details:
   - **Package:** oracle.apps.xxhr.emp.server
   - **Name:** EmpSearchAM
6. In **Step 2 of 4**, click on **Next**.

7. In **Step 3 of 4**, click **Next**.

8. In **Step 4 of 4**, check the **Generate Java File(s)** checkbox in **Application Module Class: EmpSearchAMImpl** to generate the `EmpSearchAMImpl` java class. (It is already checked by default.)

9. In the **Finish** window, select the **Finish** button.

10. Click on the **Save All** button from the toolbar.

In the navigator, expand the **Application Sources** node and we can see our package. However, we can only see part of the package, that is, `oracle.apps.xxhr`. To see the full package, click the level buttons to show six levels as shown in the following screenshot:

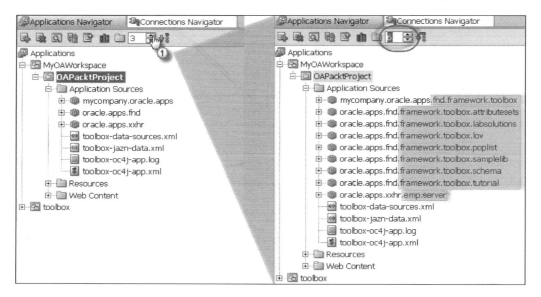

How it works...

We have now created the application module as shown in the following screenshot:

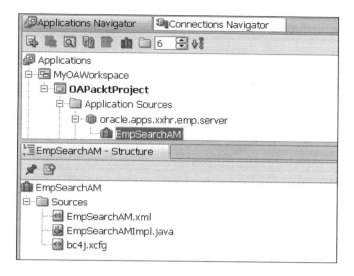

If we click on **EmpSearchAM**, we can see in the **Structure** pane for the **EmpSearchAM** application module, that there have been three files created by the wizard associated with the application module.

Creating a view object (VO)

We are now going to create the view object for our page. The view object will use the view that we created at the beginning of the recipe called XXHR_EMP_SEARCH_VL.

How to do it...

To create the view object, perform the following steps:

1. Right-click the OAPacktProject.jpr and select **New** from the pop-up menu.
2. Navigate to **Business Tier | ADF Business Components** and select **View Object**.
3. Click on **OK**.

> Dismiss the **Create View Object** welcome page, if it appears, by clicking on **Next**. (Check the **Skip this Page Next Time** checkbox so that the welcome page does not appear each time the wizard is invoked.)

4. In **Step 1 of 7**, enter the following details:
   - **Package:** oracle.apps.xxhr.emp.server
   - **Name:** EmpSearchVO

The package is the same as the one where the **EmpSearchAM** application module resides and the VO name is exactly the same as the AM, but with VO at the end. This conforms to the naming conventions we need to use in OA Framework.

5. Select the **Rows Populated by a SQL Query, with:** radio button and select the **Read-only Access** radio button as shown in the following screenshot:

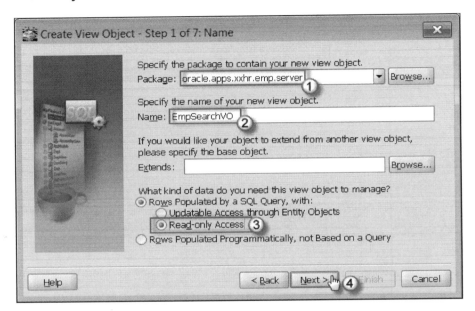

We can select the **Read-only Access** radio group, as we are not going to be performing any database transactions on this page because it is a query page.

6. Click **Next**.

7. In **Step 2 of 7**, enter the following query in the **Query Statement** field:

```
select * from XXHR_EMP_SEARCH_VL
```

8. Click the **Test** button to test the query (click on **OK** when prompted for the username and password *apps/<apps>*).

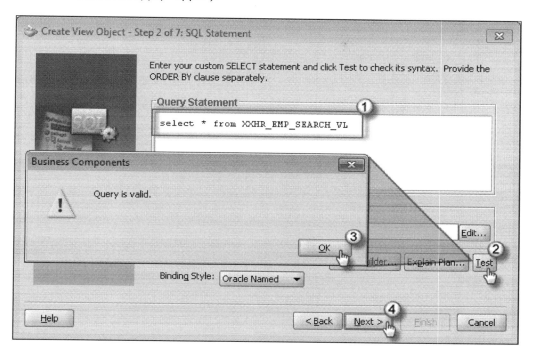

9. Click on **OK** when the **Query is valid** message is displayed.
10. Click on **Next**.

 We will not always need to do anything in some of the pages the wizard presents to us. This is why we will skip through the next few pages.

11. In **Step 3 of 7**, click on **Next**.
12. In **Step 4 of 7**, click on **Next**.
13. In **Step 5 of 7**, click on **Next**.

14. In **Step 6 of 7**, select the **Never** radio button in **Updatable** as shown in the following screenshot, and then click **Next**:

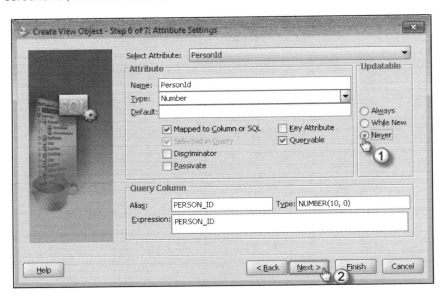

15. In **Step 7 of 7**, uncheck the **Generate Java File** checkbox in **View Object Class: EmpSearchVOImpl**.

16. Check the checkbox **View Row Class: EmpSearchVORowImpl** for both the **Generate Java File** and **Accessors** checkboxes, as shown in the following screenshot:

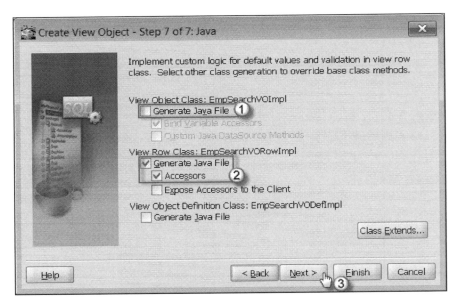

17. After completing **Step 7 of 7**, click on **Next**.

18. In the summary page, click on **Finish**.

19. Click the **Save All** button from the toolbar.

How it works...

Our view object called **EmpSearchVO** will now appear in the **Application Navigator,** as shown in the following screenshot:

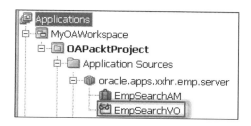

Linking the view object to the application module (VO to AM)

We are now going to link the view object to the application module. When we do this there is an instance of the view object created and it is this instance of the view object that gets linked to the application module.

How to do it...

To link the view object to the application module, perform the following steps:

1. In the **Application Navigator** tab, double-click the **EmpSearchAM** application module in the **OAPacktProject | Application Sources | oracle.apps.xxhr.emp. server** package.

2. In the **Application Module Editor** select the **Data Model** node.

3. Expand the **oracle.apps.xxhr.emp.server** package, and click on the **EmpSearchVO** view object.

4. Shift the **EmpSearchVO** from **Available View Objects:** to **Data Model:** by clicking on the **>** button as shown in the following screenshot:

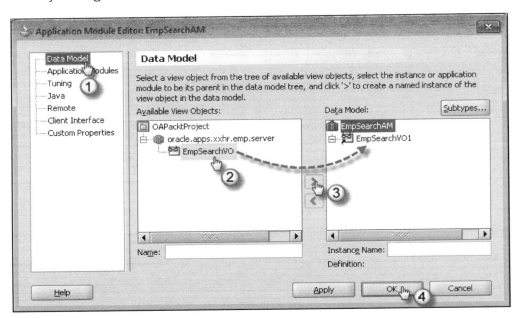

 We can see that the instance of the view object linked to the application module is called **EmpSearchVO1**.

5. Click on **OK**.

6. Click the **Save All** button from the toolbar.

How it works...

We have now linked the **EmpSearchAM application module with the EmpSearchVO** *view object. The name given to the instance of the view object is* **EmpSearchVO1**. This is provided when we shift the view object over to the application module.

Testing the application module (AM)

Now we can test how the application module brings back data from the view object.

How to do it...

We will test that the view object has been linked to the application module successfully.

1. Open SQL*Plus or SQL Developer, and log on with the `apps` user.

2. Check that the query used in the view object brings back data by typing the following SQL query:

   ```
   SELECT * FROM xxhr_emp_search_vl
   ```

 Queries may behave differently when run in SQL*Plus from how they behave in EBS. In many real world examples, it is advisable to set up your context by initializing the session by calling the `fnd_global.apps_initialize` package before testing the query.

3. In JDeveloper, right-click the **EmpSearchAM** application module.

4. Select **Test** from the pop-up menu.

5. Click on the **Connect** button when the following **Oracle Business Component Browser - Connect** window appears:

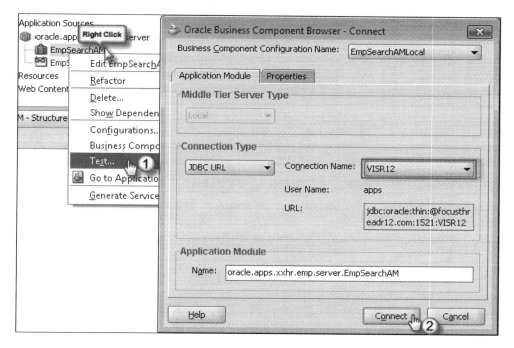

 The Oracle Business Component Browser allows us to check the application module and view object have been linked correctly. We will use this, as we have not yet created a user interface and, it is important to test if our link is working correctly before we go on to create our UIX components.

6. After a short while, the **Oracle Business Component Browser (Local)** window will appear.

7. Double-click on the **EmpSearchVO1** node and the browser will bring back data from the view object as shown in the following screenshot:

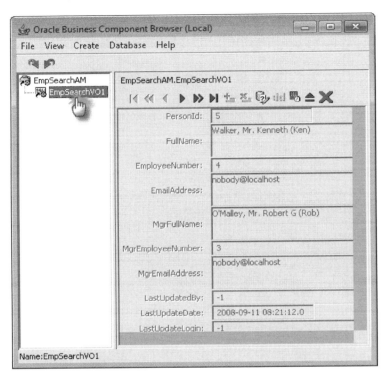

How it works...

We have tested that we have linked the application module with the view object. This is an important step, because if no data is returned at this stage, it would be pointless going on to build the user interface as it will not bring back any data either.

Creating the view layer for a query page

Now that we have created our application module and successfully tested it, we will go on to create our user interface. We will create a page that allows us to query data based upon the attributes in our application module. The page we create will look as follows at the end of this recipe:

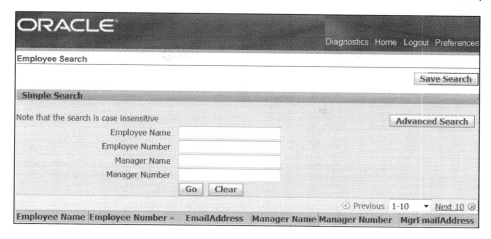

To achieve this we will perform the following tasks:

- ▸ Adding a page (PG)
- ▸ Adding a query region (RG)
- ▸ Adding a results region (RG)
- ▸ Setting attribute properties
- ▸ Testing the page

Adding a page (PG)

We need to create the page first before we can add any regions. A default OA Framework page will already have the corporate branding. We will create a page with just the corporate branding and a line of text to test the page.

How to do it...

To create a page object, perform the following steps:

1. In the **Application Navigator** tab, right-click on **OAPacktProject**.
2. Select **New** from the pop-up menu.

3. In the **New Gallery** window, navigate to **Web Tier | OA Components** and select **Page** from the **Items:** list as shown in the following screenshot:

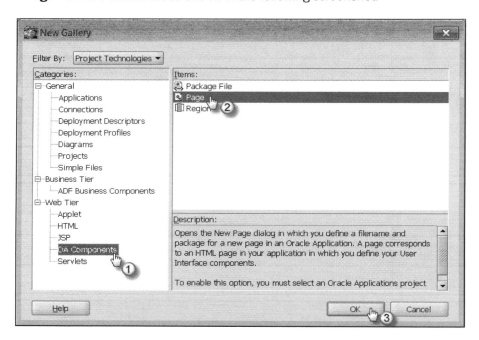

4. In the **New Page** window, set the following page details:

   ❑ **Name:** EmpSearchPG

   ❑ **Package:** oracle.apps.xxhr.emp.webui

5. Click on the **OK** button.

How it works...

We have now created a page called EmpSearchPG.xml. This is the page definition file and cannot be edited in JDeveloper. There are no drag-and-drop features in OA Framework pages, so we add pages by adding regions and items through the **Structure** pane.

Renaming the default region (PG)

The page has been created and there will be a default region called **region1**. We are going to rename the region and set some properties to link the page to our application module and name the window titles.

How to do it...

To set the page properties, perform the following operations:

1. In the **Application Navigator** tab, click on the **EmpSearchPG.xml** page.

 The items visible in the **Structure** pane are dependent upon the object selected in the **Application Navigator** tab. So, if the items in the **Structure** pane change, just click back on the **EmpSearchPG.xml** page in the **Application Navigator** tab.

2. In the **Structure** pane, click on the item **EmpSearchPG | region1** node.
3. Now in the **Property Inspector**, set the following properties:
    - **ID**: PageLayoutRN
    - **AM Definition**: oracle.apps.xxhr.emp.server.EmpSearchAM
    - **Window Title**: Employee Search Window
    - **Title**: Employee Search

A summary of the steps is displayed in the following screenshot:

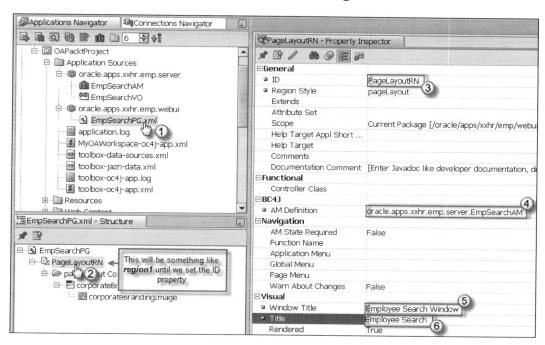

4. Click on the **Save All** button from the toolbar.

How it works...

We have now set the properties of our top most region and linked the application module to the page. We can now run the page to test what we have done so far.

1. In the **Application Navigator** tab, right click the **EmpSearchPG.xml** page and select **Run** from the pop-up menu.

The following page will appear with an empty **Employee Search** region, as we have not added any items to the page just yet. You can see that the page automatically inherits the Oracle EBS branding, look, and feel of other OA Framework pages.

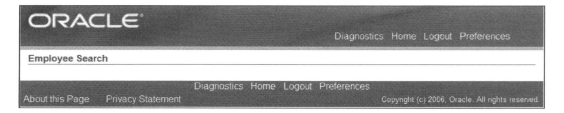

Adding a query region (RG)

We are now going to create a new region, which is a container for our search region.

How to do it...

To create a search region, perform the following steps:

1. Click the **EmpSearchPG.xml** in the **Applications Manager** and the page components will appear in the **Structure** pane.

2. In the **Structure** pane, right-click **PageLayoutRN** and select **New | Region** from the pop-up menu.

3. In the **Property Inspector**, set the following properties:

   - **ID**: EmpQueryRN
   - **Region Style**: query
   - **Construction Mode**: resultsBasedSearch
   - **Include Simple Panel**: True
   - **Include Views Panel**: True
   - **Include Advanced Panel**: True

4. Click on the **Save All** button from the toolbar.

If you click on a property in the **Property Inspector**, a description of the property is displayed in a pane at the bottom of the **Property Inspector** as shown in the following screenshot:

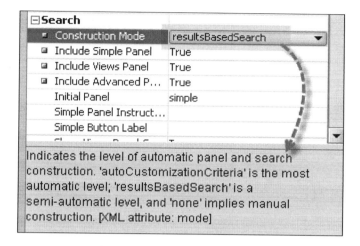

How it works...

We have now created a region that is a container for our search parameters.

Adding a results region (RG) using a wizard

We are now going to create a results region and then add items to our region, which will display the results of a search.

How to do it...

To create a results region, perform the following steps:

1. Right-click on **EmpQueryRN** in the **Structure** pane, and select **New | Region Using Wizard** from the pop-up menu.

2. In **Step 1 of 4**, select the **oracle.apps.xxhr.emp.server.EmpSearchAM** application module from the drop-down list.

3. Click on **EmpSearchVO1** from the **Available View Usages** pane, and click on **Next**.

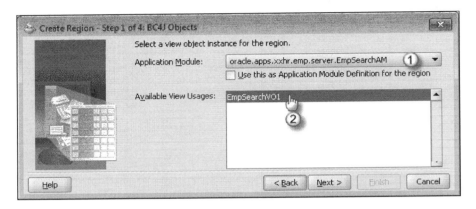

4. In **Step 2 of 4**, set the following values:

   ❑ **Region ID**: EmpResultsRN

   ❑ **Region Style**: table

5. In **Step 3 of 4**, shift the following attributes from the **Available View Attributes** to the **Selected View Attributes** pane by clicking on the **>** button:

   ❑ FullName

   ❑ EmployeeNumber

   ❑ MgrFullName

   ❑ MgrEmployeeNumber

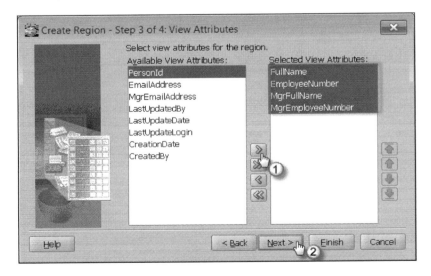

6. In **Step 4 of 4**, set the following values:

ID	Prompt	Style	Datatype
FullName	Employee Name	messageStyledText	VARCHAR2
EmployeeNumber	Employee Number	messageStyledText	VARCHAR2
MgrFullName	Manager Name	messageStyledText	VARCHAR2
MgrEmployeeNumber	Manager Number	messageStyledText	VARCHAR2

7. Click on **Next** and then **Finish**.

8. In the **Structure** pane, click on the **EmpResultsRN** and set the following properties in the **Property Inspector**:

    - **Width**: 100%
    - **User Personalization**: True
    - **Additional Text**: Employee Search Results

Let's suppose we forgot to add the e-mail address field when we created the region using the wizard. We are now going to add the e-mail address fields to the region as we forgot to put them in when we created the region with the wizard. We are just going to edit the region and add the two e-mail addresses we forgot about the first time.

1. In the **Structure** pane, right-click the **EmpResultsRN** and select **Edit Region** from the pop-up menu.

2. Click on the **View Attributes** tab and shift the **EmailAddress** and **MgrEmail Address** fields over to the **Selected View Attributes** pane as shown in the following screenshot:

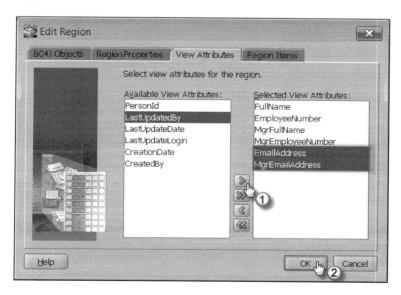

3. Set the properties of the two items as follows:

ID	Prompt	Style	Datatype
EmailAddress	Employee Email	messageStyledText	VARCHAR2
MgrEmailAddress	Manager Email	messageStyledText	VARCHAR2

4. Click on the **OK** button.

We can reorder the items in the region by clicking and dragging them in the **Structure** pane as shown in the following screenshot:

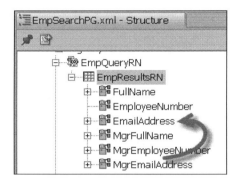

How it works...

We have now added the items that we want to display in the results region of our search page.

Setting item properties

We will now set the properties of some of the items in our query region as query items by setting their item properties. We will also set other properties, which allow sorting and set the initial sort sequence.

How to do it...

To set the properties of the items in our region, perform the following steps:

1. In the **Structure** pane, click on the **FullName** attribute and set the following properties:

    ❑ **Search Allowed**: True

    ❑ **Sort Allowed**: yes

2. In the **Structure** pane, click on the **EmployeeNumber** attribute and set the following properties:

- ❏ **Search Allowed**: True
- ❏ **Sort Allowed**: yes
- ❏ **Initial Sort Sequence**: first

3. In the **Structure** pane, click on the **MgrFullName** attribute and set the following properties:

- ❏ **Search Allowed**: True
- ❏ **Sort Allowed**: yes

4. In the **Structure** pane, click on the **MgrEmployeeNumber** attribute and set the following properties:

- ❏ **Search Allowed**: True
- ❏ **Sort Allowed**: yes

5. Click the **Save All** button from the toolbar.

How it works...

We have now set the properties of the items we are displaying on our page. The **Search Allowed** property is set to True to allow the item to be used in the search criteria.

Testing the page

We are now going to run the page to test the changes we have made.

How to do it...

To test the page, perform the following steps:

1. Right-click on the EmpSearchPG.xml page and select **Run** from the pop-up menu.

2. Enter some search criteria in the **Simple Search** parameters region, and click on the **Go** button as shown in the following screenshot:

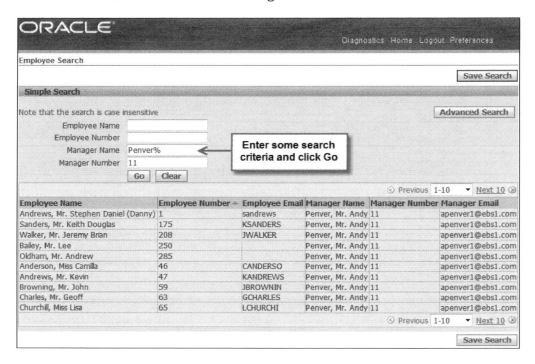

How it works...

We have now created a simple query screen. We have created a screen without having to write any java code (or controller). The page is based upon a view object that is based upon a query and not from an entity object, as we will not need to perform any database transactions; so we don't need an entity object.

3

Creating a Master Detail Page in OA Framework

In this chapter, we will cover the following recipes:

- ▶ Creating the model layer for a master detail page
- ▶ Creating a master region
- ▶ Creating a detail region
- ▶ Deploying a page to EBS

Introduction

In this chapter, we will be creating a master detail page in OA Framework. We will expand on what we have already learnt in the previous chapter.

At the end of the chapter, readers will have an understanding of how we can create master detail pages in OA framework. Readers will understand how we can create view objects and link them together. We will be creating a page that is based upon an entity object, as in the next chapter we will be performing database transactions. Finally, at the end of the chapter, we will go through the process of deploying our page in Oracle E-Business Suite (EBS) and running it through the application.

In the code bundle, there is also a zip file called `oafch3.zip` provided. This is a complete version of the examples that we develop throughout this chapter.

To open the contents of the examples for this chapter, unzip the `oafch2.zip` file to the directory `C:\oaf\jdevhome\jdev\myprojects\`.

Now in JDeveloper, open the `C:\oaf\jdevhome\jdev\myprojects\OAPacktWorkspace.jws` file, and the completed contents of this chapter will be loaded into JDeveloper for you to reference.

Creating the model layer for a master detail page

We are now going to create a new page that uses an entity object (EO). We need to define an entity object, if we intend our page to perform database transactions, such as inserts, updates, and deletes. In the scenario where we are going to implement only for the purposes of this book, we are going to demonstrate building a page that performs database transactions and later show how to develop more advanced features using OA Framework. What we are going to do is create a page that will display societies or clubs that an employee belongs to that are either internally run by our organization or externally run. We will also link up with the query page we have already created in the later recipes.

In this section, we will cover the following tasks

- Creating the entity object (EO)
- Creating the application module (AM)
- Creating the view object (VO)
- Editing the view object (VO)
- Linking the view object (VO) to application module (AM)
- Testing the application module (AM)
- Creating the view link (VL)
- Adding the view link (VL) to the application module (AM)
- Testing the application module (AM)

Creating the entity object (EO)

We are now going to create the entity object. The entity object will represent the database table for the page we are going to create.

How to do it...

To create the entity object, perform the following:

1. Right-click on the **OAPacktProject** project in the navigator and select **New** from the pop-up menu.

2. Navigate to **Business Tier | ADF Business Components** and select **Entity Object,** as shown in the following screenshot:

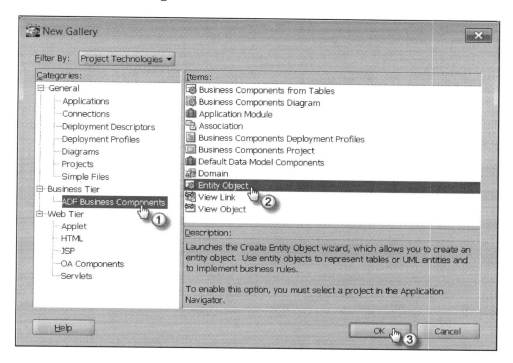

3. Click on **OK**.

   The **Create Entity Wizard** will appear. Click on **Next** on the welcome page if it appears.

4. In **Step 1 of 5**, enter the following details:

   - **Name:** EmpSocietiesEO
   - **Package:** oracle.apps.xxhr.emp.schema.server
   - **Schema Object:** XXHR.XXHR_PER_SOCIETIES
   - **Database Schema:** XXHR

The entry for the package field will need to be typed in manually as the directory does not exist in our local PC as yet. JDeveloper will automatically generate the directory structure for us in our should be project's directory (C:\oaf\jdevhome\jdev\myprojects).

The following is a summary of the screen:

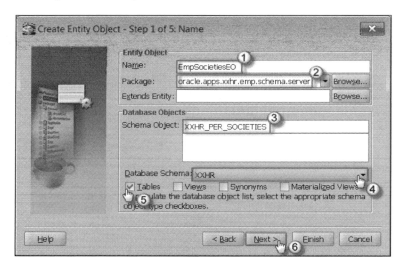

5. Click on **Next**.

6. In **Step 2 of 5**, click on **Next**.

> If there are no attributes displayed in the **Entity Attributes** pane, click the **New from Table** button.

7. Shift all of the attributes by clicking on the **>>** button from the **Available:** pane to the **Selected:** pane, and click on **OK** as shown in the following screenshot:

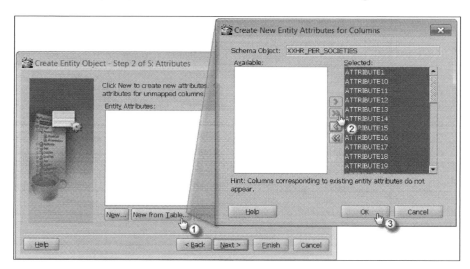

8. In **Step 3 of 5**, check the **Primary Key**, and **Update** and **Insert** checkboxes in **Refresh** as shown in the following screenshot. Then click on **Next**.

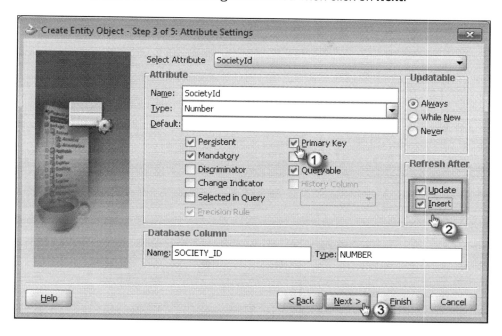

9. In **Step 4 of 5**, for the **Entity Object Class: EmpSocietiesEOImpl** class, check the following boxes:

   ❑ **Generate Java File**

   ❑ **Accessors**

   ❑ **Create Method**

   ❑ **Remove Method**

   ❑ **Validation Method**

When we create entity objects it is Oracle standard practice as per their development standards that we create the entity object class methods as we have done above. Checking these options will create the java classes and methods within them. If we do not create them at this point we can always generate them as required at a later stage.

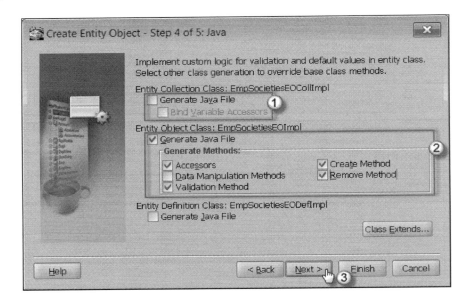

10. Click on **Next**.

11. Finally, in **Step 5 of 5**, click on **Finish**.

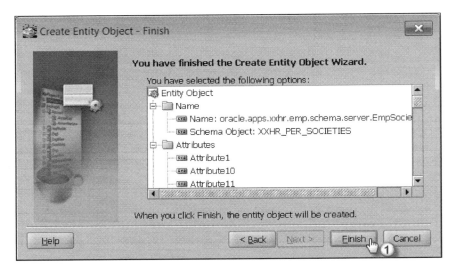

How it works...

We have now created our entity object based upon the XXHR_PER_SOCIETIES table. Our entity object has been created in a package with the same extension as our application module, but with .schema between the emp and server. This is to follow Oracle development standards.

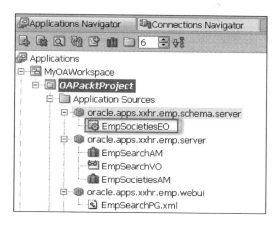

There's more...

If you are seeing lots of other packages in the **Applications Navigator** tab, we can restrict what is available in our view. We can do this by double-clicking the **OAPacktProject** to bring up the **Project Properties** window. Click on **Project Content** on the left navigation pane, and on the right at the bottom of that page we can see two tabs called **Included** and **Excluded**. The **Included** tab will have **All** checked, which means we will see all of the packages in our **Application Navigator** window. Click on the **Add** button, choose the directory we want to view (in this case, **oracle | apps | xxhr | emp**), and click the **OK** button.

The directory will be added to the **Included** tab as shown in the following screenshot. Only the files in this directory and subdirectories will be displayed in the **Application Navigator** tab.

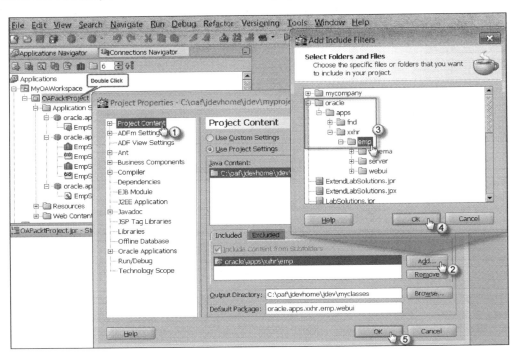

Creating the application module (AM)

We will now create the application module that will be based upon our entity object. We will link to the entity object this time, as we will be creating a page that will insert, update, and delete records to the **XXHR_PER_SOCIETIES** table.

How to do it...

To create the application module, perform the following:

1. Right-click the **OAPacktProject** project in the **Applications Navigator** tab and select **New** from the pop-up menu.

2. Navigate to **Business Tier | ADF Business Components** and select **Application Module**.

3. Click on **OK**.

4. In **Step 1 of 4**, enter the following details, and click on **Next**:

   - **Package:** `oracle.apps.xxhr.emp.server`

   - **Name:** `EmpSocitiesAM`

5. In **Step 2 of 4**, click on **Next**.

6. In **Step 3 of 4**, click on **Next**.

7. In **Step 4 of 4**, check the **Generate Java File(s)** checkbox in **Application Module Class: EmpSocietiesAMImpl** to generate the EmpSocietiesAMImpl java class.

8. In the **Finish** window, click on the **Finish** button.

9. Click the **Save All** button from the toolbar.

How it works...

We have now created the application module for the societies screen.

Creating the view object (VO)

We are now going to create our view object, and this will be based upon our entity object we have just created.

How to do it...

To create the view object, perform the following:

1. Right-click the **OAPacktProject** and select **New** from the pop-up menu.

2. Navigate to **Business Tier | ADF Components** and select **View Object**.

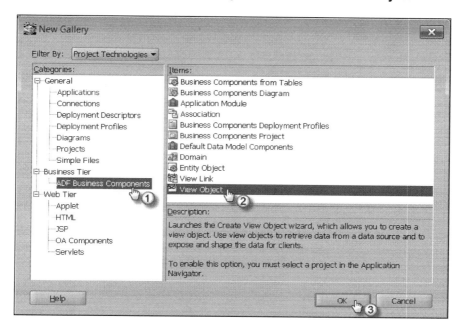

3. Click on **OK**.

4. If the **Create View Object** welcome page opens, click on **Next**.

5. In **Step 1 of 7**, enter the following details:

   ❑ **Package:** oracle.apps.xxhr.emp.server

   ❑ **Name:** EmpSocietiesVO

6. Select the **Rows Populated by a SQL Query, with:** radio button, and select the **Updatable Access through Entity Objects** radio button as shown in the following screenshot:

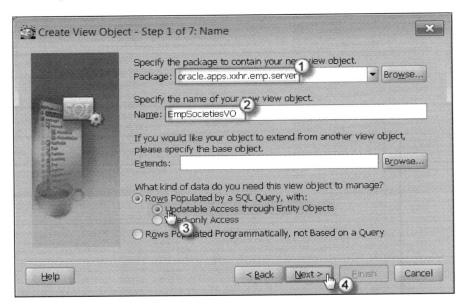

7. Click on **Next**.

8. In **Step 2 of 7**, select the **EmpSocietiesEO** entity object from the **Available:** pane, and shift it to the **Selected:** pane as shown in the following screenshot:

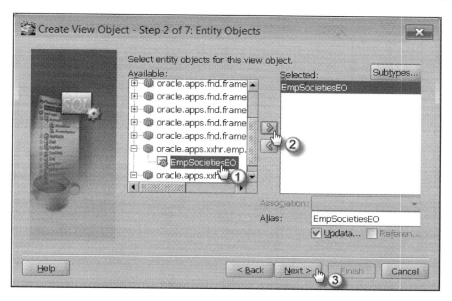

9. Click on **Next**.

10. In **Step 3 of 7**, shift the following items from the **Available:** pane to the **Selected:** pane by clicking the **>** button:

   - **SocietyId**
   - **PersonId**
   - **Code**
   - **DateStart**
   - **DateEnd**
   - **SubsPeriod**
   - **SubsAmount**
   - **SubsTotal**
   - **SubsHold**

Now we can order the items by using the up and down arrows as shown in the following screenshot:

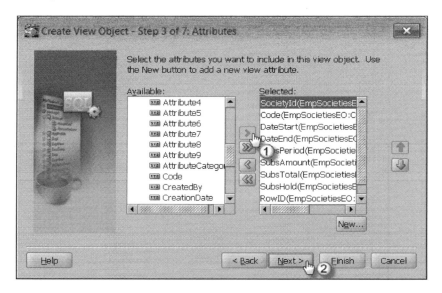

11. In **Step 4 to 6**, click on **Next**.

12. In **Step 7 of 7**, uncheck **Generate Java File** checkbox in **View Object Class: EmpSocietiesVOImpl**.

13. Check the checkbox for the **View Row Class: EmpSocietiesVORowImpl** for both the **Generate Java File** and **Accessors** checkboxes, as shown in the following screenshot:

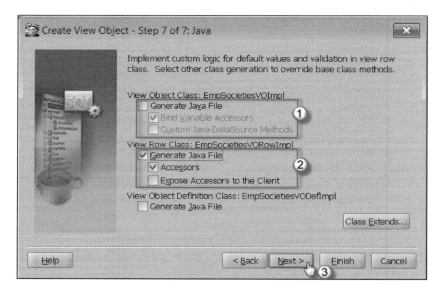

14. Click on **Next**.

15. Click on **Finish**.

16. Click the **Save All** button from the toolbar.

How it works...

We have created the view object that is based upon the entity object.

Editing the view object (VO)

Now we will edit the view object. The XXHR_PER_SOCIETIES table contains a field which is a code that is based upon a lookup value. We created the lookup when we ran the script for the database objects at the beginning of the chapter. Next we will add the lookup value that we want displayed to the user.

How to do it...

To edit the view object, perform the following:

1. Double-click on the **EmpSocietiesVO** view object in the **Application Navigator** tab.

2. In the **View Object Editor**, click on **SQL Statement** and check the **Expert Mode** checkbox as shown in the following screenshot:

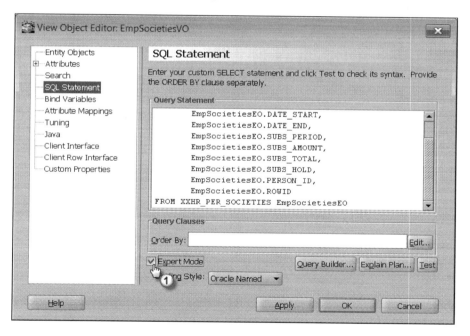

3. Edit the **Query Statement** with the following query, and click on **OK**:

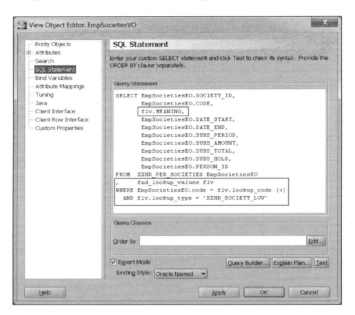

4. Click **Save All** from the toolbar menu to save the changes we have made.

How it works...

We have now amended the view object to add a lookup value to the data that is displayed to the user when we build our page later on.

Linking the view object (VO) to the application module (AM)

We will now link the view object to the application module. The application module will be referenced when we build our user interface later in the chapter. Before we build the user interface, we will check that the application module returns data from the database.

How to do it...

To link the view object to the application module, perform the following:

1. In the **Application Navigator** tab, double-click the **EmpSocietiesAM** application module.

2. In the **Application Module Editor**, select the **Data Model** node.

3. Shift the **EmpSocietiesVO** from **Available View Objects:** to **Data Model:** by clicking the **>** button as shown in the following screenshot:

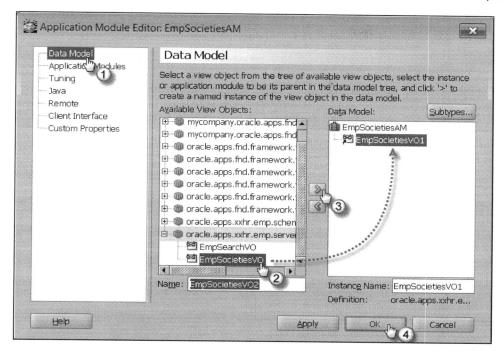

4. Click on **OK**.

5. Click the **Save All** button from the toolbar.

How it works...

We have now linked the view object to the application module.

Testing the application module (AM)

Now that we have created the entity object, view object, and application module and linked them, we need to test that the data returned by the application module is returned before we create the user interface. If it is not returned at this stage when we test the application module, it will not be returned when we create the page. That is, assuming that there is data in the database.

How to do it...

To test the application module, perform the following:

1. Right-click the **EmpSocietiesAM** application module.

2. Select **Test** from the pop-up menu.

3. Click the **Connect** button when the **Oracle Business Component Browser - Connect** window appears.

4. Double-click on the **EmpSocietiesVO1** node and the browser will bring back data from the view object as shown in the following screenshot:

As we have not developed an insert page yet, we will not have any data in the **EmpSocietiesVO1** view object. There is a procedure, which was created when we built the database object that allows us to add some test data while we develop the page. Call the following procedure to create a test detail record, passing in the person_id. Open a SQL Developer or SQL Plus session, and make a call to the procedure to insert a test record.

```
BEGIN
    XXHR_PER_SOCIETIES_PVT.insert_test_record(p_person_id => 374);
END;
```

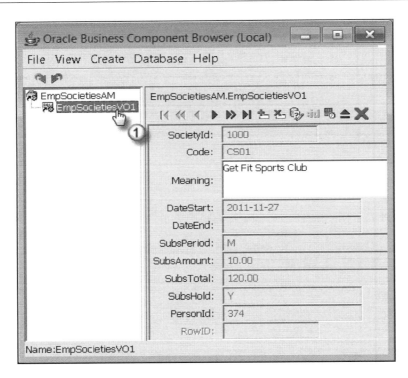

How it works...

We have now created our entity object, application module, and view object. The objects in our **Application Module** tab should resemble the objects in the following screenshot:

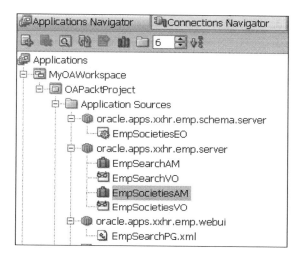

Creating the view link (VL)

We will now create a view link. The view link will allows us to create a relationship between our master block and our detail block.

How to do it...

To create the view link, perform the following:

1. Right-click the **OAPacktProject** and select **New** from the pop-up menu.

2. Navigate to **Business Tier | ADF Business Components** and select **View Link**.

 You can also right-click the **oracle.apps.xxhr.emp.server** package and select **New View Link** from the pop-up menu.

3. If the **Welcome** page appears, click on **Next**.

4. In **Step 1 of 4**, enter the following details:

    ❑ **Package:** `oracle.apps.xxhr.emp.server`

    ❑ **Name:** `EmpSocietiesVL`

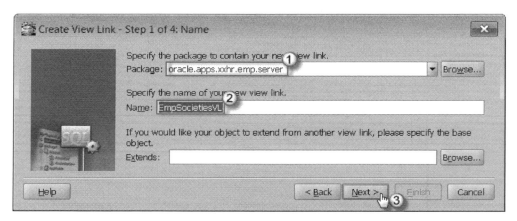

5. In **Step 2 of 4**, in the **Select Source Attribute:** pane, expand the **EmpSearchVO** view object and select the **PersonId** attribute. In the **Select Destination Attribute:** pane, expand the **EmpSocietiesVO** view object and select the **PersonId** attribute.

6. Click on the **Add** button as shown in the following screenshot:

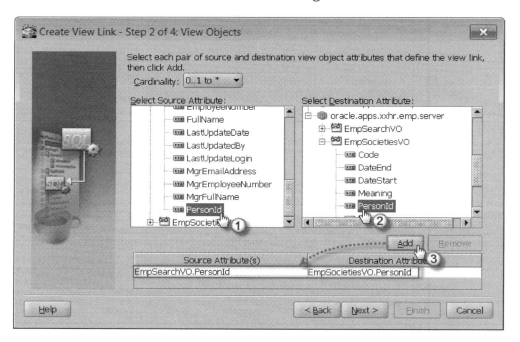

7. In **Step 3 and 4**, click on **Next**.

8. In the **Finish** window, click on the **Finish** button.

How it works...

We have now created a link between our master view object and our detail view object. The views are linked by the **PersonId** attribute and the relationship is one to many.

Adding the view link (VL) to the application module (AM)

We will now add the view link to the application module. This will represent the relationship between the master and detail view objects, and we will be able to test the relationship before we go on to create the user interface.

How to do it...

To add the view link to the application module, perform the following:

1. Double-click the **EmpSearchAM** application module.

2. In the **Data Model:** pane, click on the **EmpSearchVO1** view object instance.

3. In the **Available View Objects:** pane, select the **EmpSocietiesVO via EmpSocietiesVL view object** in **oracle.apps.xxhr.emp.server | EmpSearchVO**, and shift it to the right-hand pane by clicking the **>** button as shown in the following screenshot:

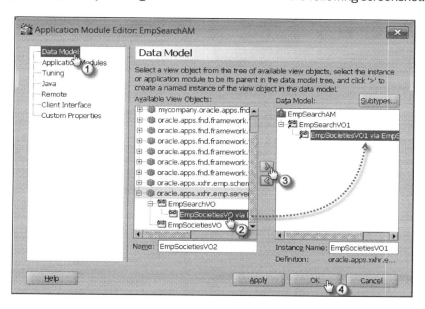

4. Click on **OK**.

How it works...

We can see that the master view object is now linked to the detail view object via the view object that we have created.

Testing the application module (AM)

We will now test that the master-detail relationship, which we have created, brings back data as we expect it to. We will do this test before we go on to create the user interface to check that the data is being returned as we expect it to be.

How to do it...

To test the application module, perform the following:

1. Right-click on the **EmpSearchAM** application module.

2. Select **Test** from the pop-up menu.

3. Click the **Connect** button when the **Oracle Business Component Browser - Connect** window appears.

4. Double-click on the **EmpSearchVO1** as shown in the following screenshot:

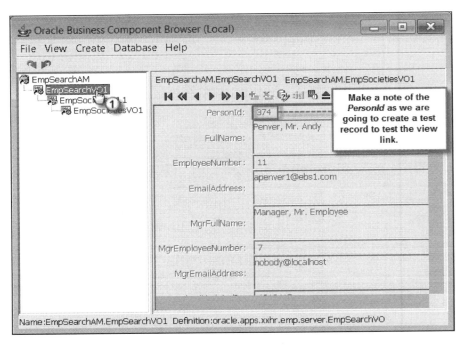

Make a note of the **PersonId** from the data in **EmpSearchVO1**. In the previous screenshot, the value of **PersonId** is **374**. Now open an SQL*Plus session or SQL Developer, log on as the apps user, and call the procedure to create a test record as shown in the following screenshot:

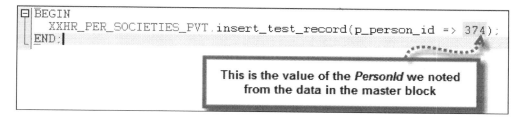

This is the value of the *PersonId* we noted from the data in the master block

Now that we have created a test detail record, it should appear when we double-click the **EmpSocietiesVO1** view object as shown in the following screenshot. We can call this procedure to create as many records as desired—just pass in the `person_id` of the relevant master record.

5. Double-click on **EmpSocietiesVO1** as shown in the following screenshot:

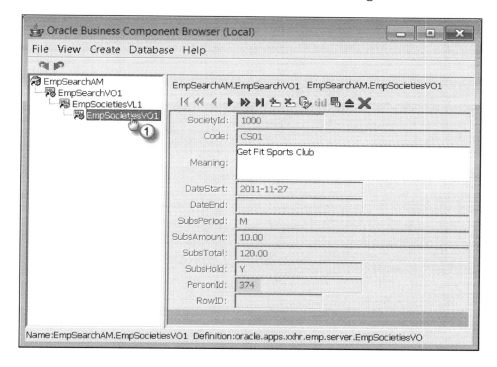

Data will be returned in the **EmpSocietiesVO1** view object only if there is data in the table that is linked (via the **PersonId** attribute) to the master view. If you created some dummy records for an employee using the script provided for the chapter in the download bundle, you will retrieve some data; otherwise you may not see any data here.

How it works...

We have tested and found that the master-detail relationships between our view objects that we had created have been created successfully.

Creating a master region

We will now create the view objects and also the controller for the page. The page will consist of a master and detail regions based upon the application module we have just created. We will perform the following tasks to create the view and controller layers for the page:

- ▸ Adding a master region (RN)
- ▸ Creating the master region (RN) items
- ▸ Creating the Controller (CO)
- ▸ Testing the page

Adding a master region (RN)

Okay, now we need to create a region to display the master region. First we will create the page, and then we will add our master region to the page.

How to do it...

To create the master region, perform the following:

1. In the **Application Navigator** tab, right-click on **OAPacktProject**.
2. Select **New** from the pop-up menu.
3. In the **New Gallery** window, navigate to **Web Tier | OA Components** and select **Page** from the **Items** list.
4. In the **New Page** window, set the following page details:
    - ❑ **Name:** EmpSocietiesPG
    - ❑ **Package:** oracle.apps.xxhr.emp.webui

5. Click on the **OK** button.

6. In the **Structure** pane, click on the item **EmpSecietiesPG | region1** node.

7. Now in the **Property Inspector** window, set the following properties:

   ❑ **ID**: PageLayoutRN

   ❑ **AM Definition**: oracle.apps.xxhr.emp.server.EmpSearchAM

   ❑ **Window Title**: Employee Societies Window

   ❑ **Title**: Employee Societies

A summary of the steps is displayed in the following screenshot:

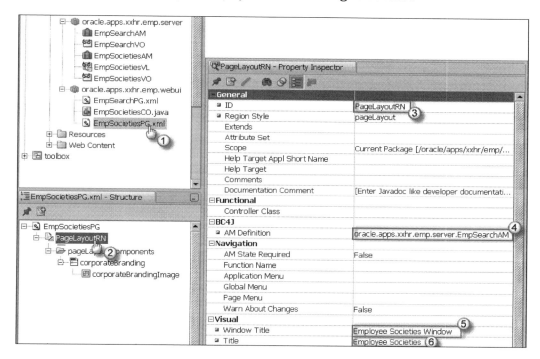

8. Right-click on the **PageLayoutRN** region in the **Structure** pane, and select **New | Region** from the pop-up menu.

9. In the **Structure** pane, click on the **EmpSocietiesPG | PageLayoutRN | region1** region.

10. Now in the **Property Inspector** window, set the following properties:

- ❏ **ID**: EmpMasterRN
- ❏ **Region Style**: advancedTable
- ❏ **View Instance**: EmpSearchVO1

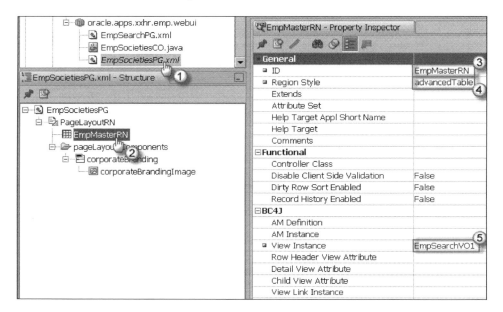

11. Click on **Save All** from the toolbar to save the changes we have made.

How it works...

We have now created the page and set the properties of the page. We have also created our header region, which will be an advanced table style and based upon the **EmpSearchVO1** view object instance.

Creating the master region (RN) items

We will now create the items for our master region.

How to do it...

To create the items in our master region, perform the following:

1. Right-click on the **EmpMasterRN** region and select **New | Column** from the pop-up menu.

2. Click on **column1** and set the **ID** property to `MasterPersonIdCol`.

3. Right-click on the **MasterPersonIdCol** column, and select **New | Item** from the pop-up menu.

4. Click on the item we have just added (**item1**) and set the following properties:
   - **ID**: `PersonId`
   - **Item Style**: `messageStyledText`
   - **View Attribute**: `PersonID`

   The following screenshot shows the screen with the properties set:

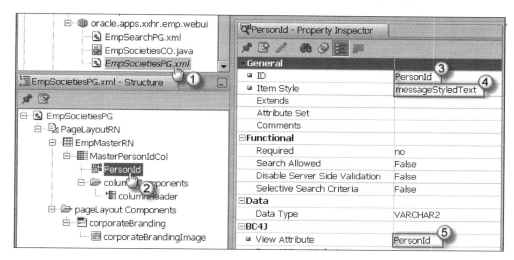

5. Now right-click the **columnHeader** column component, and select **New | sortableHeader** from the pop-up menu.

6. Click on the **sortableHeader1** header and set the following properties:

   ❑ **ID**: personIdHdr

   ❑ **Prompt**: Person ID

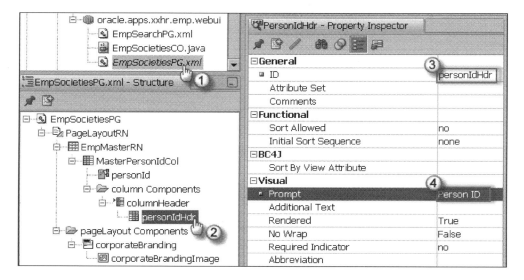

Now we are going to create the remaining items for the master region.

Creating columns

To create the columns for each of our items for the master region, perform the following.

1. Right-click on the **EmpMasterRN**, and select **New | Column** from the pop-up menu.

2. Repeat step 1 four times to create four new items, and set the **ID** property of the four new items as follows:

   ❑ FullNameCol

   ❑ EmployeeNumberCol

   ❑ EmailAddressCol

   ❑ MgrFullNameCol

After adding the columns for these items, the screen will have the column placeholders defined as shown in the following screenshot:

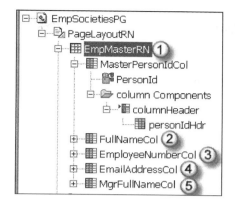

Creating column items

To create the items for each column, perform the following:

1. For each of the columns, right-click on the column and select **New | Item** from the pop-up menu.

2. Set the properties of the **FullNameCol** item as follows:
   - **ID**: FullName
   - **Item Style**: messageStyledText
   - **View Attribute**: FullName

3. Set the properties of the **EmployeeNumberCol** item as follows:
   - **ID**: EmployeeNumber
   - **Item Style**: messageStyledText
   - **View Attribute**: EmployeeNumber

4. Set the properties of the **EmailAddressCol** item as follows:
   - **ID**: EmailAddress
   - **Item Style**: messageStyledText
   - **View Attribute**: EmailAddress

5. Set the properties of the **EmailAddressCol** item as follows:
   - **ID**: MgrFullName
   - **Item Style**: messageStyledText
   - **View Attribute**: MgrFullName

Now, each column will have an item defined, as shown in the following screenshot:

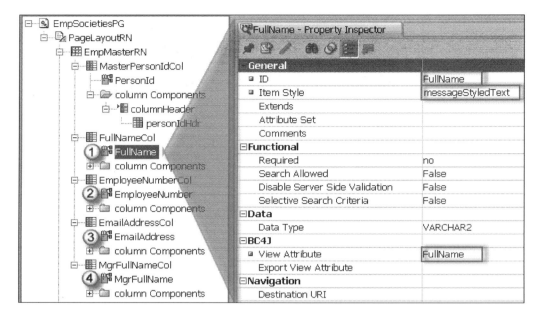

We will now create the column headers for each of the items.

Creating column headers

To create the column headers for each of our columns, perform the following:

1. Expand the **column Components** folder for the **FullNameCol item**.

2. Right-click on the **columnHeader** node, and select **New | sortableHeader** from the pop-up menu.

3. Set the properties of **sortableHeader** as follows:

   - **ID**: FullNameHdr
   - **Prompt**: Employee Name

4. Expand the **column Components** folder for the **EmployeeNumberCol** item.

5. Right-click on the **columnHeader** node, and select **New | sortableHeader** from the pop-up menu.

6. Set the properties of **sortableHeader** as follows:

   - **ID**: EmployeeNumberHdr
   - **Prompt**: Employee Number

7. Expand the **column Components** folder for the **EmailAddressCol** item.

8. Right-click the **columnHeader** node, and select **New | sortableHeader** from the pop-up menu.

9. Set the properties of **sortableHeader** as follows:

    ❑ **ID**: EmailAddressHdr

    ❑ **Prompt**: Email Address

10. Expand the **column Components** folder for the **MgrFullNameCol** item.

11. Right-click the **columnHeader** node, and select **New | sortableHeader** from the pop-up menu.

12. Set the properties of **sortableHeader** as follows:

    ❑ **ID**: MgrFullNameHdr

    ❑ **Prompt**: Manager Name

The column headers will now be defined as shown in the following screenshot:

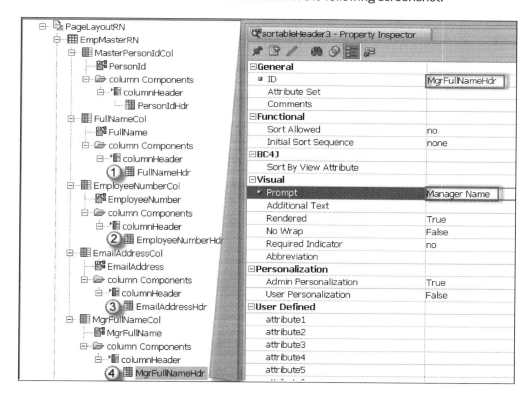

How it works...

We have now created all of the elements for our master region. The advanced table has the columns defined, the items associated with each item, and the column headings. The items are mapped to a view object attribute.

Creating the controller (CO)

We are now going to create the controller for the page. The controller has two key classes that we need to understand. The first is a java class called `processRequest` or `pr`, which will be executed each time the page is rendered. Note: if you are familiar with Oracle Forms, this would be the equivalent to a WHEN-NEW-FORM-INSTANCE trigger in Oracle forms. We code here to perform activities we want to perform, when the page is opened. We would normally set properties here for other activities, such as executing a query to retrieve data. We may even perform activities, such as amending the where clause of our view object. The second java method we need to discuss is called the `processFormRequest` or `pfr`, and this fires whenever an event is triggered after the page has been rendered. This may be a user clicking a button for example. We need to capture the event we want to perform activities for, and then code the activity. If you are familiar with Oracle Forms, it is similar to the event triggers. However, remember that we need to code the event we want to capture in the java class.

How to do it...

To create a new controller, perform the following:

1. In the **Structure** pane, right-click the **PageLayoutRN** region and select **Set New Controller** from the pop-up menu.

2. When the **New Controller** window appears, set the following values:

   □ **Package Name**: `oracle.apps.xxhr.emp.webui`

   □ **Class Name**: `EmpSocietiesCO`

By default, JDeveloper automatically adds a `.webui` to the package name. It would be easy to just click on **OK**, but be careful to remove the additional webui that is added to the package name (if it has been automatically added by JDeveloper). For example, the package name may well be defaulted to `oracle.apps.xxhr.emp.webui.webui`. We would need to edit the package name, by removing the second webui to read `oracle.apps.xxhr.emp.webui`.

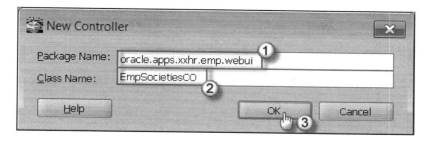

3. In the **Application Navigator** tab, in the `oracle.apps.xxhr.emp.webui` package, double-click on the `EmpSocietiesCO.java` controller.

4. Add the following import statements to the `EmpSocietiesCO.java` code:

```
import oracle.apps.fnd.framework.OAApplicationModule;
import oracle.apps.fnd.framework.OAViewObject;
```

We have imported these two packages, as we want to create an instance of the application module and view object the methods we are going to edit. We will discuss an easy way to add the `import` statements later on. The `import` statements have now been added to the controller as shown in the following screenshot:

```
EmpSocietiesCO.java
/*=============================================================+
  |   Copyright (c) 2001, 2005 Oracle Corporation, Redwood Shores, CA, USA  |
  |                        All rights reserved.                              |
  +=============================================================+
  |  HISTORY                                                                 |
  +=============================================================*/
package oracle.apps.xxhr.emp.webui;

import oracle.apps.fnd.common.VersionInfo;
import oracle.apps.fnd.framework.webui.OAControllerImpl;
import oracle.apps.fnd.framework.webui.OAPageContext;
import oracle.apps.fnd.framework.webui.beans.OAWebBean;
import oracle.apps.fnd.framework.OAApplicationModule;
import oracle.apps.fnd.framework.OAViewObject;
```

5. Scroll down to the `processRequest` class and add the following lines of code:

```
public void processRequest(OAPageContext pageContext, OAWebBean webBean)
{
  super.processRequest(pageContext, webBean);
  OAApplicationModule am = (OAApplicationModule)pageContext.getApplicationModule(webBean);
  OAViewObject vo = (OAViewObject)am.findViewObject("EmpSearchVO1");
  if(vo != null) {
      vo.executeQuery();
  }
}
```

The code that we have added creates an instance of the application module and an instance of the view object. The view object is based upon the **EmpSearchVO** view object. We have checked that instance of the view object exists and if so we execute a query which will return the records associated with the view defined in the view object.

6. Click the **Save All** button from the toolbar to save all of the changes made.

How it works...

We have created the controller for the **EmpSocietiesPG** page. The controller will have automatically generated the `processRequest` and `processFormRequest` classes. We have amended the `processRequest` class, so that when we open the page, the view object will automatically execute a query.

Testing the page

We will now test the page we have created so far.

How to do it...

To test the page, right-click on the **oracle.apps.xxhr.emp.webui | EmpSocietiesPG.xml** page in the **Application Navigator** tab, and select **Run** from the pop-up menu.

How it works...

The following page will appear, and a query will automatically be performed when we enter the page:

ORACLE°

Diagnostics Home Logout Preferences

Employee Societies

⊙ Previous 1-10 ▾ Next 10 ⊙

Person ID	Employee Name	Employee Number	Email Address	Manager Name
5	Walker, Mr. Kenneth (Ken)	4	nobody@localhost	O'Malley, Mr. Robert G (Rob)
11	Heiden, Ms. Camille Serena (Cammie)	10	nobody@localhost	Colby, Ms. Sharon
12	Daniels, Britta Michelle (Britta)	11	nobody@localhost	Bradford, Ms. Carol (Carol)
15	Peters, Ms. Tracy Marie (Tracy)	14	nobody@localhost	Douglas, Mr. Carl Lawrence (Carl)
21	Douglas, Mr. Carl Lawrence (Carl)	20	nobody@localhost	Bradford, Ms. Carol (Carol)
24	Green, Mr. Terry	23	nobody@localhost	Johnson, Ms. Alex
25	Stock, Ms. Pat	24	nobody@localhost	Brown, Ms. Casey
26	Black, Mr. Chris	25	nobody@localhost	Smith, Mr. Jonathan
27	Johnson, Ms. Alex	26	nobody@localhost	Horton, Ms. Connor Esq.
28	Peters, Mr. Samuel	27	nobody@localhost	Brock, Mr. Kim

⊙ Previous 1-10 ▾ Next 10 ⊙

Diagnostics Home Logout Preferences

About this Page   Privacy Statement

Creating a detail region

We will now create the detail region for our page. The detail page will be based upon our **EmpSocietiesVO1** view instance, and will be linked to the master region by the view link we defined earlier on in the chapter.

In this section, we will cover the following tasks

- ▶ Adding a detail region (RN)
- ▶ Creating the detail region (RN) items
- ▶ Adding a show/hide attribute
- ▶ Adding sortable headers

Adding a detail region (RN)

We are now going to create the detail region and items.

How to do it...

To create a detail region, perform the following:

1. Click on the **EmpSocietiesPG.xml** page in the **Application Navigator** tab.

2. In the **Structure** pane, right-click on the **EmpMasterRN** region and select **New | detail** from the pop-up menu as shown in the following screenshot:

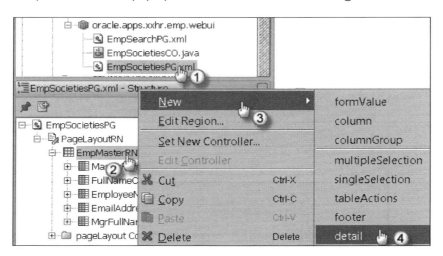

3. Click on the new region (**region1**) in the **Structure** pane, and set the following properties:

- ❏ **ID**: EmpDetailRN
- ❏ **Region Style**: header
- ❏ **Text**: Clubs and Societies

The following detail pane will now appear:

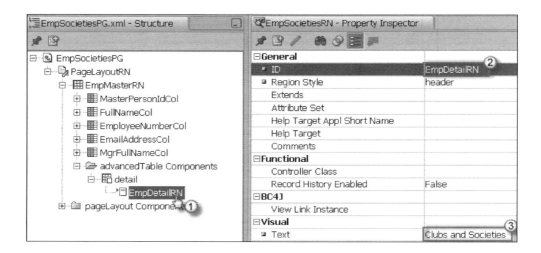

4. Right-click on the **EmpDetailRN** region, and select **New | Region** from the pop-up menu.

5. Set the following properties for the new region:

   ❑ **ID**: EmpSocietiesRN

   ❑ **Style**: advancedTable

   ❑ **View Object Instance**: EmpSocietiesVO1

The properties of the EmpSocietiesRN region will be set as shown in the following screenshot:

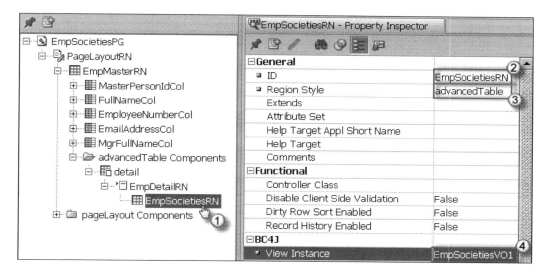

6. Click the **Save All** button from the toolbar to save all of the changes made.

How it works...

We have now created our detail region. The detail region has a header region called **EmpDetailRN** and a region to display the data called **EmpSocietiesRN**. The **EmpSocietiesRN** style is another advanced table and this is based upon the **EmpSocietiesVO1** view object instance.

Creating the detail region (RN) items

In the same way as we did for the master region, we are going to create the components of the advanced table so we will create the columns, the items, and the sortable headers.

How to do it...

Now we are going to create the columns and then the items associated with each item. The following explains the steps we will perform for each item:

1. Right-click on the **EmpSocietiesRN** region, and select **New | Column** from the pop-up menu.

2. Click on **column1** and set the **ID** property to DetPersonIdCol.

3. Right-click on the **DetPersonIdCol** column, and select **New | Item** from the pop-up menu.

4. Click on the item we have just added (**item1**), and set the following properties:

   - ❑ **ID**: DetPersonId
   - ❑ **Item Style**: messageStyledText
   - ❑ **View Attribute**: PersonID

5. Now right-click on the **columnHeader** column component, and select **New | sortableHeader** from the pop-up menu.

6. Click on the **sortableHeader1** header, and set the following properties:

   - ❑ **ID**: DetPersonIdHdr
   - ❑ **Prompt**: Person ID

Creating columns

Now we are going to create the remaining items for the master region:

1. Right-click on the **EmpSocietiesRN** and select **New | Column** from the pop-up menu.

2. Create six new columns, and set the **ID** property for each of the new columns as follows:

   - ❑ SocietyIdCol
   - ❑ MeaningCol
   - ❑ DateStartCol
   - ❑ DateEndCol
   - ❑ SubsPeriodCol
   - ❑ SubsAmountCol
   - ❑ SubsTotalCol

The columns will now have been created and will appear as shown in the following screenshot:

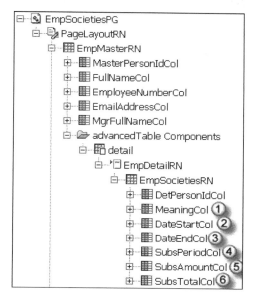

Creating column items

We will now create the items for each of the columns we have defined. To do this, perform the following:

1. For each of the columns, right-click the column and select **New | Item** from the pop-up menu.

2. Set the properties of the **SocietyIdCol** item as follows :

   - **ID**: SocietyId
   - **Item Style**: messageStyledText
   - **View Attribute**: SocietyId

3. Set the properties of the **MeaningCol** item as follows :

   - **ID**: Meaning
   - **Item Style**: messageStyledText
   - **View Attribute**: Meaning

4. Set the properties of the **DateStartCol** item as follows:

    ❑   **ID**: DateStart

    ❑   **Item Style**: messageStyledText

    ❑   **View Attribute**: DateStart

5. Set the properties of the **DateEndCol** item as follows:

    ❑   **ID**: DateEnd

    ❑   **Item Style**: messageStyledText

    ❑   **View Attribute**: DateEnd

6. Set the properties of the **SubsPeriodCol** item as follows:

    ❑   **ID**: SubsPeriod

    ❑   **Item Style**: messageStyledText

    ❑   **View Attribute**: SubsPeriod

7. Set the properties of the **SubsAmountCol** item as follows:

    ❑   **ID**: SubsAmount

    ❑   **Item Style**: messageStyledText

    ❑   **View Attribute**: SubsAmount

8. Set the properties of the **SubsTotalCol** item as follows:

    ❑   **ID**: SubsTotal

    ❑   **Item Style**: messageStyledText

    ❑   **View Attribute**: SubsTotal

9. Click the **Save All** button from the toolbar to save all of the changes made.

The items for each column will now have been created and will appear as shown in the following screenshot:

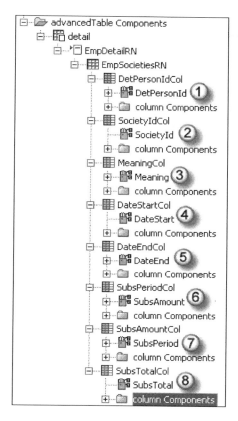

Creating column headers

We will now create the column headers for each of the items. To do this, perform the following:

1. Expand the **column Components** folder for the **MeaningCol** item.

2. Right-click on the **columnHeader** node, and select **New | sortableHeader** from the pop-up menu.

3. Set the properties of **sortableHeader** as follows:

   ❑ **ID**: MeaningHdr

   ❑ **Prompt**: Club \ Society

4. Expand the **column Components** folder for the **DateStartCol** item.

5. Right-click the **columnHeader** node and select **New | sortableHeader** from the pop-up menu.

6. Set the properties of **sortableHeader** as follows:

    ❑ **ID**: DateStartHdr

    ❑ **Prompt**: Date Start

7. Expand the **column Components** folder for the **DateEndCol** item.

8. Right-click the **columnHeader** node and select **New | sortableHeader** from the pop-up menu.

9. Set the properties of the sortableHeader as follows:

    ❑ **ID**: DateEndHdr

    ❑ **Prompt**: Date End

10. Expand the **column Components** folder for the **SubsPeriodCol** item.

11. Right-click the **columnHeader** node and select **New | sortableHeader** from the pop-up menu.

12. Set the properties of **sortableHeader** as follows:

    ❑ **ID**: SubsPeriodHdr

    ❑ **Prompt**: Period

13. Expand the **column Components** folder for the **SubsAmountCol** item.

14. Right-click the **columnHeader** node, and select **New | sortableHeader** from the pop-up menu.

15. Set the properties of **sortableHeader** as follows:

    ❑ **ID**: SubsAmountHdr

    ❑ **Prompt**: Amount

16. Expand the **column Components** folder for the **SubsTotalCol** item.

17. Right-click the **columnHeader** node, and select **New | sortableHeader** from the pop-up menu.

18. Set the properties of **sortableHeader** as follows:

    ❑ **ID**: SubsTotalHdr

    ❑ **Prompt**: Total

19. Click the **Save All** button from the toolbar to save all of the changes made.

The sortable headers for each column will now have been created and will appear as shown in the following screenshot. The screenshot shows the first three but we will need to create headers for all items.

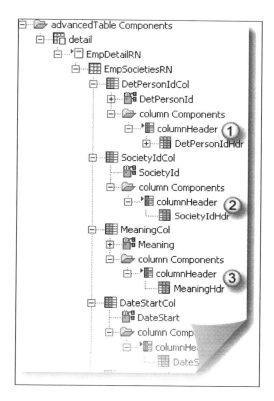

How it works...

We have now created all of the components for our detail region. We first created the columns we are going to display in the table and then attached an item to each column. Each item is associated with an attribute from the **EmpSocietiesVO1** view instance. Finally, we create the sortable header for each column.

Adding a show/hide attribute

We will now create a new attribute, which we will use to expand the records in our master region. When we click on the attribute, the detail records (if there are any) will be displayed below it.

How to do it...

To add a **Show\Hide** attribute, perform the following:

1. Double click on the **EmpSearchVO** view.

2. Expand the **Attributes** node, and click on the **New** button to create a new attribute.

3. In the **New View Attribute** window, set the following details:

    □ **Name:** ShowHide

    □ **Type:** String

    □ **Updateable:** Always

    The steps we need to take are summarized in the following screenshot. We have not mapped the item to a column (that is, checked the **Mapped to Column or SQL** checkbox) and therefore, it is *not* based upon a view attribute.

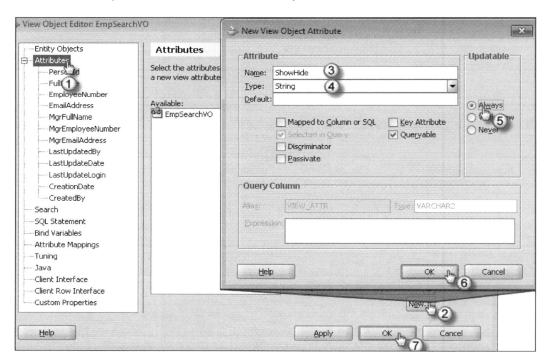

4. Click on **OK**.

5. Click on **Save All**.

6. Click the `EmpSocietiesPG.xml` file so that the **EmpSocietiesPG** page appears in the **Structure** pane.

7. Click the **EmpMasterRN** and set the following properties:

   ❑ **Detail View Attribute**: `ShowHide`

   ❑ **Child View Attribute**: `PersonId`

   ❑ **View Link Instance**: `EmpSocietiesVL1`

> For **Child View Attribute**, type in `PersonId`.

EmpSocietiesVO	
⊟ oracle.apps.xxhr.emp.webui	
EmpSearchPG.xml	
EmpSocietiesCO.java	
EmpSocietiesPG.xml	

EmpMasterRN - Property Inspector

General	
ID	EmpMasterRN
Region Style	advancedTable
Extends	
Attribute Set	
Help Target Appl Short Name	
Help Target	
Comments	
Functional	
Controller Class	
Disable Client Side Validation	False
Dirty Row Sort Enabled	False
Record History Enabled	False
BC4J	
AM Definition	
AM Instance	
View Instance	EmpSearchVO1
Row Header View Attribute	
Detail View Attribute	ShowHide
Child View Attribute	PersonId
View Link Instance	EmpSocietiesVL1

EmpSocietiesPG.xml - Structure

- EmpSocietiesPG
  - PageLayoutRN
    - EmpMasterRN
      - MasterP...IdCol
      - FullNameCol
      - EmployeeNumberCol
      - EmailAddressCol
      - MgrFullNameCol
      - advancedTable Components
        - detail
          - EmpDetailRN
            - EmpSocietiesRN
              - DetPersonIdCol
              - MeaningCol
              - DateStartCol
              - DateEndCol

8. Click on **EmpSocietiesRN** and set the following properties:

   □ **View Link Instance**: EmpSocietiesVL1

   □ **Empty Table Text**: No records found.

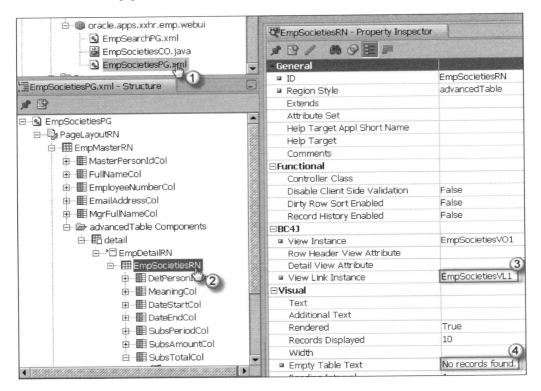

9. Click on the **Save All** button from the toolbar to save all of the changes made.

How it works...

We have now created a new attribute in our view object. When we run the page, the header now has the new **Show\Hide** attribute. When we click the **Show\Hide** attribute the following detail records will be displayed (that's if any detail records exist for the master record):

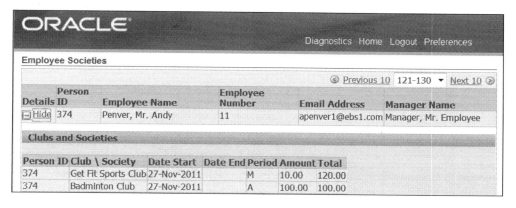

Adding sortable headers

We are now going to enable users to sort on the column in the master region. We can do this by setting the properties of the sortable header item.

How to do it...

To set the column as a sortable column, perform the following:

1. Click the EmpSocietiesPG.xml file so that the **EmpSocietiesPG** page appears in the **Structure** pane.

2. In the **Structure** pane, navigate to the **EmployeeNumberHdr** sortable header, and set the following properties:

   □ **Sort Allowed**: yes

   □ **Initial Sort Sequence**: first

The screen will show sortable header properties as shown in the following screenshot:

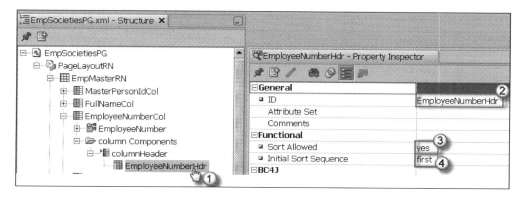

3. Save all the changes and run the form.

When we click on the sortable header, we get the following error message. To prevent this message appearing, we need to edit the java class for the row of the view object.

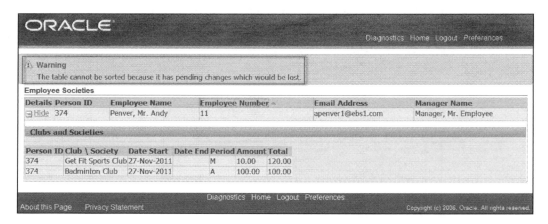

To edit the code for the **EmpSearchVO** view object, perform the following:

1. Right-click on the **EmpSearchVO** node, and select the **Go to View Row Class** from the pop-up menu as shown in the following screenshot:

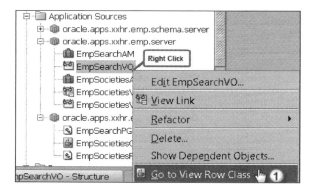

2. Scroll to the bottom of the EmpSearchVORowImpl.java file and edit the `setShowHide` class by editing the code as shown in the next screenshot.

    The EmpSearchVORowImpl.java file will open up in JDeveloper. Edit the code as shown in the following screenshot. Comment out the call to `setAttributeInternal` and add this line to the `populateAttribute` classes.

```
EmpSearchVORowImpl.java
        public void setShowHide(String value) {
            //setAttributeInternal(SHOWHIDE, value);
            populateAttribute(SHOWHIDE, value);
        }
    }
```

3. Click on **Save All**.

How it works...

We have edited the row implementation java class for the view object row setter method to prevent the error appearing when we click on the sortable header.

Deploying a page to EBS

We are now going to be deploying the page to Oracle EBS and perform the configuration required to run the page from within Oracle EBS. When we deploy the files to the server we need to transfer all the files to the application server. We will also import the PG.xml file to the MDS repository and this has to be run for all the pages. At runtime, EBS accesses our page from the MDS repository (that is, the database) and not from the application server. The `PG.xml` file does not have to be stored on the application server, but it is a good practice to maintain a copy of any `PG.xml` and `RN.xml` files on the application server.

If we look at the different layers, we will see that the files that are generated for each layer are as follows:

- **User interface XML (UIX)** creates an xml file (`PG.xml` or `RN.xml`)
- **Controller (CO)** creates a java class file (`.java`)
- **Application module (AM)** creates an xml file (`AM.xml`) and a java file (`AMImpl.java`)
- **View object (VO)** creates an xml file (`VO.xml`) and two java files (`VOImpl.java` and `VORowImpl.java`)
- **Entity object (EO)** creates an xml file (`EO.xml`) and a java file (`EOImpl.java`)

In the upcoming recipes, we will perform the following tasks to deploy the page in EBS:

▸ Copy the files to the application server

▸ Set the permissions of the .class files on the application server

▸ Importing the page definition

▸ Creating a function

▸ Configure a menu

▸ Creating a custom responsibility

▸ Adding our responsibility to a user

▸ Run the OAF page

Copy the files to the application server

The first task we need to perform is to copy all of the files over to the application server. Specifically, we put them in the $JAVA_TOP/oracle/apps directory.

How to do it...

To copy the files of the page over to the application server, perform the following:

1. Log in to the application server with your preferred FTP client (the screenshots use **WinSCP**) with the application tier owner.

2. Copy the xxhr directory from the local PC to $JAVA_TOP/oracle/apps as shown in the following screenshot:

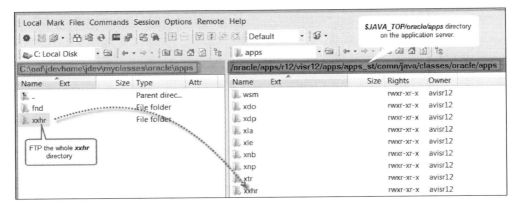

We have transferred all of the files for our page to the application server. However, the java class files need to be transferred in binary mode as they are executable files, so we will transfer these again. The `.class` files are in the following directories on our local PC:

```
C:\oaf\jdevhome\jdev\myprojects\oracle\apps\xxhr\emp\
schema\server

C:\oaf\jdevhome\jdev\myprojects\oracle\apps\xxhr\emp\
server

C:\oaf\jdevhome\jdev\myprojects\oracle\apps\xxhr\emp\
webui
```

3. In **WinSCP**, navigate to the `C:\oaf\jdevhome\jdev\myprojects\oracle\apps\xxhr\emp\schema\server` directory on the local PC.

4. On the server side, navigate to the `$JAVA_TOP/oracle/apps/xxhr/emp/schema/server` directory and copy the `EmpSocietiesEOImpl.class` file from the local PC to the application server. Ensure that the transfer is done in binary mode.

> Overwrite the existing file when prompted.

We will now transfer the class files in binary mode to the $JAVA_TOP/oracle/apps/xxhr/emp/server directory.

1. In **WinSCP**, navigate to the C:\oaf\jdevhome\jdev\myprojects\oracle\apps\xxhr\emp\server directory on the local PC.

2. On the server side, navigate to the $JAVA_TOP/oracle/apps/xxhr/emp/server directory and copy all of the *.class from the local PC to the application server. Ensure that the transfer is done in binary mode.

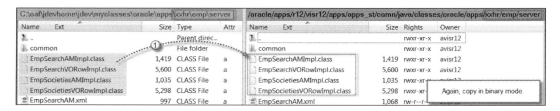

We will now transfer the class files in binary mode to the $JAVA_TOP/oracle/apps/xxhr/emp/webui directory.

1. In **WinSCP**, navigate to the C:\oaf\jdevhome\jdev\myprojects\oracle\apps\xxhr\emp\webui directory on the local PC.

2. On the server side, navigate to the $JAVA_TOP/oracle/apps/xxhr/emp/webui directory and copy all of the *.class files from the local PC to the application server. Ensure that the transfer is done in binary mode.

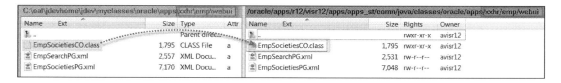

How it works...

We have just copied all of the .class files from the local PC to the application server in binary mode, as the class files are executable binary files.

Set the permissions of the .class files on the application server

We need to set the permissions of the .class files on the application server that we have just transferred to the application server. The files are in the following locations:

- ▶ $JAVA_TOP/oracle/apps/xxhr/emp/schema/server
- ▶ $JAVA_TOP/oracle/apps/xxhr/emp/server
- ▶ $JAVA_TOP/oracle/apps/xxhr/emp/webui

How to do it...

To set the properties of the .class files, perform the following:

1. Open Putty to connect to the application server with the application user.
2. Navigate to $JAVA_TOP/oracle/apps/xxhr/emp/schema/server with the command cd $JAVA_TOP/oracle/apps/xxhr/emp/schema/server.
3. Now set the permission with the command chmod 755 *.class.
4. Navigate to $JAVA_TOP/oracle/apps/xxhr/emp/server with the command: cd $JAVA_TOP/oracle/apps/xxhr/emp/server.
5. Now set the permission with the command chmod 755 *.class.
6. Navigate to $JAVA_TOP/oracle/apps/xxhr/emp/server with the command cd $JAVA_TOP/oracle/apps/xxhr/emp/webui.
7. Now set the permission with the command chmod 755 *.class.

How it works...

We have now set the permissions of all of the .class files of our page on the application server. This assumes that the e-business suite instance has been installed on a UNIX type operating system.

Importing the page definition

We will now import the page into the MDS repository. The syntax for importing the page is as follows on a Unix based environment:

```
java oracle.jrad.tools.xml.importer.XMLImporter $JAVA_TOP/oracle/apps/
xxhr/emp/webui/<PageNamePG.xml>

-username <username> -password <password>

-rootdir $JAVA_TOP

-dbconnection "(DESCRIPTION=(ADDRESS=(PROTOCOL=tcp)(HOST=<host name>)
(PORT=<port>))(CONNECT_DATA=(SID=<SID>)))"
```

How to do it...

To import our page into the database, perform the following:

1. Open a Putty session on the application tier and log on as the application tier user.

2. Navigate to the $JAVA_TOP directory by typing cd $JAVA_TOP.

3. At the prompt type the following command:

    ```
    java oracle.jrad.tools.xml.XMLImporter $JAVA_TOP/oracle/apps/
    xxhr/emp/webui/EmpSocietiesPG.xml -username apps -password
    apps -rootdir $JAVA_TOP -dbconnection "(DESCRIPTION=(ADDRESS
    =(PROTOCOL=tcp)(HOST=MyR12Instance.com)(PORT=1521))(CONNECT_
    DATA=(SID=VISR12)))"
    ```

> Replace the highlighted text in the above command with the details of the R12 environment you are using.

How it works...

We have now run the command to import the page. We can see that the following page has been imported successfully:

```
APPS Tier>cd $JAVA_TOP
APPS Tier>java oracle.jrad.tools.xml.importer.XMLImporter $JAVA_TOP/oracle/apps/xxhr/emp/webui/EmpSoci
etiesPG.xml -username apps -password apps -rootdir $JAVA_TOP -dbconnection "(DESCRIPTION=(ADDRESS=(PRO
TOCOL=tcp)(HOST=MyR12Instance.com)(PORT=1521))(CONNECT_DATA=(SID=VISR12)))"

Importing file "/oracle/apps/r12/visr12/apps/apps_st/comn/java/classes/oracle/apps/xxhr/emp/webui/EmpS
ocietiesPG.xml" as "/oracle/apps/xxhr/emp/webui/EmpSocietiesPG".

Import completed.
APPS Tier>
```

Creating a function

We will now create the function that calls the OAF page.

How to do it...

To create the function, perform the following:

1. Log in to Oracle and select the Application Developer responsibility.

2. Navigate to **Application | Function** and the **Form Functions** window will open.

3. Add a record with the following data to the **Description** tab:

Function	XXHR_EMP_SOCIETIES
User Function Name	XXHR OAF Employee Societies
Description	XXHR OAF Employee Societies Example

4. Add a record with the following data to the **Properties** tab:

5. Type: `SSWA jsp function`

6. Add a record with the following data to the Web HTML tab:

7. `HTML Call: OA.jsp?page=/oracle/apps/xxhr/emp/webui/`
   `EmpSocietiesPG`

 The `EmpSocietiesPG` HTML Call has been defined without the `.xml`
extension.

8. Click on the **Save** button in the toolbar (or *Ctrl + S*) to save the record.

9. Exit the form.

How it works...

The function is what we call to launch the page. We add the function to a menu to make it available to a responsibility.

Configure a menu

The following recipe will configure a menu which will be attached to our new responsibility we are going to create. This will determine the concurrent programs and forms we will be able to access.

How to do it...

To create a menu, perform the following:

1. Log in to Oracle e-business suite (EBS) with the Application Developer responsibility.

2. Navigate to **Application | Menu** and the **Menus** window will open.

3. Enter data as in the following table for the master record:

Item Name	Item Value
Menu	XXHR_TEST_O_AFMENU
User Menu Name	XXHR Test OAF Menu
Menu Type	Standard
Description	XXHR Test OAF Menu

4. Enter data as in the following table for the detail records:

Seq	Prompt	Submenu	Function	Description
10	OAF Employee Societies		XXHR OAF Employee Societies	

5. Click the **Save** button in the toolbar (or *Ctrl* + *S*) to save the record.

   The screen will now appear as in the following screenshot:

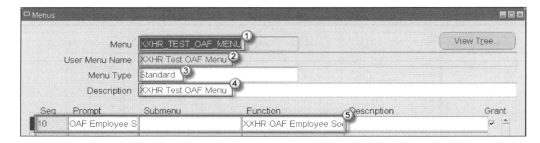

6. Exit the form.

How it works...

The menu is what a user will see when they are assigned a responsibility. More specifically the user will see the prompt value, which when selected will launch the function assigned to it. The menu can also be assigned a submenu. If you add a submenu the whole menu will be inherited and any functions it contains. We have created a simple menu that has the standard concurrent request functions added to it so that we can run and view our concurrent program.

Creating a custom responsibility

Now to create our new responsibility that we will use to access core HR screens, we will create a test employee record and ensure that the employee is a manger of other employees. This will be used to access some of the self-service screens, where we will create some personalizations in the upcoming recipes.

How to do it...

Follow the next steps to create a new responsibility called **XX Test OAF**:

1. Log in to Oracle with the System Administrator responsibility.

2. Navigate to **Security | Responsibility | Define** and the **Responsibilities** window will open.

3. Enter data as shown in the following table:

Item Name	Item Value
Responsibility Name	XX Test OAF
Application	Human Resources
Responsibility Key	XXTESTOAF
Description	XX Test OAF Responsibility
Data Group: Name	Standard
Application	Human Resources
Menu	XXHR Test OAF Menu
Request Group: Name	

The **Responsibilities** screen should now look like the following screenshot:

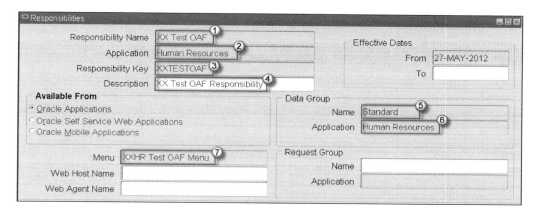

4. Click the **Save** button in the toolbar (or *Ctrl + S*) to save the record.
5. Exit the form.

How it works...

We have now created a new responsibility where we can access the OAF page we have created.

Adding our responsibility to a user

We are going to add the responsibility to our user we created in *Chapter 1, Personalizing OA Framework Pages*, called XXUSER.

How to do it...

To add the responsibility to the user, perform the following:

1. Log in to EBS with the SYSADMIN user (or a user that has access to the System Administrator responsibility)

2. Navigate to **Security | User | Define**.

3. Press *F11* to query the XXUSER in the **User Name** field.

4. Add the responsibility: XX Test OAF.

   The **Users** screen should now look similar to the following screenshot:

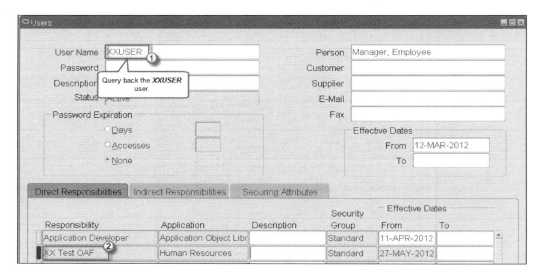

5. Save the form.

How it works...

We have now added the responsibility to our user called **XXUSER**. The user has access to the responsibilities we are going to need to test the OAF page.

Run the OAF page

We are now going to run the page from within EBS.

How to do it...

To run the page, perform the following:

1. Log in to Oracle EBS with **XXUSER** and select the **XX Test OAF** responsibility.

2. Click on the **OAF Employee Societies** link as shown in the following screenshot:

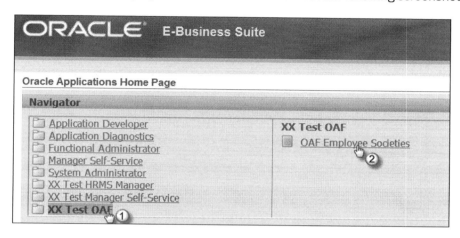

How it works...

The following OAF page will now be displayed:

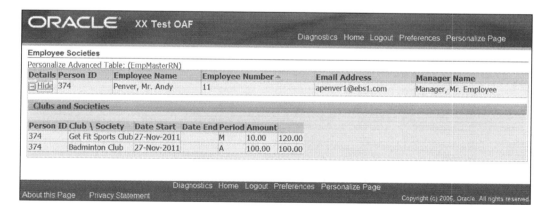

4

Adding a Creation Page and LOV Region in OA Framework

In this chapter, we will cover the following recipes:

- ► Creating a page to insert and update records
- ► Passing parameters
- ► Creating a list of values
- ► Adding a link to a region
- ► Running a page in debug mode

Introduction

In this chapter, we will be looking at making changes to the OA Framework pages we have created so far. We are going to add to this by creating a page that allows us to insert and update records to the database. Also, we will show how we can add default values such as a sequence, and how we can pass parameters from one page to another.

At the end of the chapter, you will have an understanding of how we can create pages that interact with the database, how we can create lists of values, and how we can pass parameters. You will also know how to use the debugger that is provided in JDeveloper, which developers will find to be an essential tool for developing pages using OA Framework.

Creating a page to insert and update records

We are now going to create a new page that will create a new society. We will look at the steps we need to take to build the page, and then the code we need to add to insert a record in the database table.

In this recipe, we will be performing the following tasks:

- ▶ Creating a view object
- ▶ Linking the view object to an application module
- ▶ Creating a page to insert data
- ▶ Adding a page status region
- ▶ Creating a page buttons region
- ▶ Creating and editing the page controller
- ▶ Capturing an event
- ▶ Editing the application module class
- ▶ Editing the entity object class

Creating a view object

The first step we are going to perform when building our page will be to add a new view object.

How to do it...

To create the view object, perform the following:

1. In **Applications Manager**, right-click the `oracle.apps.xxhr.emp.server` package and select **New View Object** from the pop-up menu.

2. If the **Create View Object** welcome page opens, click on **Next**. (Check the **Skip this Page Next Time** checkbox so that the welcome page does not appear each time the wizard is invoked.)

3. In **Step 1 of 7**, enter the following details:

   ❑ **Package**: oracle.apps.xxhr.emp.server

   ❑ **Name**: EmpSocietiesCreateVO

4. Select the **Rows Populated by SQL Query, with:** radio button, and then the **Updateable Access through Entity Objects** radio button as shown in the following screenshot:

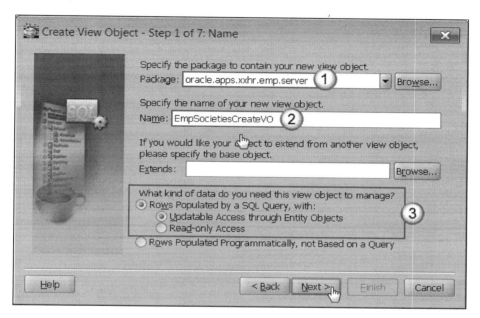

5. Click on **Next**.

6. In **Step 2 of 7**, shift the **EmpSocietiesEO** entity object from the **Available:** pane in the `oracle.apps.xxhr.emp.schema.server` package, to the **Selected:** pane by clicking on **>** as shown in the following screenshot:

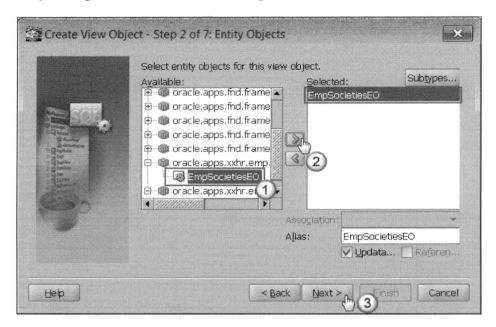

7. Click on the **Next** button.
8. In **Step 3 of 7**, shift all of the attributes from the **EmpSocietiesEO** entity object to the **Selected:** pane as shown in the following screenshot:

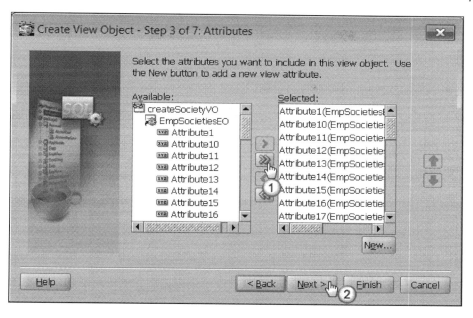

9. Click on **Next**.

10. In **Step 3 of 7**, click on **Next**.

11. In **Step 4 of 7**, click on **Next**.

12. In **Step 5 of 7**, click on **Next**.

13. In **Step 6 of 7**, click on **Next**.

14. In **Step 7 of 7**, uncheck the **Generate Java File** checkbox in **View Object Class: EmpSocietiesCreateVOImpl**.

15. Check the **Generate Java File** and **Accessors** checkboxes in the **View Row Class: EmpSocietiesCreateVORowImpl** checkbox.

16. Click on **Finish**.

17. Click on the **Save All** button from the toolbar.

How it works...

We have now created the view object called EmpSocietiesCreateVO that we are going to use for our create societies page. Next we will need to associate the view object with the application module. The view object will be used to query data based upon the **EmpSocietiesEO** entity object. It needs to be based upon an entity object as we are interacting with a database object.

Linking the view object to an application module

We will now link the view object we have created to the application module that we created in *Chapter 3, Creating a Master Detail Page in OA Framework.*

How to do it...

To link the view object to the application module, perform the following:

1. In the **Application Navigator** tab, right-click the **EmpSocietiesAM** application module and select **Edit EmpSocietiesAM** from the pop-up menu as shown in the following screenshot:

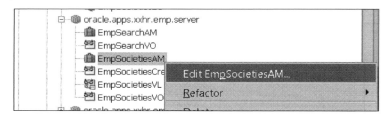

2. In the **Application Module Editor** window select the **Data Model** node.

3. Expand the `oracle.apps.xxhr.emp.server` package and click on the **EmpSocietiesCreateVO** view object.

4. Shift the **EmpSocietiesCreateVO** from **Available View Objects:** to **Data Model:** by clicking the **>** button as shown in the following screenshot:

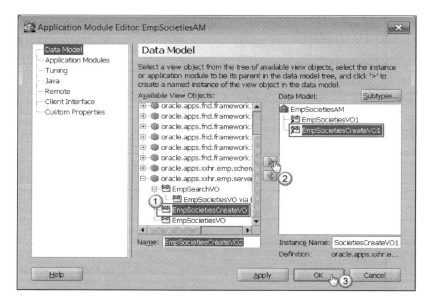

5. Click on **OK**.

6. Click on the **Save All** button from the toolbar.

How it works...

We have now linked the **EmpSocietiesAM** application module with the **EmpSocietiesCreateVO** view object. The name given to the instance of the view object is **EmpSocietiesCreateVO1**. This is provided when we shift the view object over to the application module.

There's more

If you remember from the previous chapter, we should always test our application module. Right-click on the **EmpSocietiesAM** application module in **Applications Navigator** and select **Test** from the pop-up menu. In the **Connect** dialog box, select the **Connect** button. When the **Oracle Business Component Browser** window opens, double-click the **EmpSocietiesCreateVO1** object. The attributes are displayed in alphabetical order, so scroll down to view the attributes, which will contain data as shown in the following screenshot:

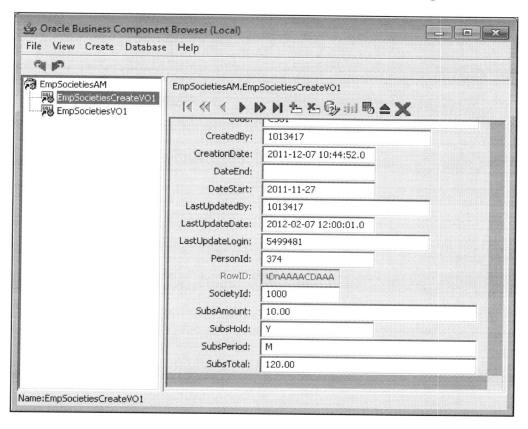

Creating a page to insert data

We are now going to create the page that will allow users to enter new societies and commit the record to the database.

How to do it...

To create a new page, perform the following:

1. In the **Application Navigator** tab, right-click on `oracle.apps.xxhr.emp.webui`.

2. Select **New** from the pop-up menu.

3. In the **New Gallery** window, navigate to **Web Tier | OA Components** and select **Page** from the **Items** list.

4. In the **New Page** dialog box, set the following attributes:

   ❑ **Name:** `CreateSocietyPG`

   ❑ **Package:** `oracle.apps.xxhr.emp.webui`

   The **New Page** dialog window will look like the following:

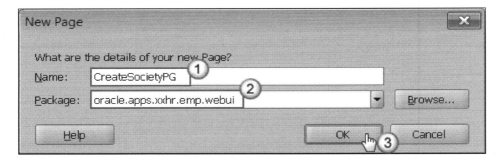

5. Click on **OK**.

6. In the **Application Structure** menu, click on the page called `CreateSocietyPG.xml` page we have just created.

7. In the **Structure** pane, click on **region1** and set the following properties:

   ❑ **ID**: `PageLayoutRN`

   ❑ **AM Definition**: `oracle.apps.xxhr.emp.server.EmpSocietiesAM`

   ❑ **Window Title**: `Employee Societies`

   ❑ **Title**: `Create \ Update Society`

The steps are summarized in the following screenshot:

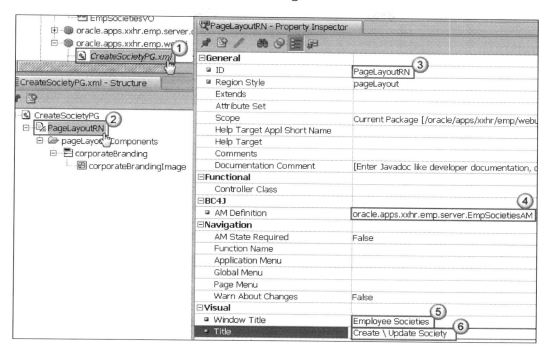

8. Right-click on the **PageLayoutRN** region we have just set the properties for and navigate to **New | Region Using Wizard** from the pop-up menu as shown in the following screenshot:

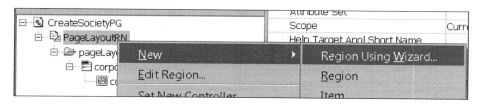

9. In **Step 1 of 4**, select the **oracle.apps.xxhr.emp.server.EmpSocietiesAM** application module from the drop-down list.

10. Click on **EmpSocietiesCreateVO1** from the **Available View Usages:** and click on **Next** as shown in the following screenshot:

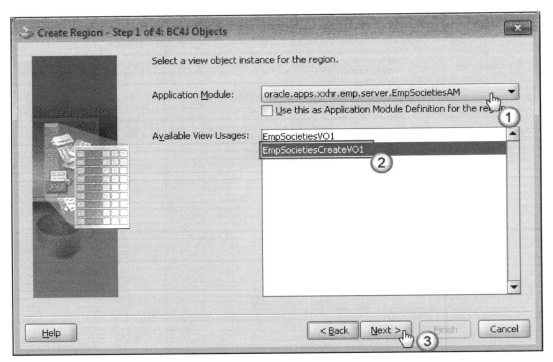

11. In **Step 2 of 4**, set the following values:
   - **Region ID:** EmpSocietiesCreateRN
   - **Region Style: defaultSingleColumn**

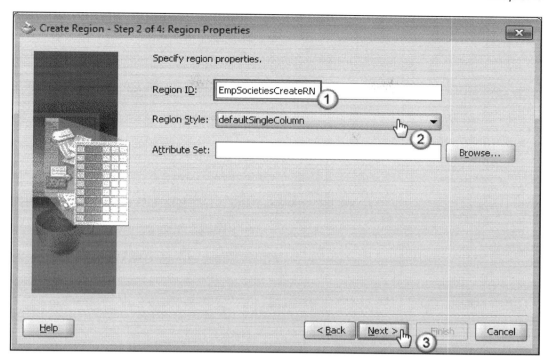

12. In **Step 3 of 4**, shift the following attributes from the **Available View Attributes:** pane to the **Selected View Attributes:** pane:

- ❑ PersonId
- ❑ SocietyId
- ❑ Code
- ❑ DateStart
- ❑ DateEnd
- ❑ SubsAmount
- ❑ SubsPeriod
- ❑ SubsTotal
- ❑ SubsHold

The steps are summarized as shown in the following screenshot:

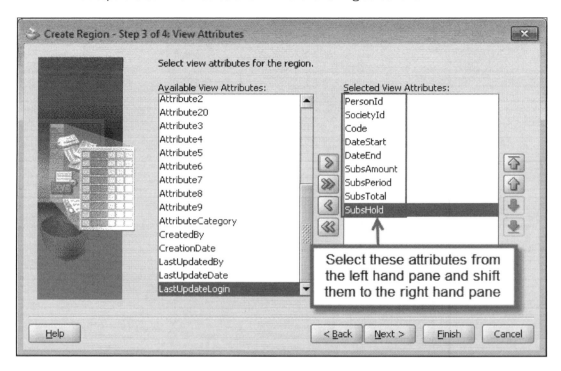

13. Click on **Next**.
14. In **Step 4 of 4**, set the following values:

ID	Prompt	Style	Datatype
PersonId	Person ID	messageStyledText	VARCHAR2
SocietyId	Society ID	messageStyledText	VARCHAR2
Code	Society Code	messageTextInput	VARCHAR2
DateStart	Start Date	messageTextInput	DATE
DateEnd	End Date	messageTextInput	DATE
SubsPeriod	Period	messageTextInput	VARCHAR2
SubsAmount	Amount	messageTextInput	VARCHAR2
SubsTotal	Total	messageTextInput	VARCHAR2
SubsHold	On-Hold	messageCheckBox	VARCHAR2

The following screenshot shows the screen after entering the data from the previous table:

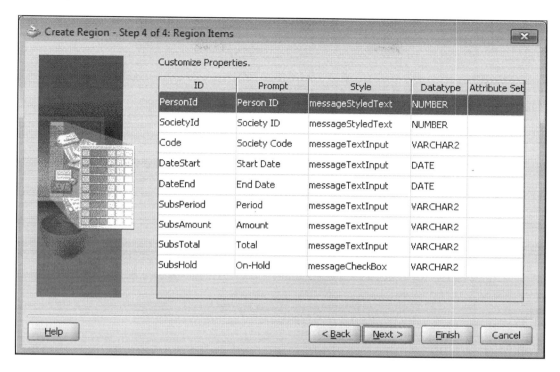

15. Click on **Next** and then on **Finish**.

We will display the SocietyId and PersonId items until we have completed development of the page. After we have completed development we will hide them from the user. Next we are going to set the properties of the checkbox item on the page.

16. In the **Structure** pane, navigate to **CreateSocietiesPG | PageLayoutRN | EmpSocietiesCreateRN | PersonId** and set the following properties:

    □ **Required**: yes

17. In the **Structure** pane, navigate to **CreateSocietiesPG | PageLayoutRN | EmpSocietiesCreateRN | SocietyId** and set the following properties:

    □ **Required**: yes

18. In the **Structure** pane, navigate to **CreateSocietiesPG | PageLayoutRN | EmpSocietiesCreateRN | SubsHold** and set the following properties:

    □ **Checked Value**: Y

    □ **Unchecked Value**: N

The **Subs Hold** properties will appear as shown in the following screenshot:

CreateSocietyPG.xml - Structure		SubsHold - Property Inspector	
□ ⓐ CreateSocietyPG		⊟**General**	
⊟ PageLayoutRN		▪ ID	SubsHold
⊟ EmpSocietiesCreateRN		▪ Item Style	messageCheckBox
⊞ PersonId		Extends	
⊞ SocietyId		Attribute Set	
⊞ Code		Comments	
⊞ DateStart		⊟**Functional**	
⊞ DateEnd		Required	no
⊞ SubsPeriod		Read Only	False
⊞ SubsAmount		Disabled	False
⊞ SubsTotal		Search Allowed	False
⊞ SubsHold		Sort Allowed	no
⊟ pageLayout ⓵ mponents		Initial Sort Sequence	none
⊟ corporate ding		Disable Server Side Validation	False
corporateBrandin		Selective Search Criteria	False
		⊟**Data**	
		▪ Data Type	VARCHAR2
		Initial Value	
		▪ Checked Value	Y ⓶
		▪ Unchecked Value	N ⓷
		Initially Checked	False

19. Click on the **Save All** button from the toolbar.

How it works...

We have now added the items that will be displayed to the user to enter data for the **Create Societies** page. The items are rendered on the screen at runtime. They are rendered in the order in which they appear in the **Structure** tab, as there is no user interface to allow us to move the objects around. We set properties of the items to define how we want the items to behave and how we want them to be displayed.

Adding a page status region

We are now going to add a page status region to display a message if there are any required fields that have not been populated. We are going to inherit this by extending an existing region from the FND framework components.

How to do it...

To add a page status region, perform the following:

1. In **Applications Navigator**, click on the `CreateSocietyPG.xml` page.

2. In the **Structure** pane, right-click on the **PageLayoutRN** region and navigate to **New | pageStatus** from the pop-up menu as shown in the following screenshot:

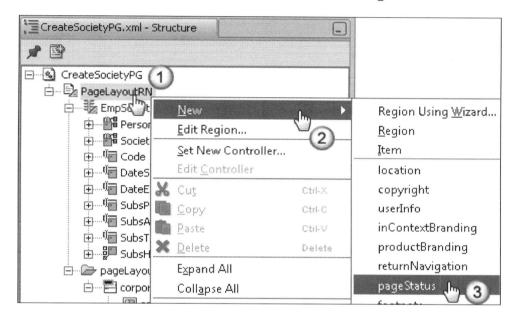

3. Click on **region1**.

4. Set the **ID** property to `PageStatusRN`.

5. Click on the **Extends** property and select the Edit icon.

6. In the **Package:** field, click on the **Browse** button and select `oracle/apps/fnd/framework/webui` from the package browser, and click on **OK**.

7. Now select the **Entire MDS XML Path** radio button.

8. Click on the **Search** button.

9. Select the **OAReqFieldDescRG** from the results as shown in the following screenshot:

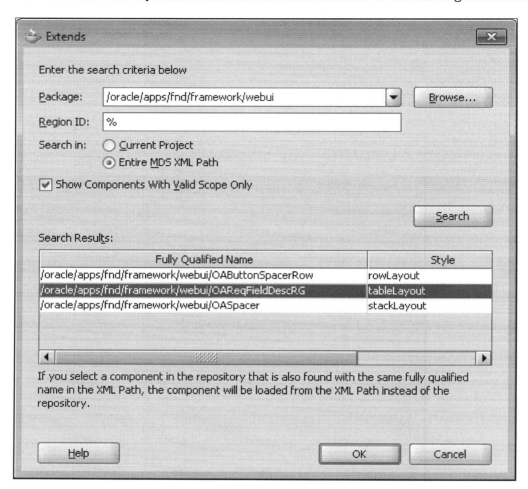

10. Click on **OK**.

How it works...

We have now added a page status region to our page. We can add components that Oracle has created and add them to our pages as we have done here. Oracle has created many generic objects that we can add to our pages when required.

Creating a page buttons region

We are now going to add a new region to which we will add two buttons. One button is called Apply, which will commit any data to the database, and the other button is called Cancel, which will cancel any changes.

How to do it...

To add a buttons region, perform the following:

1. In the **Application Navigator** tab, click on the `CreateSocietyPG.xml` page.

2. In the **Structure** pane, right-click on the **PageLayoutRN** region and select **New | Region** from the pop-up menu as shown in the following screenshot:

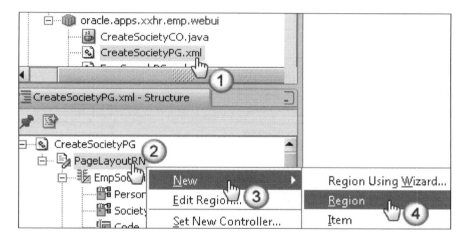

3. Click on the region we have just created called **region1** and set the following properties:

   ❑ **ID**: `PageButtonRN`

   ❑ **Region Style**: `pageButtonBar`

4. Right-click on the **PageButtonBarRN** and select **New | Item** from the pop-up menu.

5. Click on **item1** and set the following properties:

   ❑ **ID**: `Apply`

   ❑ **Item Style**: `submitButton`

The screen should look like the following:

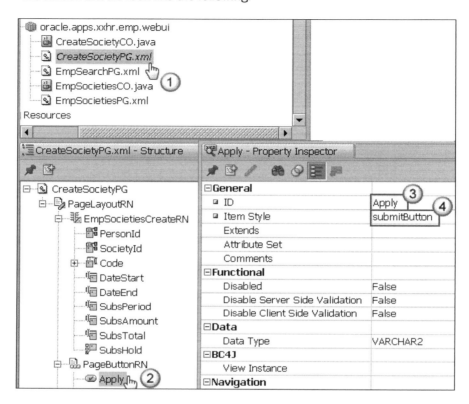

Now we are going to set the **Attribute Set** property to inherit standards for the object. To do this, perform the following:

1. Click on the **Attribute Set** property and click on the Edit icon (⬚).
2. In the **Attribute Set** field, type in %Apply% and click on the **Search** button.

3. Select the Apply fully qualified name from the results and click on the **OK** button as shown in the following screenshot:

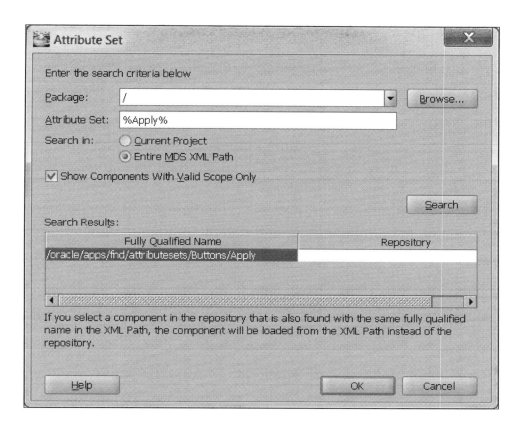

The property will be added as follows:

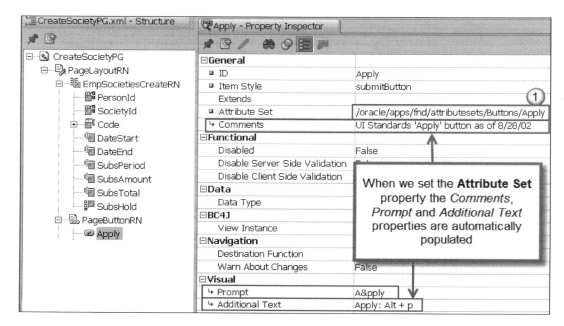

4. Right-click the **PageButtonBarRN** and select **New | Item** from the pop-up menu.

5. Click on **item1** and set the following properties:
   - **ID**: Cancel
   - **Item Style**: submitButton
   - **Attribute Set**: /oracle/apps/fnd/attributesets/Buttons/Cancel

6. Click on the **Save All** button from the toolbar.

How it works...

We have now created the items that we want displayed on our page. In the **Application Navigator** tab, right-click on the CreateSocietyPG.xml and select **Run** from the pop-up menu.

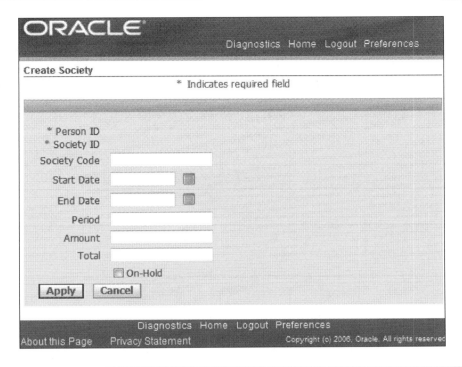

Creating and editing the page controller

Now that we have created the page we will need to code the controller to capture events, such as clicking the buttons and adding code to the application module and entity object layers to perform logic and transactions to the database. First of all, we will create the controller for the page.

How to do it...

To create the controller, perform the following steps:

1. In **Applications Navigator**, click on the `CreateSocietyPG.xml` page.

2. In the **Structure** pane, right-click the **PageLayoutRN** region, and select **Set New Controller...** from the pop-up menu.

3. In the **New Controller** dialog window, set the following item values:

   ❑ **Package Name:** `oracle.apps.xxhr.emp.webui`

   ❑ **Class Name:** `CreateSocietyCO`

The steps are summarized in the following screenshot:

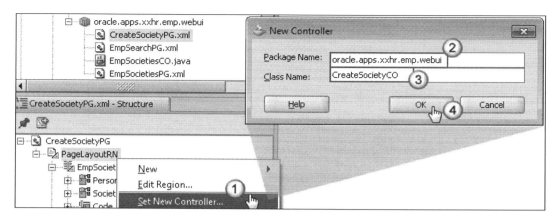

When the dialog window appears, the package name is pre-populated and you will see that `.webui` will be appended to the current package name. Therefore, you would see `oracle.apps.xxhr.emp.webui.webui` in the package name field. Remember to remove the additional `.webui` from the package name as shown in the next screenshot.

The following screenshot shows how the dialog box appears, and highlighted is the duplicate .webui entry that needs to be removed:

4. Click on **OK**.

5. In the **Applications Navigator** tab, double-click `CreateSocietiesCO.java` to open the controller in the editor pane.

   We are now going to add some code to the controller so that when the `processRequest` class is executed, we will generate a new sequence number for our record. Later, we will add to this to put in some conditions but for now we are just going to generate a new sequence whenever we enter the screen.

6. Navigate to the `processRequest` method and add two lines below the `super.processRequest(pageContext, webBean);` line as shown in the following screenshot:

```
public void processRequest(OAPageContext pageContext, OAWebBean webBean)
{
  super.processRequest(pageContext, webBean);
  OAApplicationModule am = pageContext.getApplicationModule(webBean);
  am.invokeMethod("createNewSociety", null);
}
```

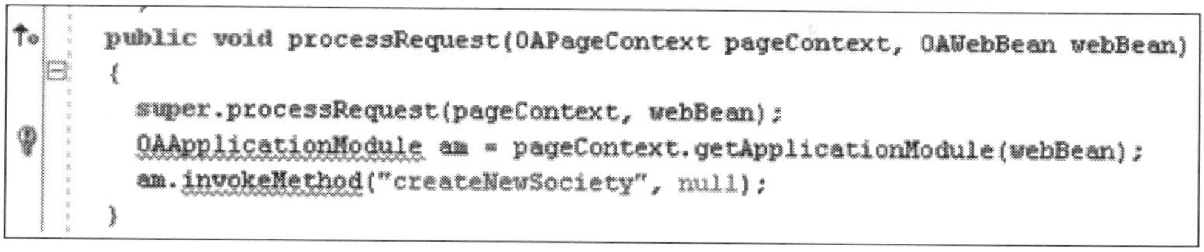

Now in the first line of code, we are creating an instance of the application module. The instance of the application module is called `am`. In the second line of code, we will call a method called `createNewSociety`. We will add the method to the `application module` class.

However, before we do that you will see that some of the code has red lines underneath it. If you hover over the text with red lines in it, the JDeveloper editor will provide information as to why the red line is there. It may be that there is a syntax error, or as in this case, the reference to OAApplicationModule is not valid, as the package is not local and needs to be imported into our class. JDeveloper makes it easy for us to add the package into the import section of the class. To do this, when the balloon message appears, press *Alt + Enter* as shown in the following screenshot:

```
public void processRequest(OAPageContext pageContext, OAWebBean webBean)

 import oracle.apps.fnd.framework.OAApplicationModule; ... (Alt-Enter)

  OAApplicationModule am = pageContext.getApplicationModule(webBean);
  am.invokeMethod("createNewSociety", null);
}
```

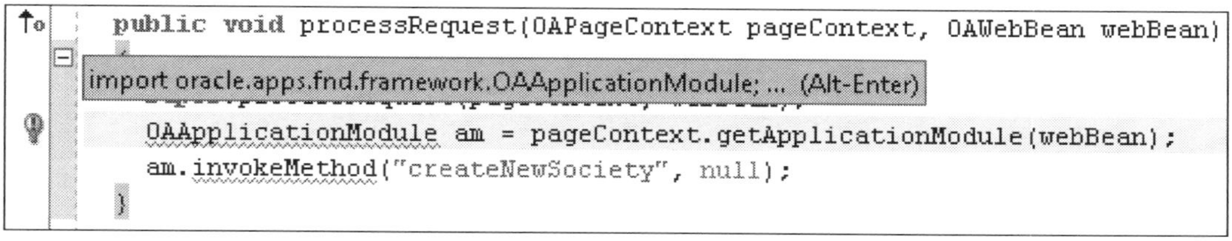

A context menu will appear prompting us what to do as follows:

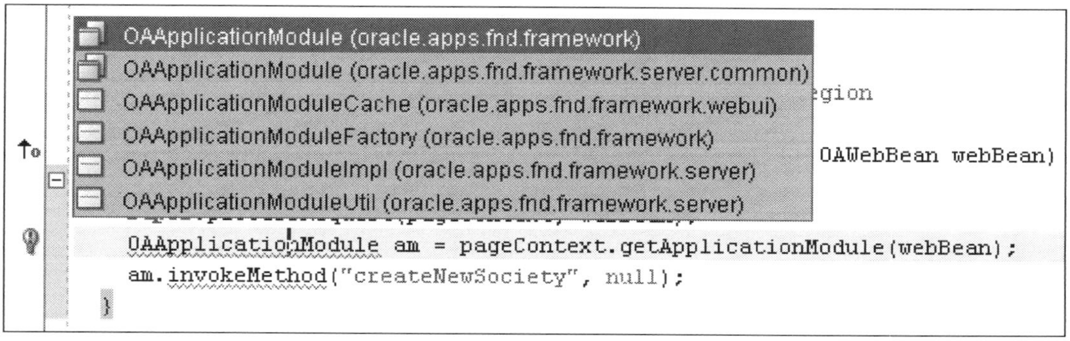

```
OAApplicationModule (oracle.apps.fnd.framework)
OAApplicationModule (oracle.apps.fnd.framework.server.common)
OAApplicationModuleCache (oracle.apps.fnd.framework.webui)      egion
OAApplicationModuleFactory (oracle.apps.fnd.framework)
OAApplicationModuleImpl (oracle.apps.fnd.framework.server)       OAWebBean webBean)
OAApplicationModuleUtil (oracle.apps.fnd.framework.server)

  OAApplicationModule am = pageContext.getApplicationModule(webBean);
  am.invokeMethod("createNewSociety", null);
}
```

If we double-click on the **OAApplicationModule (oracle.apps.fnd.framework)** in the list, the package automatically gets added to the import section.

Alternatively, we can click on the light bulb in the left-hand side of the code to see various options available in relation to the perceived problem. In this case, we would select the **Import 'oracle.apps.fnd.framework.OAApplicationModule'** from the list as shown in the following screenshot:

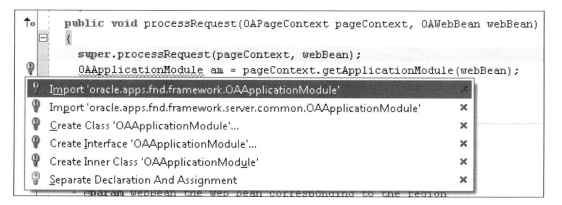

How it works...

If we now scroll up to the `import` section of the class, we will see that the package has been added automatically as shown in the following screenshot:

```
CreateSocietyCO.java
/*==============================================================+
 |   Copyright (c) 2001, 2005 Oracle Corporation, Redwood Shores, CA, USA  |
 |                        All rights reserved.                     |
 +==============================================================+
 |   HISTORY                                                       |
 +==============================================================*/
package oracle.apps.xxhr.emp.webui;

import oracle.apps.fnd.common.VersionInfo;
import oracle.apps.fnd.framework.OAApplicationModule;
import oracle.apps.fnd.framework.OAException;
import oracle.apps.fnd.framework.webui.OAControllerImpl;
import oracle.apps.fnd.framework.webui.OAPageContext;
import oracle.apps.fnd.framework.webui.OAWebBeanConstants;
import oracle.apps.fnd.framework.webui.beans.OAWebBean;
```

Capturing an event

We capture events that occur during runtime in the `processFomRequest` method. Now we are going to add code to the `processFormRequest` method to capture the event when the **Apply** button is pressed.

How to do it...

To do this, scroll down to the `processFormRequest` method and add the code as shown in the following screenshot:

```
public void processFormRequest(OAPageContext pageContext, OAWebBean webBean)
{
    super.processFormRequest(pageContext, webBean);
    OAApplicationModule am = pageContext.getApplicationModule(webBean);

    // Capturing the event when the Apply button is clicked
    if (pageContext.getParameter("Apply") != null) {
        // Call a method to commit the transaction and display a message
        am.invokeMethod("commitTransaction");
        throw new OAException("Society successfully created");
    }
}
```

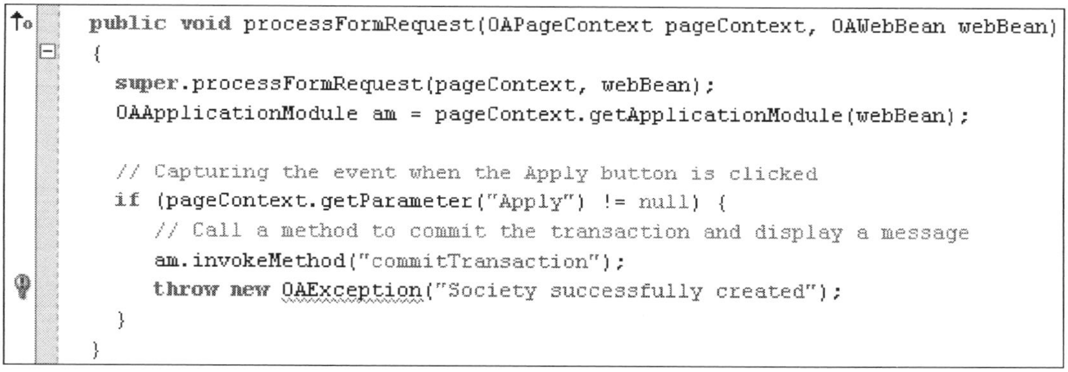

In this method, we again create an instance of the application module called `am`. We will then check if the event calling `processFormRequest` is the **Apply** button being pressed. If it is, we will call a method in our application module to commit the record to the database. After the commit, we will display a message to the user to inform them that the record has been saved successfully.

Again, you will see that `OAException` is underlined, so we need to add the package to the import section. As we did before, click the light bulb and select **Import 'oracle.apps.fnd. framework.OAException'** as shown in the following screenshot:

```
        if (pageContext.getParameter("Apply") != null) {

            am.invokeMethod("commitTransaction");
            throw new OAException ("Society successfully created"); :
```

Import 'oracle.apps.fnd.framework.OAException'	✕
Create Class 'OAException'...	✕
Create Inner Class 'OAException'	✕

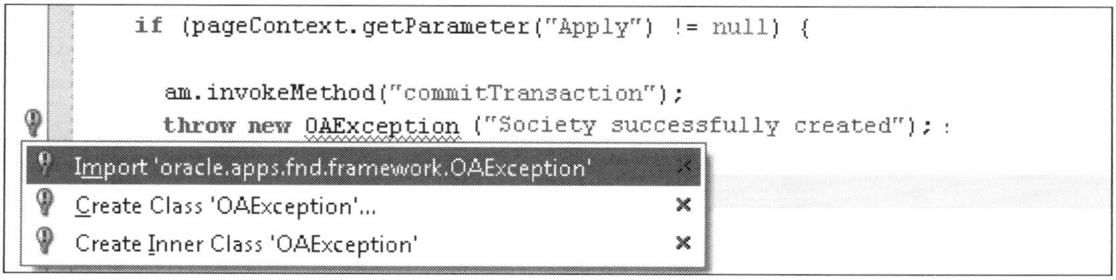

How it works...

We have now captured the user clicking the Apply button on the screen. When the user does this, we call a method in the application method java class called `commitTransaction` and then display a message to the user that the transaction has completed successfully.

Editing the application module class

We are now going to add the class we call from the `processRequest` method to the application module class.

How to do it...

To add the method to the application module class, perform the following:

1. In **Applications Navigator**, right-click on the **EmpSocietiesAM** application module and select **Go to Application Module Class** from the pop-up menu as shown in the following screenshot:

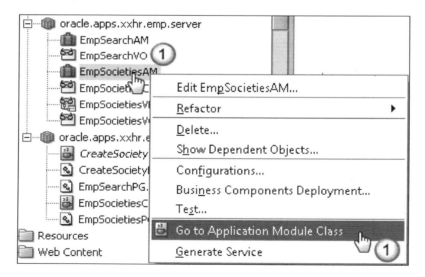

2. Scroll down to the end of the class and add the `createNewSociety` method we call from the controller as shown in the following screenshot:

```
/**
 * createNewSociety method
 */
public void createNewSociety(String paramPersonId) {
    // Create an instance of the view object and call it vo
    EmpSocietiesCreateVOImpl vo = getEmpSocietiesCreateVO1();

    // We need to do this on a VO that has not been queried before we insert
    // our first row.  We don't want to do it for subsequent inserts.
    if (vo.getFetchedRowCount() == 0)
    {
        vo.setMaxFetchSize(0);
    }
    // We are now going to create a record in the view object
    Row row = vo.createRow();
    row.setAttribute("PersonId", paramPersonId);
    // Now we will call the standard method to insert the record
    vo.insertRow(row);
    // Required as per OA Framework Model Coding Standard M69
    row.setNewRowState(Row.STATUS_INITIALIZED);
}
```

3. Now add the following method called `commitTransaction`, directly after the `createNewSociety` method to commit the transaction.

```
/** commitTransaction method
 */
public void commitTransaction() {
    // Commit the transaction
    getTransaction().commit();
}
}
```

4. Click on the **Save All** button from the toolbar.

How it works...

We have added two methods to the application module `EmpSocietiesAMImpl` class. We are going to edit the create method to generate a sequence number for the society record when we enter the page.

Editing the entity object class

We will now edit the entity object which interacts with the database table.

How to do it...

To add methods to the entity object class, perform the following:

1. In **Applications Navigator**, right-click the **EmpSocietiesEO** entity object and select **Go to Entity Object Class** from the pop-up menu as shown in the following screenshot:

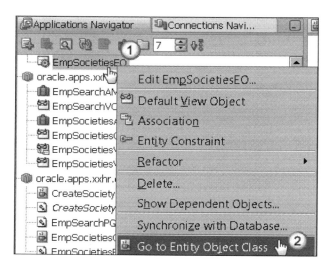

2. Scroll down and edit the `create` method to get a new sequence number for the **Society ID**.

   You can select **Search** from the menu and type `void create` in the **Text to Search For:** field as shown in the following screenshot:

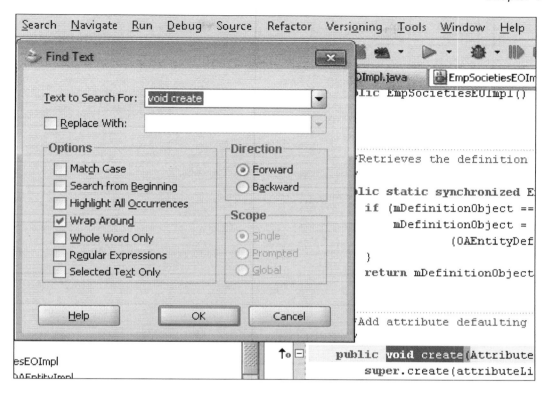

3. Amend the create method with the following code:

```
/**Add attribute defaulting logic in this method.
 */
public void create(AttributeList attributeList) {
    super.create(attributeList);

    // To access database, we need the class - OADBTransaction
    OADBTransaction txn = getOADBTransaction();

    // SocietyId is obtained from the SEQUENCE called XXHR_PER_SOCIETIES_SEQ
    // and then we set the societyId by calling the setter method
    Number societyId = txn.getSequenceValue("XXHR_PER_SOCIETIES_SEQ");
    setSocietyId(societyId);

}
```

As we did earlier, if we have any red underlined text we need to import the package (OADBTransaction) into the class by clicking the light bulb icon and selecting the `Import 'oracle.apps.fnd.framework.server.OADBTransaction'` item as shown in the following screenshot:

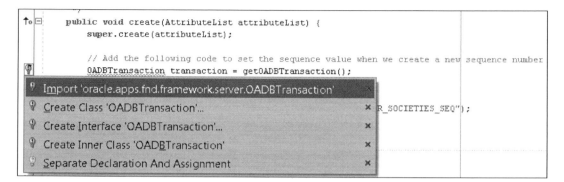

If we scroll to the top and look at the import section, we can see that the package has been added to the class.

```
EmpSocietiesEOImpl.java

    package oracle.apps.xxhr.emp.schema.server;

    import oracle.apps.fnd.framework.server.OADBTransaction;
    import oracle.apps.fnd.framework.server.OAEntityDefImpl;
    import oracle.apps.fnd.framework.server.OAEntityImpl;

    import oracle.jbo.AttributeList;
    import oracle.jbo.domain.Date;
    import oracle.jbo.domain.Number;
    import oracle.jbo.domain.RowID;
    import oracle.jbo.server.AttributeDefImpl;
    import oracle.jbo.server.EntityDefImpl;
```

How it works...

If we now run the page we can see that the **Society ID** is populated with a value from our database sequence as shown in the following screenshot. We need to create a unique identifier when we insert records. The next available number is obtained from the **EMP_PER_SOCIETIES_SEQ** sequence we created at the start of the chapter.

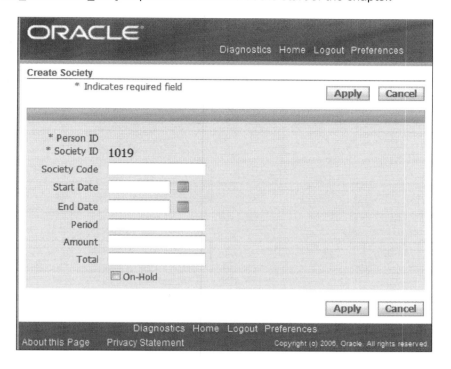

There's more...

If we want to default any other values, we can do this in the entity object. Let's say for example, we want to default the start date item to the current date. We can add two lines to the code to the `create` method as follows:

```
public void create(AttributeList attributeList) {
    super.create(attributeList);

    // To access database, we need the class - OADBTransaction
    OADBTransaction txn = getOADBTransaction();

    // SocietyId is obtained from the SEQUENCE called XXHR_PER_SOCIETIES_SE
    // and then we set the societyId by calling the setter method
    Number societyId = txn.getSequenceValue("XXHR_PER_SOCIETIES_SEQ");
    setSocietyId(societyId);

    // Set the default start date
    Date startDate = txn.getCurrentDBDate();
    setDateStart(startDate);
}
```

If we now run the form, we can see that the start date is now defaulted to the current date.

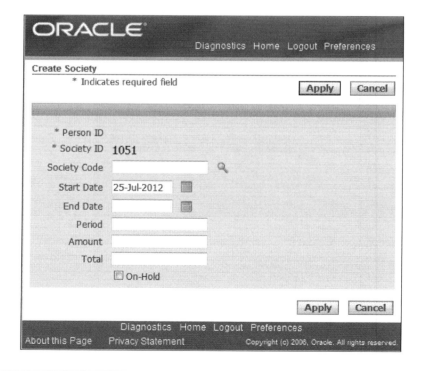

Passing the parameters

When we call the page, we will pass a value in for the Person ID field. You will notice that at present the value is empty. Therefore, we need to populate this with the value of the PersonId parameter we are using to call the page. In preparation for this, we will set a default value of 1234 in the controller. Later on when we add the code to call this page from our **EmpSocietiesPG**, we will add the PersonId parameter that is passed.

How to do it...

To set a default value, perform the following:

1. Open the CreateSocietyCO.java controller and edit the processRequest method. Remember the processRequest method executes when the page is initialized, so this is where we will set the default value.

2. Create a parameter list that we can pass to our createNewSociety method by adding the following code:

```
public void processRequest(OAPageContext pageContext, OAWebBean webBean)
{
  super.processRequest(pageContext, webBean);
  OAApplicationModule am = pageContext.getApplicationModule(webBean);
  // for now we are going to set teh personId parameter to a dummy value of 1234
  String paramPersonId = "1234"; (1)
  // add a parameter list that we can use to pass parameters
  // into our createNewSociety method
  Serializable[] params = {paramPersonId}; (2)
  am.invokeMethod("createNewSociety", params); (3)
}
```

 Add any new packages to the import statement by clicking on the light bulb in the margin as we have previously.

First, we create a parameter that we will add to a parameter list. We then add the parameter to the parameter list. Finally, we will edit the call to the createNewSociety method to add the parameter list called params that we pass in the call to the createNewSociety method. Next we need to amend the createNewSociety method to accept the parameters we pass in the parameter list. Perform the following steps:

1. Open the `EmpSocietiesAMImpl.java` java class and edit the `createNewSociety` method.

```java
/** createNewSociety method
 */
public void createNewSociety(String paramPersonId) {
  // Create an instance of the view object and call it vo
  EmpSocietiesCreateVOImpl vo = getEmpSocietiesCreateVO1();

  // We need to do this on a VO that has not been queried before we insert
  // our first row.  We don't want to do it for subsequent inserts.
  if (vo.getFetchedRowCount() == 0)
  {
    vo.setMaxFetchSize(0);
  }
  // We are now going to create a record in the view object
  Row row = vo.createRow();
  // Set the PersonId field to the paramPersonId we have passed
  // in the parameter list called params to the method
  row.setAttribute("PersonId", paramPersonId);

  // Now we will call the satndard method to insert the record
  vo.insertRow(row);
  // Required as per OA Framework Model Coding Standard M69
  row.setNewRowState(Row.STATUS_INITIALIZED);
}
```

2. Click on **Save All**.

How it works...

We have now added code to the call to the `createNewSociety` method to pass parameters. When we run the page, we can see that the **Person ID** is populated with a dummy static value of **1234**. We will be editing the code later on to pass the `PersonId` value, which will be passed as a parameter from the calling page.

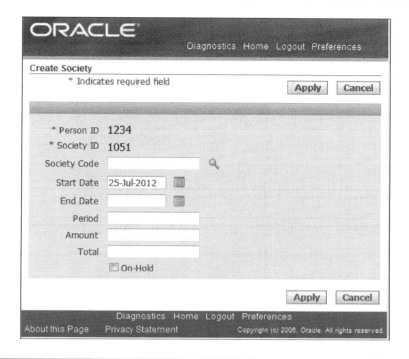

Creating a list of values

Okay, now that we have populated the primary and foreign keys on our page, we will add a list of values for the **Society Code** field. When we create a list of values, we will create a new region. To create a list of values we will perform the following tasks:

- ▶ Creating an application module for LOV
- ▶ Creating a view object for LOV
- ▶ Linking the application module to the view object
- ▶ Creating a region for the list of values
- ▶ Linking the LOV region to an item

Creating the application module

First of all we are going to create the application module for the list of values. We only need an application module and view object, as we are not dealing with database transactions and therefore, do not need to create an entity object. The advantage of creating an application module for the **list of values** (**LOV**) specifically means that we will avoid caching of the LOV object and therefore, it should be independent of the application module associated with the page.

How to do it...

To create an application module for a list of values, perform the following:

1. In **Applications Navigator**, right-click on **OAPacktProject** and navigate to **New | Business Tier | ADF Business Components | Application Module** from the pop-up menu, as shown in the following screenshot:

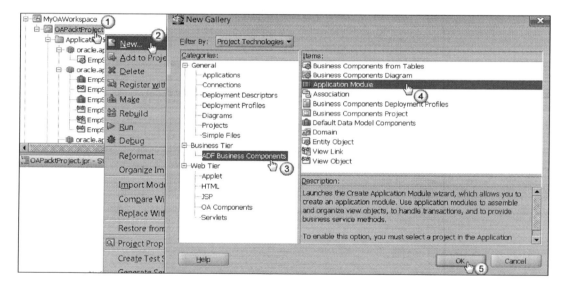

2. Click on **OK** to launch the **Create Application Module** wizard.

3. In **Step 1 of 4**, set the following values and click on **Next** as shown in the following screenshot:

    ▫ **Package:** `oracle.apps.xxhr.emp.lov.server`

    ▫ **Name:** `SocietyNameLovAM`

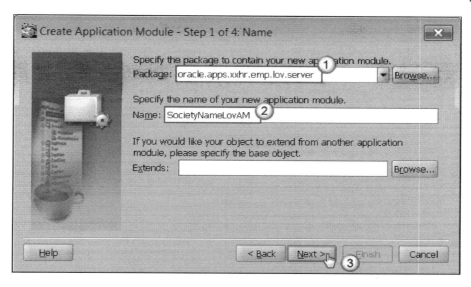

4. In **Step 2 of 4**, click on **Next**.

5. In **Step 3 of 4**, click on **Next**.

6. In **Step 4 of 4**, uncheck the **Generate Java Files checkbox** and click on **Finish**.

How it works...

The application module will be created in the new package as shown in the following screenshot. It is standard to create the list of values in its own package as follows:

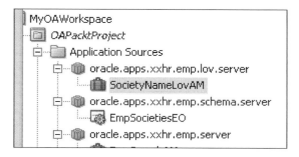

Creating the view object

We are now going to create the view object for the list of values. Our list of values is based upon a lookup called XXHR_SOCIETY_LOV. We created this earlier in the book and we are going to query this list to populate the **Society Code** field.

How to do it...

Now we will create the view object for the list of values. To do this, perform the following:

1. Right-click on the `oracle.apps.xxhr.emp.lov.server` package and select **New View Object...** from the pop-up menu.

2. In **Step 1 of 7** of the **Create View Object** wizard, set the following values:

   - **Package:** `oracle.apps.xxhr.emp.lov.server`
   - **Name:** `SocietyNameLovVO`

3. Select the **Read-only Access** radio button and click on Next.

   A summary of the steps is shown in the following screenshot:

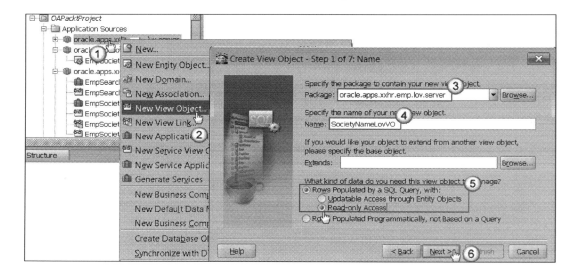

4. In **Step 2 of 7**, add the following query in the **Query Statement** field:

```
SELECT flv.lookup_code,
       flv.meaning
  FROM fnd_lookup_values flv
 WHERE flv.lookup_type = 'XXHR_SOCIETY_LOV'
```

Test the query by clicking on the **Test** button as shown in the following screenshot:

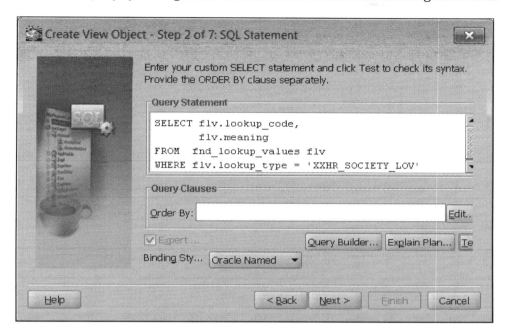

5. Click on **Next**.

6. In **Step 2 of 7**, click on **Next**.

7. In **Step 3 of 7**, click on **Next**.

8. In **Step 4 of 7**, click on **Next**.

9. In **Step 5 of 7**, click on **Next**.

10. In **Step 6 of 7**, click on **Next**.

11. In **Step 7 of 7**, uncheck **Generate Java File** in **View Object Class: SocietyNameLovVOImpl** and check **Generate Java File** in **View Row Class: SocietyNameLovVORowImpl**, as shown in the following screenshot:

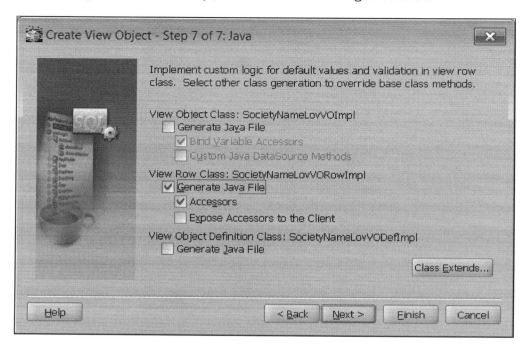

12. Click on **Finish**.

How it works...

We have now created the view object for the list of values. This will provide the query for the data that will be displayed when the list of values is initiated by a user.

Linking the application module to the view object

We now need to link the view object and application module.

How to do it...

To link the view object and application module, perform the following:

1. In **Applications Navigator**, double-click the **SocietyNameLovAM** application module.

2. When the **Application Module Editor: SocietyNameLovAM** window opens, click on **Data Model**.

3. Shift **SocietyNameLovVO** from the **Available View Objects:** pane to the **Data Model:** pane as shown in the following screenshot:

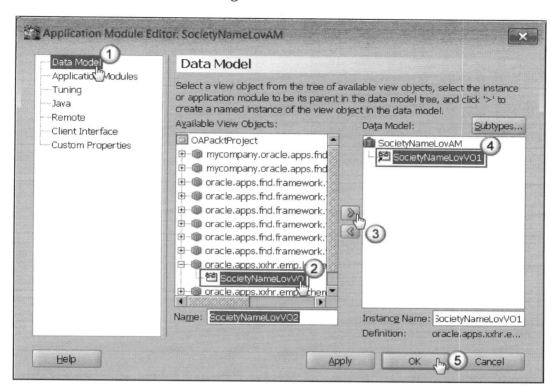

4. Click on **OK**.
5. Click on **Save All** from the toolbar menu.

How it works...

We have now linked the application module with the view object. We should test our application module. As we have done before, right-click on the application module, connect to the database, and double-click the **SocietyNameLovVO1** instance as shown in the following screenshot:

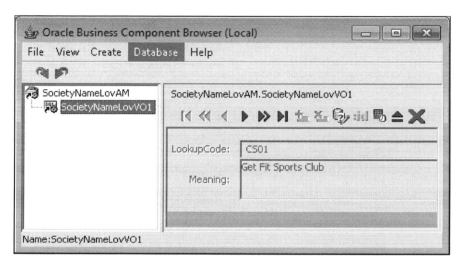

Creating the region for the list of values

We will now create the **User Interface XML** (**UIX**) layer for the list of values. We will first of all create a region to contain all of the UIX components.

How to do it...

To create the region for the list of values, perform the following:

1. In **Applications Navigator**, right-click on the **OAPacktProject** project and navigate to **New | Web Tier | OA Components | Region**.

2. In the **New Region** dialog window set the following fields:

   ▫ **Name:** SocietyNameLovRN

   ▫ **Package:** oracle.apps.xxhr.emp.lov.webui

   ▫ **Style: listOfValues**

3. Click on **OK** as shown in the following screenshot:

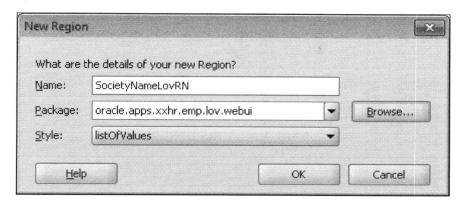

4. Click on **SocietyNameLovRN** in **Applications Navigator**.

5. In the *Structure* window, click on **SocietyNameLovRN** and set the following properties:

   - **Scope**: Public

   - **Advanced Search Allowed**: True

   - **AM Definition**: oracle.apps.xxhr.emp.lov.server. SocietyNameLovAM

The properties should now be set as follows:

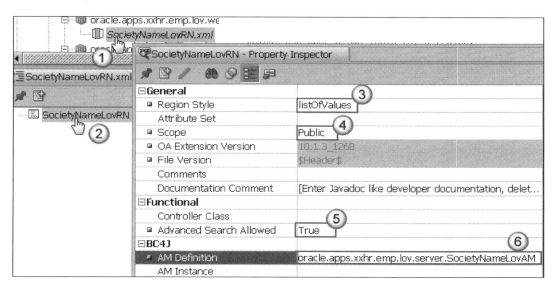

6. In the **Structure** window, right-click on **SocietyNameLovRN** and navigate to **New | Table Using Wizard** from the pop-up menu.

7. In **Step 1 of 4**, set the **Application Module:** field to `oracle.apps.xxhr.emp.lov.server.SocietyNameLovAM`, and then click on **SocietyNAmeLovVO1** from the **Available View Usages:** pane as shown in the following screenshot:

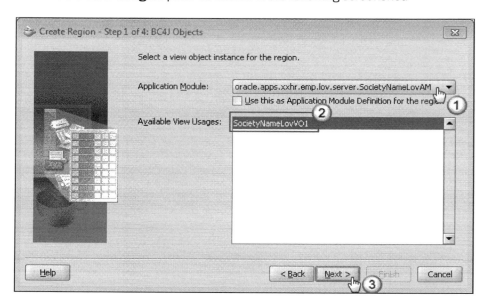

8. Click on **Next**.

9. In **Step 2 of 4**, set the following values:

    □ **Region ID:** `SocietyNameResultsRN`

    □ **Region Style:** `table`

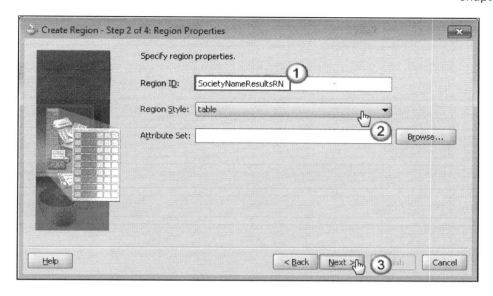

10. Click on **Next**.

11. In **Step 3 of 4**, shift the following fields from the **Available View Attributes:** pane to the **Selected View Attributes:** pane:

    ❑ LookupCode

    ❑ Meaning

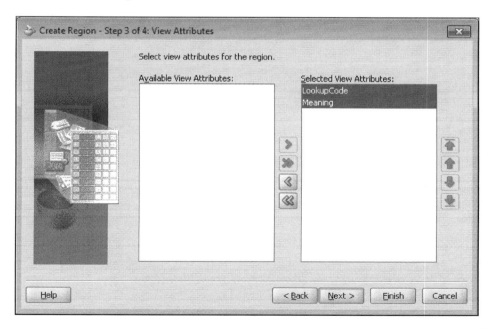

12. Click on **Next**.

13. Set the prompts as shown in the following screenshot:

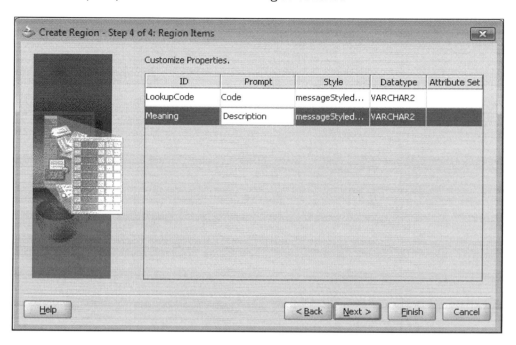

14. Click on **Finish**.

15. In the **Structure** window, navigate to **SocietyNameLovRN | SocietyNameResultsRN | LookupCode** and set the following properties:

    - **Selective Search Criteria**: True
    - **Prompt**: Society Code

16. In the **Structure** window, navigate to **SocietyNameLovRN | SocietyNameResultsRN | Meaning** and set the following properties:

    - **Selective Search Criteria**: True
    - **Prompt**: Description

17. Click on **Save All** from the toolbar menu.

How it works...

We have now created the region for the list of values. Now we need to link the list of values to an item in our **CreateSocietiesPG** page.

Linking the LOV region to an item

We are now going to link the LOV we have just created to the Society Code field in our create Societies page.

How to do it...

To link the LOV region to an item, perform the following:

1. In **Applications Navigator**, click on the `CreateSocietyPG.xml` page in `oracle.apps.xxhr.emp.webui`.

2. In the **Structure** window, navigate to **CreateSocietiesPG | PageLayoutRN | EmpSocietiesCreateRN | Code** and set the following properties:

   - **Item Style**: `messageLovInput`
   - **External LOV**: `/oracle/apps/xxhr/emp/lov/webui/SocietyNameLovRN`

> Dismiss any message that warns of removing any existing LOV mappings. These messages are warning messages and we do not want to retain the existing mappings.

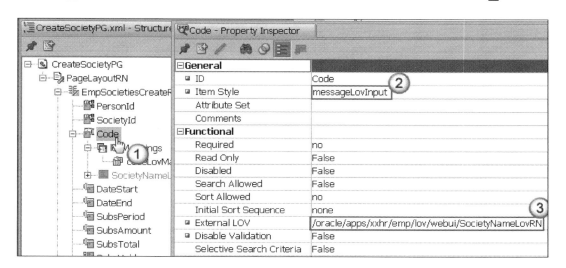

3. Expand the **lovMappings** objects in **Code** and set the following properties of the **lovMap1** item as follows:

   ❑ **ID**: codeLovMap

   ❑ **LOV Region Item**: LookupCode

   ❑ **Return Item**: Code

   ❑ **Criteria Item**: Code

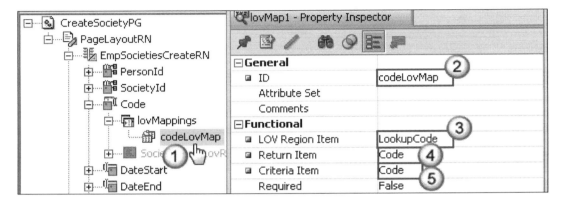

4. Click on **Save All** from the toolbar menu.

How it works...

We have now linked the LOV to the item. Now, an icon will appear next to the field to show that there is a list of values available. The user will be able to select a value from the LOV associated with the item.

Adding a link to a region

In this recipe, we are going to add an item to the records returned in the Employee Societies page. When a user clicks the button we will capture some key attributes from the row and pass them to the create society page.

To create a link item, we will perform the following actions:

▶ Creating a link item

▶ Capturing the create item event

Creating a link item

We are now going to add an item to the row, which will display a create icon on each row of the employee records in the **EmpMasterRN** region.

How to do it...

To add an item to create a new society record, perform the following:

1. In **Applications Navigator**, click on the EmpSocietiesPG.xml page.

2. In the **Structure** tab, right-click the **EmpMasterRN** and navigate to **New | column** from the pop-up menu.

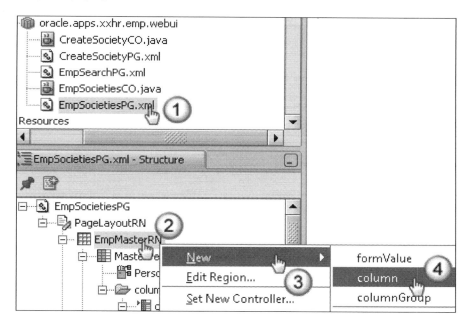

3. Click the item created and set the **ID** property of the column to AddSocietyCol.

4. Right-click on the AddSocietyCol column and navigate to **New | Item** from the pop-up menu. Set the following properties:

    ❑ **ID**: AddSociety

    ❑ **Item Style**: link

    ❑ **ActionType**: fireAction

    ❑ **Event**: addSociety

5. Now we will add the parameter details, so click on the edit icon in the **Parameters** property.

6. When the **Parameters** screen opens, click on the **Add Parameters** button.

7. Add the following parameters:

  ❑ **Name**: `paramMasterPersonId`

  ❑ **Value**: `${oa.EmpSearchVO1.PersonId}`

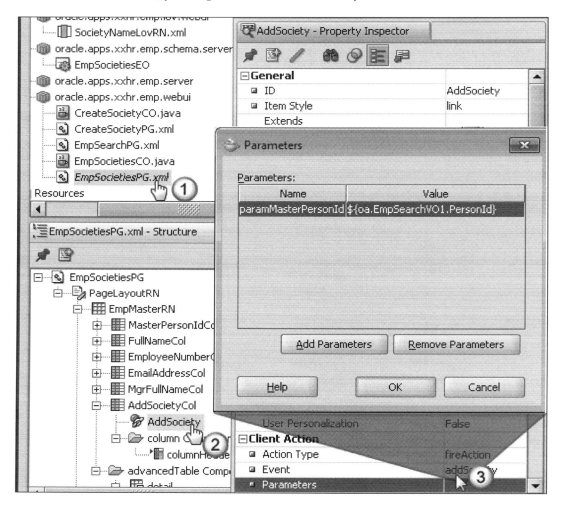

8. Click on **OK**.

9. Right-click the **AddSociety** item and navigate to **New | Image** from the pop-up menu.

10. Set the following properties of the new item:

   ❑ **ID**: `AddSocietyImage`

   ❑ **Item Style**: `image`

   ❑ **Image URI**: `addicon_enabled.gif`

The steps are summarized in the following screenshot:

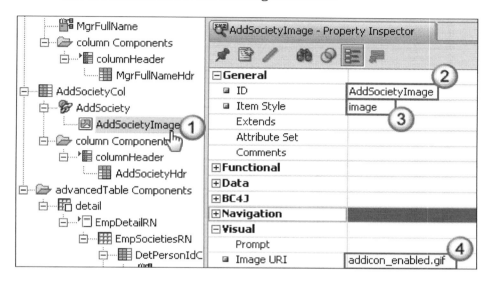

11. Right-click on **columnHeader** in **AddSocietyCol | column Components |** and navigate to **New | sortableHeader1** from the pop-up menu.

12. Set the following properties of the **sortableHeader1** item:

   ❑ **ID**: `AddSocietyHdr`

   ❑ **Prompt**: `Add Society`

13. Click on **Save All** from the toolbar menu.

How it works...

The new item components will now be created and the structure should appear as follows:

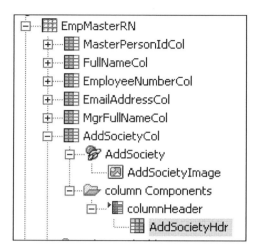

Capturing the create item event

We are now going to capture the `PersonId` of the record on which the create society icon was clicked by the user. We will then display a message to show that we have captured the value.

How to do it...

To capture the event and display a message, perform the following:

1. In **Applications Navigator**, double-click on the `EmpSocietiesCO.java` file.

2. Scroll down the controller to the `processFormRequest` method.

3. Add the following code to capture the event, capture the `PersonId`, and display it in a message when the user clicks the icon:

```
public void processFormRequest(OAPageContext pageContext, OAWebBean webBean)
{
    super.processFormRequest(pageContext, webBean);

    // Get the action in the employee region
    String actionInEmpRegion = pageContext.getParameter(EVENT_PARAM);

    // Perform logic for clicking the addSociety image
    if (actionInEmpRegion.equals("addSociety")){
        // Get the personId of the employee we clicked the crete society ocon for
        String actionPersonId = pageContext.getParameter("paramMasterPersonId");
        // Display the action and the personId in a message on the screen
        throw new OAException("Action triggered is " + actionInEmpRegion
                        + " and the PersonId captured is " + actionPersonId
                        , OAException.CONFIRMATION);
    }
}
```

4. Click on **Save All** from the toolbar menu.

How it works...

We have now added the code that will capture the parameter value that we want to pass to our create society page and now we are going to test it.

Right-click on the `EmpSocietiesPG.xml` page and select **Run** from the pop-up menu. The page will be displayed. Now we will see that we have a new column called **Add Society**. If we click on the icon, we will get the confirmation message displayed that will show us the event that was triggered (`addSociety`) and the value of the parameter `paramPersonId`. The screen will look similar to the page in the following screenshot:

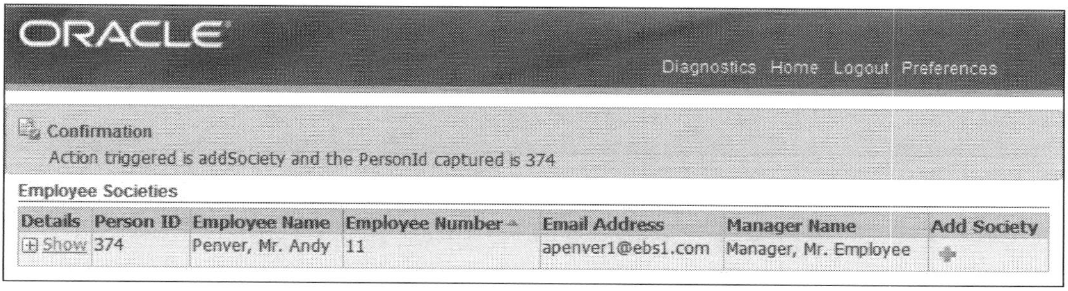

ORACLE

Diagnostics   Home   Logout   Preferences

Confirmation
Action triggered is addSociety and the PersonId captured is 374

Employee Societies

Details	Person ID	Employee Name	Employee Number ▲	Email Address	Manager Name	Add Society
⊞ Show	374	Penver, Mr. Andy	11	apenver1@ebs1.com	Manager, Mr. Employee	✛

Running a page in the debug mode

This next recipe is going to use the debugger within JDeveloper. This is invaluable when developing and when we want to debug our code, as it is laborious to keep putting debug messages in the code. Using the debugger will make life much easier for us during development.

How to do it...

To run the page in the **Debug** mode, perform the following:

1. In JDeveloper, open the `EmpSocietiesCO.java` file if it is not already open.

2. Scroll down the controller to the `processFormRequest` method and click on the left-hand side column to add some break points, as shown in the following screenshot:

```java
public void processFormRequest(OAPageContext pageContext, OAWebBean webBean)
{
    super.processFormRequest(pageContext, webBean);
    OAApplicationModule am = pageContext.getApplicationModule(webBean);

    String actionInEmpRegion = pageContext.getParameter(EVENT_PARAM);
    String actionPersonId = pageContext.getParameter("paramMasterPersonId");

    // Handle the submit button press actions.
    if (actionInEmpRegion.equals("addSociety"))
    {
        throw new OAException("Action triggered is " + actionInEmpRegion
                        + " and the PersonId Captured is " + actionPersonId
                        , OAException.CONFIRMATION);
```

3. Now when we run the page, we will select **Debug** from the pop-up menu instead of **Run,** as shown in the following screenshot:

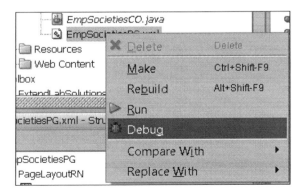

4. When the page opens as shown in the following screenshot, click on **+** icon in the **Add Society** column:

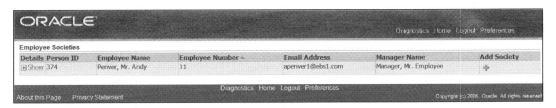

At this point, go back to JDeveloper and we can see that the debugger has stopped at our first break point. The line the debugger has stopped on is highlighted in blue in the following screenshot:

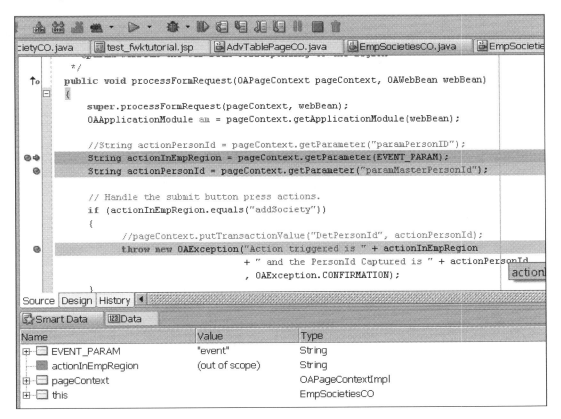

If we click on the **Resume** button, the debugger will jump to the next breakpoint in the code. If we look at the **Smart Data** tab, we can also see that the `actionInEmpRegion` and `actionInPersonId` variables have been created and the current values are populated as shown in the following screenshot. We can also add or remove breakpoints while the page is running rather than restarting the debugger.

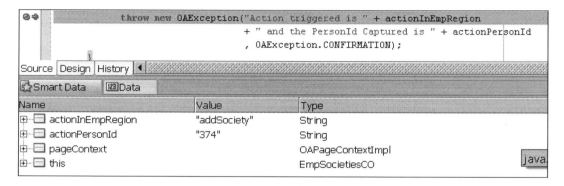

How it works...

We need to use the debugger when we develop pages in OA Framework. It is an easy way to establish what is happening at specific points in the code.

5
Advanced OA Framework

In this chapter we will cover:

- ▶ Navigating between OA Framework pages
- ▶ Updating records
- ▶ Adding a validation to the page
- ▶ Calling PL/SQL from the OAF Page
- ▶ Adding a decision message
- ▶ Partial Page Rendering
- ▶ Viewing a page from EBS
- ▶ Transferring the files

Introduction

In this chapter, we will get into some more advanced features of OA Framework pages, which include much more coding. The chapter will continue to develop the pages we have worked on so far.

Navigating between OA Framework pages

We are now going to add code that will navigate between pages. We will also pass parameters so that we can pass data from one page to another. We are going to show how we can pass parameters in different ways. We will perform the following actions in this recipe:

- ▶ Adding logic to navigate between pages and pass parameters
- ▶ Adding code to the destination page to capture the parameters passed
- ▶ Creating a dictionary message
- ▶ Adding logic and calling a dictionary message
- ▶ Adding logic for a `Cancel` button
- ▶ Adding a method to roll back a transaction

Adding logic to navigate between pages and pass parameters

The method that we are going to use to call our create society page is `pageContext.setForwardURL`. We are going to pass parameters in the URL, and as a parameter list, in the following recipe.

How to do it...

To navigate to the **createSocietiesPG** page, perform the following steps:

1. Under the **Applications Navigator** tab, double click on the **EmpSocietiesCO.java** file, and in the editor, scroll down to the `processFormRequest` method.

2. Comment out the exception that displays a confirmation message (starting `throw new OAException`...). We put the exception to raise a message, but if we leave it here, the exception will always exit the method before we reach any code after the exception. This was done previously to show how we could display the values of variables in the method. Going forward we will use the debugger.

3. Define a hash map to store parameters that will be passed with the forward URL method.

4. Add a new parameter to the HashMap.

5. Call the `createSocietyPG` page by calling the method `pageContext.setForwardURL`.

6. Click on **Save All** from the toolbar menu.

The code is shown in the following screenshots, which has a summary of the actions performed. Notice that in calling the URL of the create society page, we have passed parameters in two ways. Firstly, through the URL, we have added the parameter called `urlActionParam`. Secondly, we can add parameters to the HashMap we defined. In this case, we are passing `personId` of the employee for which we want to create a new society:

```java
public void processFormRequest(OAPageContext pageContext, OAWebBean webBean){
    super.processFormRequest(pageContext, webBean);
    OAApplicationModule am = (OAApplicationModule)pageContext.getApplicationModule(webBean);

    // Get the action in the employee region
    String actionInEmpRegion = pageContext.getParameter(EVENT_PARAM);
```

```java
    // Perform logic for clicking the addSociety image
    if (actionInEmpRegion.equals("addSociety")){
        // Display the action and the personId in a message on the screen
        // throw new OAException("Action triggered is " + actionInEmpRegion
        //                       + " and the PersonId captured is " + actionPersonId
        //                       , OAException.CONFIRMATION);

        // Get the personId of the employee we clicked the crete society ocon for
        String actionPersonId = pageContext.getParameter("paramMasterPersonId");
        // Handle the submit button press actions.
        HashMap map = new HashMap();
        map.put("mapParam1", actionPersonId);
```

```java
// We are calling the Create employee page and we are going to pass parameters through the URL
// and also through a HashMap to pass the personId
pageContext.setForwardURL("OA.jsp?page=/oracle/apps/xxhr/emp/webui/CreateSocietyPG&urlParam=Create",
                null, // String functionName
                OAWebBeanConstants.KEEP_MENU_CONTEXT,
                null, // String menuName
                map, // Hashmap parameters
                true, // Retain AM
                OAWebBeanConstants.ADD_BREAD_CRUMB_SAVE, // String addBreadCrumb
                OAWebBeanConstants.IGNORE_MESSAGES // byte messagingLevel
                );
}
```

> It is equally important that we know when to retain the **application module** (**AM**) while navigating between pages. The AM should be retained whenever you are navigating away from a page and where there is a possibility to come back to the originating page again. We are doing this in this recipe. This applies to any navigation link that opens in a new page, or any navigation that has a back button to come back to the originating page.

We should not retain the AM when we are navigating between two independent pages, especially when they have common view objects. This can cause unexpected results as the view objects are cached.

How it works...

We wanted to pass parameters when we navigate to another page. To do this, we have added code to capture the user clicking on the addSociety icon in the originating page. When the icon is clicked, we need to capture the parameters we want to pass to the destination page. We can then call the setForwardURL method to navigate to a page and pass the parameter list in an object called HashMap. We have stored the data in a map object called HashMap. The map interface is a data structure used to implement an associative array, a structure that can map keys to values. This is used as a way to store data in a structured manner to be able to retrieve it later on.

Adding code to the destination page to capture the parameters passed

We will add code to capture the parameters that are passed, as part of the call to the destination page. We need to do this in the processRequest method of the destination page, as this is the method that will be executed when we navigate to the page. We will then add some logic to the method to call the createNewSociety method, if the action passed in the URL parameter is Create. Later on we are going to navigate to the page where the URL parameter is going to be updated and, in this instance we will need to perform different logic.

How to do it...

To capture the parameters and code logic, perform the following steps:

1. In the **Applications Navigator** tab, double-click on the **CreateSocietyCO.java** file, and in the editor, scroll down to the processRequest method.

2. Set the paramPersonId parameter to store the parameter passed in the HashMap called mapParam1.

3. Add a new variable called paramUrlAction to store the action we passed in the URL parameter called urlActionParam.

4. Add logic to execute the call to the createNewSociety method only when the URL action parameter is equal to Create.

   The following screenshot shows a summary of the code we are adding to the processRequest method of the CreateSocietyCO.java file.

```
public void processRequest(OAPageContext pageContext, OAWebBean webBean)
{
   super.processRequest(pageContext, webBean);
   OAApplicationModule am = pageContext.getApplicationModule(webBean);

   // String paramPersonId = "1234";
   // Capture the parameter passed in the hash
   String paramPersonId = pageContext.getParameter("mapParam1");
   // Capture the parameter passed in the URL
   String paramUrlAction = pageContext.getParameter("urlParam");
   // If the URL parameter was from the Add Society button call our create method
   if (paramUrlAction.equals("Create")) {
      Serializable[] params = {paramPersonId};
      am.invokeMethod("createNewSociety", params);
   }
}
```

5. Click on **Save All** from the toolbar menu.

6. Now, we need to edit the `createNewSociety` method to accept the parameter list called `params`.

```
public void createNewSociety(String paramPersonId) {
   // Create an instance of the view object and call it vo
   EmpSocietiesCreateVOImpl vo = getEmpSocietiesCreateVO1();

   // We need to do this on a VO that has not been queried before we insert
   // our first row.  We don't want to do it for subsequent inserts.
   if (vo.getFetchedRowCount() == 0)
   {
      vo.setMaxFetchSize(0);
   }
   // We are now going to create a record in the view object
   Row row = vo.createRow();
   row.setAttribute("PersonId", paramPersonId);

   vo.insertRow(row);
   // Required per OA Framework Model Coding Standard M69
   row.setNewRowState(Row.STATUS_INITIALIZED);
}
```

How it works...

We have added some code to the destination page that will store the parameters that have been passed and then set the values of the `personId` and `societyId` fields. The parameters were passed to the page using two methods. One in the URL string identified by an `&` (ampersand) and the other in the `HashMap` object.

We are going to run the form in the debug mode to ensure that the parameters are being passed to the destination form as desired. In the `CreateSocietyCO.java` file, which we have just edited, add some breakpoints, as shown in the following screenshot:

```
// String paramPersonId = "1234";
// Capture the parameter passed in the hash
String paramPersonId = pageContext.getParameter("mapParam1");
// Capture the paramter passed in the URL
String paramUrlAction = pageContext.getParameter("urlParam");
// If the URL parameter was from the Add Society button call our create method
if (paramUrlAction.equals("Create")) {
    Serializable[] params = {paramPersonId};
    am.invokeMethod("createNewSociety", params);
```

In the Applications Navigator, right-click on the **EmpSocietiesPG.xml** page and select **Debug** from the pop-up menu. Step through the breakpoints as shown in the following screenshot, and we can see the values of the local variables in the `processRequest` method of the page:

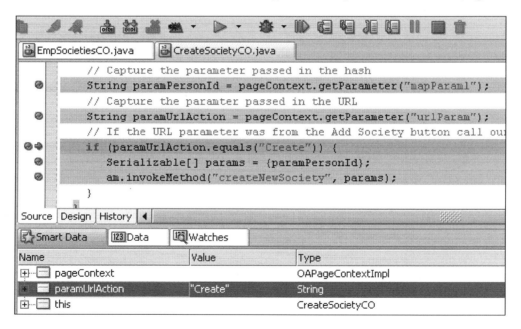

Once we have jumped through the breakpoints, we can return to our page where we will see that the `paramPersonId` variable has been displayed in the **Person ID** field.

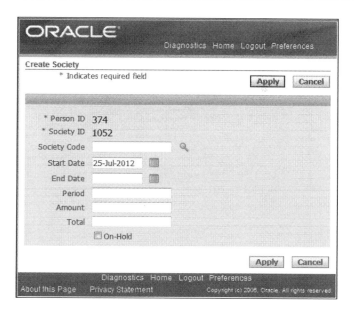

Creating a dictionary message

We will now define a message in Oracle that we can call from our OA framework page. When specifying tokens in a message, you need to start the token with & (ampersand) and the token name must be specified in uppercase.

How to do it...

To create a message, perform the following steps:

1. Log in to Oracle with the **Application Developer** responsibility.
2. Navigate to **Application | Messages** and the **Messages** window will open.
3. Enter the following data:

Item	Value
Name	FWK_TBX_T_SOC_CREATE_CONFIRM
Language	US
Application	Common Modules-AK
Number	0
Current Message Text	The society &SOC_DESC has been created.

4. Save the form.

The form should look as shown in the following screenshot:

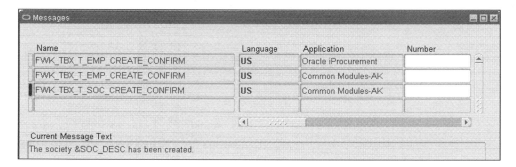

How it works...

We have now configured our message. We have also added a token to the message, which will be populated at runtime when we call the message. The message dictionary is used to store messages that can be recalled at runtime. The message is given a name, which is used to recall the message and we can also dynamically insert data into the message by using tokens that begin with an `&` (ampersand) character.

Adding logic and calling a dictionary message

Now we are going to add some logic to the `Apply` and `Cancel` buttons. We have already added the code to capture the event when a user clicks on the `Apply` button. We are going to add to that code some more functionalities and a confirmation message that appears when the user clicks on the `Apply` button. We also want to capture the event when a user clicks on the `Cancel` button. When the event occurs, we want to navigate back to the originating page without saving the changes. Remember that we capture events that occur once the page has been rendered in the `processFormRequest` method.

How to do it...

To add the logic to the buttons, perform the following steps:

1. In **Applications Navigator**, double-click on the **CreateSocietyCO.java** file.
2. Scroll down the controller to the `processFormRequest` method.

   Amend the code as follows:

```
public void processFormRequest(OAPageContext pageContext, OAWebBean webBean)
{
    super.processFormRequest(pageContext, webBean);
    OAApplicationModule am = pageContext.getApplicationModule(webBean);

    // Code logic for the Apply and Cancel buttons
    if (pageContext.getParameter("Apply") != null) {
        // Create instance of the view object
        OAViewObject vo = (OAViewObject)am.findViewObject("EmpSocietiesCreateVO1");
        // Get the value of the society code
        String societyCode = (String)vo.getCurrentRow().getAttribute("Code");
        // Commit the transaction
        am.invokeMethod("commitTransaction");

        // Set the message tokens
        MessageToken[] tokens = {new MessageToken("SOC_DESC", societyCode) };
        // Call a confirmation message
        OAException confirmMessage = new OAException("AK",
                                            "FWK_TBX_T_SOC_CREATE_CONFIRM",
                                            tokens,
                                            OAException.CONFIRMATION, null);
        pageContext.putDialogMessage(confirmMessage);
        // Navigate back to the employee societies page
        pageContext.forwardImmediately("OA.jsp?page=/oracle/apps/xxhr/emp/webui/EmpSocietiesPG",
                            null,
                            OAWebBeanConstants.KEEP_MENU_CONTEXT,
                            null,
                            null,
                            true, // retain AM
                            OAWebBeanConstants.ADD_BREAD_CRUMB_NO);
    }
}
```

3. Click on **Save All** from the toolbar menu.

How it works...

We have now added code to get `society_code` from the current record for the message token. Then, we commit the record as per the existing code. We then create an instance of an `OAException` message and call the message. Finally, once we have completed the transaction, we return to the employee society's page.

Adding logic for a Cancel button

Now we will add some logic for the `Cancel` button. If the `Cancel` button is clicked by the user, we will roll back the transaction and return to the originating page.

How to do it...

To add the logic for the `Cancel` button, perform the following steps:

1. Open the `CreateSocietyCO.java` controller.

2. Scroll down to `processFormRequest` and after the logic for the `Apply` button, add the following code:

```
}
    else if (pageContext.getParameter("Cancel") != null){

        am.invokeMethod("rollbackSociety");
        TransactionUnitHelper.endTransactionUnit(pageContext, "societyCreateTxn");

        // Navigate back to the EmpSocietiesPG if the user clicks the Cancel button
        pageContext.forwardImmediately("OA.jsp?page=/oracle/apps/xxhr/emp/webui/EmpSocietiesPG",
                                 null,
                                 OAWebBeanConstants.KEEP_MENU_CONTEXT,
                                 null,
                                 null,
                                 true, // retain AM
                                 OAWebBeanConstants.ADD_BREAD_CRUMB_NO);

    }
}
}
```

How it works...

We have now added code to the processFormRequest method to capture the user clicking on the `Cancel` button. This will roll back the transaction and navigate back to the originating page.

Adding a method to roll back a transaction

We will now define a message in Oracle. When specifying tokens in a message, you need to start the token with an `&` character and the token name must be specified in uppercase.

How to do it...

To add a method to roll back the transaction, perform the following steps:

1. Right-click on the **EmpSocietyAM** application module and select **Go to Application Module Class** to open the `EmpSocietiesAMImpl.java` class.

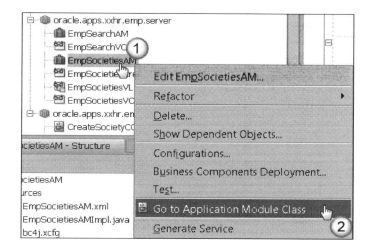

2. Scroll down to the end of the class and add the method called `rollbackSociety`, as shown in the following screenshot:

```
/**
 * rollbackSociety method
 */
public void rollbackSociety()
{
    Transaction txn = getTransaction();
    if (txn.isDirty())
    {
        txn.rollback();
    }
}
```

How it works...

We have now added the method that we execute when the `Cancel` button is clicked by the user. This will roll back the transaction.

Updating records

We are now going to create an icon that will navigate to our `createSocietyPG` page and query back the society and allow us to update it. We will perform the following tasks to update the society record:

- ▸ Adding an update icon
- ▸ Adding the logic when the update icon is clicked on
- ▸ Adding the code to process the update in the `createSocietyPG` page
- ▸ Adding the `updateSociety` method

Adding an update icon

Firstly, we will add the update icon to the master-detail page.

How to do it...

To add an icon for the updating society, perform the following steps:

1. In **Applications Navigator**, click on the **EmpSocietiesPG.xml** page.

2. In the **Structure** pane, right-click on the **EmpSocietiesRN** detail region. Select **New** and then select **column** from the pop-up menu, as shown in the following screenshot:

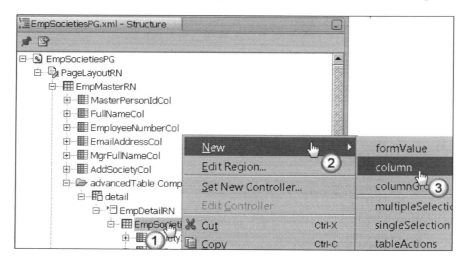

3. Set the **ID** property to **UpdateSocietyCol**.

4. Now, right-click on the **UpdateSocietyCol** item and select **New | Item** from the pop-up menu.

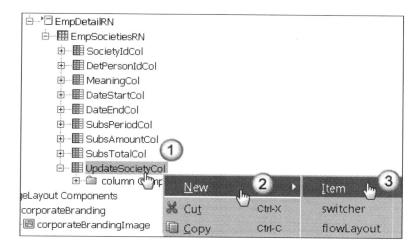

5. Set the following properties of the new item:

   ❏ **ID**: UpdateSociety

   ❏ **Item Style**: image

   ❏ **Image URI**: updateicon_enabled.gif

Now, we are going to set the properties to capture SocietyId of the record we selected:

1. Set the following properties to fire an action and capture SocietyId of the record for which we clicked on the update icon.

   ❏ **Action Type**: fireAction

   ❏ **Event**: updateSocietyAction

   ❏ **Submit**: True

2. Now click on the **Parameters** property to open the **Parameters** dialog box.

3. Click on **Add Parameter** and add the following details:

   ❏ **Name**: updateSocietyId

   ❏ **Value**: ${oa.EmpSocietiesVO1.SocietyId}

The parameter will appear as shown in the following screenshot:

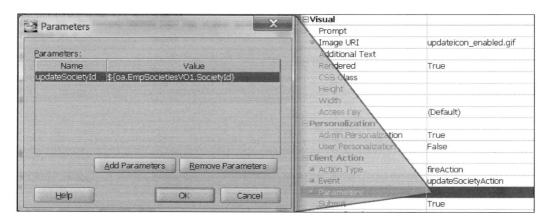

4. Click **Save All** from the toolbar menu.

Now we will add the column header.

1. Right-click on the column header for the update icon and select **New | sortableHeader** from the pop-up menu.

2. Set the properties of the header as shown in the following screenshot:

   - **ID**: updateSocietyHdr
   - **Sort Allowed: no**
   - **Prompt: Update**

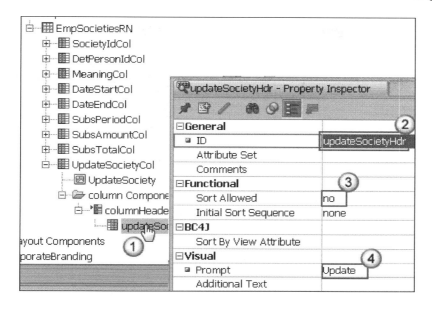

3. Click on **Save All** from the toolbar menu.

How it works...

We have now added the update icon and set the properties of the item. We want to create an update icon because we want to do two things when a user clicks on the icon. Firstly, navigate to the create/update society page. Secondly, we want to query back the society record that we want to update. To do this we must capture the society ID of the record we have clicked on so that we can query the record when we navigate to it.

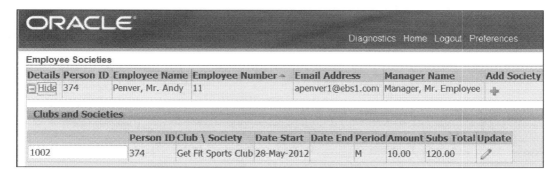

Adding the logic when the update icon is clicked on

Now that we have added the update icon to the detail records, we will add code to the controller to process the user clicking on the icon.

How to do it...

To add code to process the update item being clicked, perform the following steps:

1. In **Applications Manager**, open the `EmpSocietiesCO.java` controller.

2. Scroll down to the `processFormRequest` method and add the following logic after the `addSociety if` statement.

   The following code checks if the `updateSocietyAction` event has occurred on the page. We first create a variable called `actionSocietyId` to store the value of the `societyId` for which we clicked on the update icon. We will add the parameter to a HashMap, which will then be passed to the forward URL method to navigate to the `createSocietyPG` page. Also notice that we pass a URL parameter called `Update`, which we will use to update the logic when we navigate to the `createSocietyPG` page.

```
}
else if(pageContext.getParameter("event") != null &&                    (1)
    pageContext.getParameter("event").equals("updateSocietyAction")) {
    String actionSocietyId = pageContext.getParameter("updateSocietyId");
    // Handle the update society button press action.
    HashMap map = new HashMap();
    map.put("mapParam1", actionSocietyId);                               (2)
```

3. Now, add a call to the `setForwardURL` method.

```
// We are calling the Create employee page and we are going to pass parameters through the URL
// and also through a HashMap to pass the personId
pageContext.setForwardURL("OA.jsp?page=/oracle/apps/xxhr/emp/webui/CreateSocietyPG&urlParam=Update",
                    null, // String functionName
                    OAWebBeanConstants.KEEP_MENU_CONTEXT,
                    null, // String menuName
                    map, // Hashmap parameters
                    true, // Retain AM
                    OAWebBeanConstants.ADD_BREAD_CRUMB_SAVE, // String addBreadCrumb
                    OAWebBeanConstants.IGNORE_MESSAGES // byte messagingLevel
                    );
}
```

4. Click on **Save All** from the toolbar menu.

How it works...

We have now added code to the controller. This is done to perform the logic when an update icon is clicked on and the `updateSocietyAction` event is invoked. We capture attributes that we wish to retrieve later and then navigate to `CreateSocietyPG`. Next, we must add code to the destination page to query back the society record so that we can update it.

Adding the code to process the update in the createSocietyPG page

We will now add the code to the `processRequest` method of the controller. We want to be able to check if the action is to update the society record, and if it is, we then want to query the record back automatically for the user to update the record.

How to do it...

To update the `processRequest` method of the `CreateSocietyPG` page, performs the following steps:

1. In **Applications Navigator**, double-click on the **CreateSocietyCo.java** controller.

2. Scroll down to the `processRequest` method and add the following code to process the update action passed in from the originating page:

```
if (!pageContext.isFormSubmission()) {
    OAApplicationModule am = pageContext.getApplicationModule(webBean);

    // Capture the paramter passed in the URL
    String paramUrlAction = pageContext.getParameter("urlParam");
    // If the URL parameter was from the Add Society button call our create method
    if (paramUrlAction.equals("Create")) {
        // Capture the parameter passed in the hash
        String paramPersonId = pageContext.getParameter("mapParam1");
        Serializable[] params = {paramPersonId};
        am.invokeMethod("createNewSociety", params);
    }
    else if (paramUrlAction.equals("Update")) {
        // Capture the parameter passed in the hash
        String paramSocietyId = pageContext.getParameter("mapParam1");
        Serializable[] params = {paramSocietyId};
        am.invokeMethod("updateSociety", params);
    }
}
```

3. Click on **Save All** from the toolbar menu.

How it works...

We have now added code that will capture an update action from the `EmpSocietiesPG` page. We will add a variable to store the `societyId` parameter that is passed in through the HashMap. Note that we have also moved the variable definition into the `if` statement, as the `HashMap` parameter is based upon the context of the action that is "Create" or "Update".

Adding the updateSociety method

Now that we have added the code for entry to the page, we must add a method to automatically query back the society record that we want to update. The method we call in the `processRequest` method is called `updateSociety`. We will pass the `societyId` to this method so that we can query the society record we want to update.

How to do it...

To add the `updateSociety` method, perform the following steps:

1. In **Applications Navigator**, right-click on the **EmpSocietiesAM** application module.
2. Select **Go to Application Module Class** to open the `EmpSocietiesAMImpl` class.
3. Scroll down to the end of the class and add the following method:

```
/**
 * updateSociety method
 */
public void updateSociety(String paramSocietyId) {
  try
  {
      // Create an instance of the view object and call it vo
      EmpSocietiesCreateVOImpl vo = getEmpSocietiesCreateVO1();

      String societiesWhereClause = vo.getWhereClause();
      vo.setWhereClauseParams(null);
      vo.setWhereClause("society_id = :1");
      vo.setWhereClauseParam(0, paramSocietyId);
      vo.executeQuery();
      vo.setWhereClause(null);
      vo.setWhereClause(societiesWhereClause);
  }
  catch(Exception exception1) {

     throw OAException.wrapperException(exception1);
  }

}
```

4. Click **Save All** from the toolbar menu.

How it works...

We have added the code that will set the `where` clause of the view object and query back the society record we want to update. If we now run the `EmpSocietiesPG.xml` page and click on the update icon, the update society page will open and the society record will automatically query back the society record we wish to update, as shown in the following screenshot:

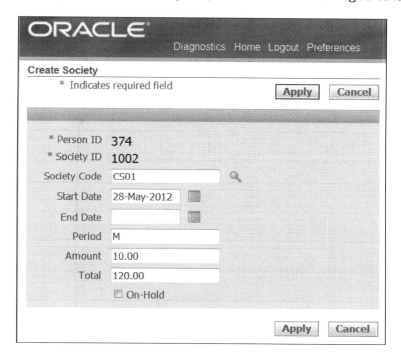

Adding a validation to the page

We are now going to add some validation to the create society page. We can add validation by adding code to the setter methods in the entity object class. In the following example, we are going to validate that a date entered in the `dateStart` field is greater than the current date.

How to do it...

To add a validation to the page, perform the following steps:

1. Right-click on **EmpSocietyEO** in **Applications Navigator**.

2. Select **Go to Entity Object Class** from the pop-up menu and scroll down to the `setDateStart` method, as shown in the following screenshot:

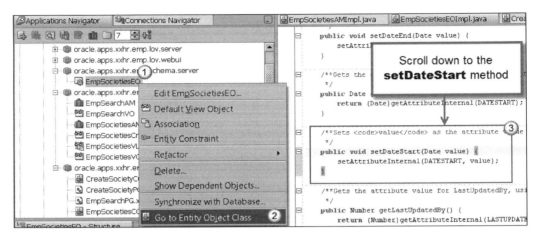

3. Add the following code before the `setAttributeInternal` line.

    i.   In the following screenshot we check to see if the value in the **Start Date** field has been entered.

    ii.   If there is a value, that is, the field is not null, we store the date in a variable called `startDate`.

    iii. We store the current date in a variable called `todaysDate`.

    iv. Finally, we check if the start date is less than today's date. If the condition is `true`, we will raise an exception and display an error message.

```
public void setDateStart(Date value) {
    if(value != null)  (1)
    {
        // Start Date cannot be earlier than today's date.
    (2) long startDate= value.dateValue().getTime();
        OADBTransaction txn = getOADBTransaction();
    (3) long todaysDate = txn.getCurrentDBDate().dateValue().getTime();

    (4) if(startDate < todaysDate)
        throw new OAException("The start date cannot be before the today's date.");
    }
    setAttributeInternal(DATESTART, value);
}
```

4. Finally, import the `OAException` method (if it is not already imported). To do this we, right-click on the light bulb and select the **Import 'oracle.apps.fnd.framework. OAException'** entry, as shown in the following screenshot:

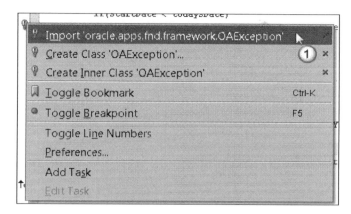

5. Click on **Save All** from the toolbar menu.

How it works...

We can edit the setter methods of objects to enter the validation logic. We only want to perform validation if the user has entered a value. When the values are committed to the database, the method will be called and will perform the logic. We can see the validation working if we enter a date and attempt to save the change to the database. To do this, open the `EmpSocietiesPG.xml` page and click on the create society icon, as shown in the following screenshot:

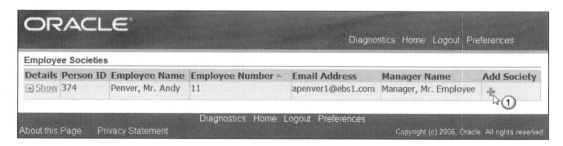

When we get to the `CreateSocietyPG` page, enter a society code using the list of values and then change the **Start Date** field to a date less than the current date, as shown in the following screenshot. Click on **Apply**:

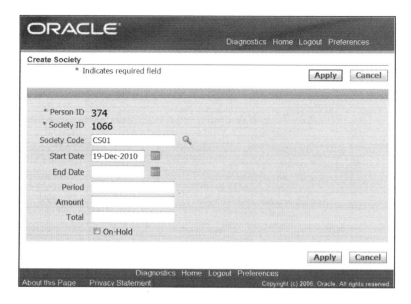

We will then see the error message appear as the validation logic we entered is triggered, as shown in the following screenshot:

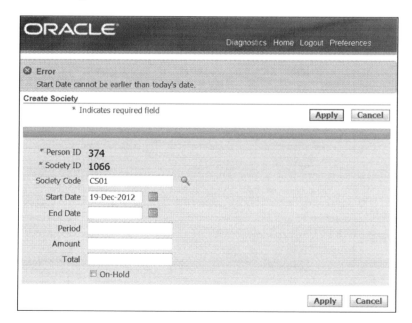

Calling PL/SQL from the OAF page

In this recipe we are going to call some SQL from our page. We will add a button to the page and when a user clicks on the button, we will call a database package that will insert a record into a database table. We will perform the following tasks:

- ▶ Adding a button to execute the SQL statement
- ▶ Creating a method in the application module
- ▶ Calling the method from the controller class

Adding a button to execute the SQL statement

We are now going to create a button. We are going to use the button to call a method that executes the piece of SQL code, which we will add afterwards.

How to do it...

To add a button, perform the following steps:

1. In the **Application Navigator** tab, click on the **CreateSocietyPG.xml** page.
2. In the **Structure** pane, navigate to **PageLayoutRN | PageButtonRN**.
3. Right-click on **PageButtonRN** and select **New | Item** from the pop-up menu:

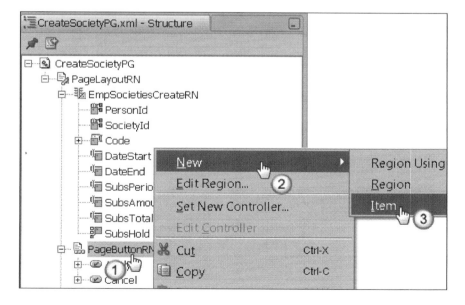

4. Click on **item1** and set the following properties:

   ❑ **ID**: plsqlButton

   ❑ **Item Style**: submitButton

   ❑ **Prompt**: Call DB Pkg

5. Now, add the following to the CreateSocietyCO.java processFormRequest method:

```
else if (pageContext.getParameter("plsqlButton") != null) {

    OAViewObject vo = (OAViewObject)am.findViewObject("EmpSocietiesCreateVO1");
    String paramSocietyId = vo.first().getAttribute("SocietyId").toString();
    throw new OAException("Society is "+ paramSocietyId);
```

How it works...

When a user clicks on the button, the controller code is executed. By clicking on the button, we will hit the else if statement and will evaluate to not null. We will then capture the societyId and display it by throwing an exception message.

If we run the EmpSocietiesPG page and navigate to the CreateSocietiesPG page, we can click on the **Call DB Pkg** button to test if we have captured the society ID. The following message should appear:

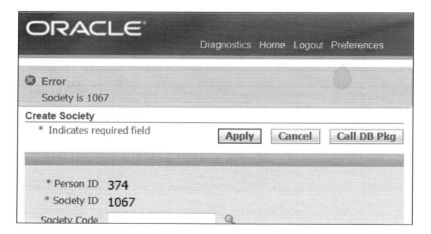

Creating a method in the application module

We will first create a method in the application module that will create and execute a SQL statement.

How to do it...

To create a method in the application module, perform the following steps:

1. In the **Application Navigator** tab, right-click on the **EmpSearchAM** node and select **Go to Application Module Class** from the pop-up menu.

2. Add the following method in the `EmpSearchAMImpl` class as shown in the following screenshot:

```
public void insertSocietyLog(String paramSocId) {        ←——— Declare the method

    // Write Action code for Yes Button
    // SQL Statement
(1) OADBTransaction txn = (OADBTransaction)getTransaction();
    String stmt = "BEGIN INSERT INTO XXHR_PER_SOCIETIES_TEST" +
            " (SOCIETY_ID, TEST_DATE) VALUES ("+paramSocId+", SYSDATE);" +
            " commit;" +
            " END;";

    try
    {
(2)     CallableStatement cs =txn.createCallableStatement(stmt,1);
        cs.execute();
        cs.close();

    }
(3) catch(Exception exception1) {

        throw OAException.wrapperException(exception1);
    }

(4) throw new OAException("Completed transaction successfully.", OAException.INFORMATION);
    }
}
```

How it works...

The first batch of code creates an instance of the database transaction. We also create a string called `stmt` that stores the SQL that we want to execute.

Note that the statement can span multiple lines by enclosing a line with
"and adding a + character so that the compiler knows that the code is
continued on the next line. Also, you can see that we have added the
parameter within the statement. This is how we can add variables to the
SQL code.

The second batch of code is the TRY statement. This executes the SQL.

The third batch of code is the CATCH statement, which will catch any errors while processing
the SQL statement.

We can display a message to show that the SQL has completed successfully.

Calling the method from the controller class

We will now call the method from the controller class. We will now call the
insertSocietyLog method in the application module to perform the SQL that will insert a
record into a database table. Now that we have checked that we are picking up societyId,
we can perform the following steps to create our new method in the application module that
will execute our SQL code.

How to do it...

To call the method from the controller class, perform the following steps:

1. In the **Application Navigator** tab, right-click on the **CreateSocietyCO.java** node
   and select **Go to Application Module Class** from the pop-up menu.

2. Scroll down to (**Step 1**), as shown in the following screenshot:

```
// Capturing the event when the Apply button is clicked
if (pageContext.getParameter("Apply") != null) {
    // Call a method to commit the transaction and display a message
    am.invokeMethod("commitTransaction");
    throw new OAException("Society successfully created");
}
// Capturing the event when the Call DB Pkg button is clicked
else if (pageContext.getParameter("plsqlButton") != null) {       (1)

    OAViewObject vo = (OAViewObject)am.findViewObject("EmpSocietiesCreateVO1");
    String paramSocietyId = vo.first().getAttribute("SocietyId").toString();
    Serializable[] params = {paramSocietyId};
    am.invokeMethod("insertSocietyLog", params);                   (2)

}
```

3. As shown in (**Step 2**), replace the following line:

```
throw new OAExcepton("Society is "+ paramSocietyId);
```

with the following line:

```
Serializable[] params = {paramSocietyId};
am.invokeMethod("insertSocietyLog", params);
```

How it works...

We want to call the method we have created for calling the SQL rather than raising an exception to display a message. `paramSocietyId` captures the `societyId` that will be passed to our method that will execute a SQL statement. The SQL statement will insert a record into a database table.

It is standard practice to write code to call a database package or SQL in the **application module (AM)** class and not in the **controller (CO)** class. The controller class should only handle events and then call methods in the application module.

If we run the `EmpSocietiesPG` page and navigate to the `CreateSocietiesPG` page, we can see that the **Call DB Pkg** button is displayed. If we click on the button, the database package will be executed and we can see that the following message is displayed on the screen:

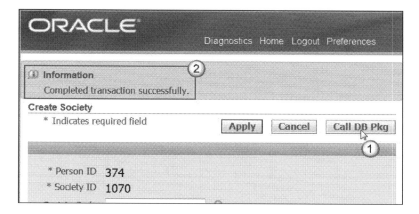

We also need to check that the transaction has actually been stored to the database. Therefore, open up the SQL Developer or tool of your choice, and query the XXHR_PER_ SOCIETIES_TEST table, as shown in the following screenshot:

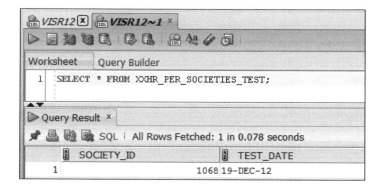

We can see that the SQL has created a record in the table and, therefore, we can see that the SQL has completed successfully. Note that we can use this method also to call a database package as desired.

Adding a decision message

We are now going to add a decision message to our page. We will use the previous recipe so that a decision message appears before executing the SQL code.

How to do it...

To add a decision message, perform the following steps:

1. In **Application Navigator**, open the **EmpSocietiesCO.java** controller.

2. In the EmpSocietiesCO.java file, scroll down to the processFormRequest method.

3. In the plsqlButton event, add a new line after the declaration of paramSocietyId, as shown in the following screenshot:

```
else if (pageContext.getParameter("plsqlButton") != null) {

    OAViewObject vo = (OAViewObject)am.findViewObject("EmpSocietiesCreateVO1");
    String paramSocietyId = vo.first().getAttribute("SocietyId").toString();
    //throw new OAException("Society is "+ paramSocietyId);
```

4. Now, we are going to comment out the call to the `insertSocietyLog` method (step 1). Then, we will define the warning message and create an instance of a dialog message (**Step 2**).

   The following code needs to be added:

```
// Capturing the event when the Call DB Pkg button is clicked
else if (pageContext.getParameter("plsqlButton") != null) {

    OAViewObject vo = (OAViewObject)am.findViewObject("EmpSocietiesCreateVO1");
    String paramSocietyId = vo.first().getAttribute("SocietyId").toString();
    //Serializable[] params = {paramSocietyId};
    //am.invokeMethod("insertSocietyLog", params);

    // **** Code for Dialog Page Starts Here ****:
    // Define the Warning Message and Initialize the Dialog Page with the Warning Message
    String msg = "You are about to call a database package for this society. Continue?";
    OAException DBWarning = new OAException(msg);
    OADialogPage dialogPage = new OADialogPage(OAException.WARNING, DBWarning, null, "", "");
```

5. Next, add two string values to define the button text for the `Yes` and `No` buttons (**Step 3**).

```
// **** Code for Dialog Page Starts Here ****:
// Define the Warning Message and Initialize the Dialog Page with the Warning Message
String msg = "You are about to call a database package for this society. Continue?";
OAException DBWarning = new OAException(msg);
OADialogPage dialogPage = new OADialogPage(OAException.WARNING, DBWarning, null, "", "");

// Set the Prompts for YES and NO button + Associate an event with YES button
String yes = pageContext.getMessage("AK", "FWK_TBX_T_YES", null);
String no = pageContext.getMessage("AK", "FWK_TBX_T_NO", null);
```

6. Next, we will add the code to create an instance of a dialog message and set the `Yes` or `No` variable for the buttons (**Step 4**).

```
// Set the Prompts for YES and NO button + Associate an event with YES button
String yes = pageContext.getMessage("AK", "FWK_TBX_T_YES", null);
String no = pageContext.getMessage("AK", "FWK_TBX_T_NO", null);

// Set the ID of the YES Button = confirmDBAction
dialogPage.setOkButtonItemName("okDBAction");
// Set the ID of the NO Button = denyDBAction
dialogPage.setNoButtonItemName("noDBAction");
```

7. Next, we will convert the `Yes` and `No` buttons to the submit buttons so that we can capture the events of them when they are clicked (**Step 5**).

```
// Set the ID of the YES Button = confirmDBAction
dialogPage.setOkButtonItemName("okDBAction");
// Set the ID of the NO Button = denyDBAction
dialogPage.setNoButtonItemName("noDBAction");          (5)

// Convert the YES and NO buttons to SUBMIT BUTTONS
dialogPage.setOkButtonToPost(true);
dialogPage.setNoButtonToPost(true);
dialogPage.setPostToCallingPage(true);
```

8. Next we will add the labels to the buttons (**Step 6**).

```
// Convert the YES and NO buttons to SUBMIT BUTTONS
dialogPage.setOkButtonToPost(true);
dialogPage.setNoButtonToPost(true);
dialogPage.setPostToCallingPage(true);

// Set the labels of the buttons
dialogPage.setOkButtonLabel(yes);                      (6)
dialogPage.setNoButtonLabel(no);
```

9. Now, we will pass the parameters to the dialog page and then redirect to the dialog page (**Step 7**).

```
// Set the labels of the buttons
dialogPage.setOkButtonLabel(yes);
dialogPage.setNoButtonLabel(no);

// Pass parameters from the page to Dialog Page and re-direct to Dialog Page
java.util.Hashtable formParams = new java.util.Hashtable(1);
formParams.put("socIdDB",paramSocietyId);
dialogPage.setFormParameters(formParams);              (7)

pageContext.redirectToDialogPage(dialogPage);
}
```

Now that we have performed the preceding steps, we need to capture the events of the `Yes` and `No` buttons on which users have clicked.

10. Create a new `else if` statement to capture the `Yes` button being clicked as follows (**Step 8**):

```
        pageContext.redirectToDialogPage(dialogPage);
    }
    // Yes button clicked                                              8
    else if (pageContext.getParameter("okDBAction") != null){

        String paramSocietyId = pageContext.getParameter("socIdDB");   9
        Serializable[] params = {paramSocietyId};
        // Call method to insert record into database
        am.invokeMethod("insertSocietyLog", params);


    }                                                                  10
    // No button clicked
    else if (pageContext.getParameter("noDBAction") != null) {
        // Write Action code for No Button
        throw new OAException("Transaction cancelled.", OAException.INFORMATION);
    }

    }
}
```

We then add the code to call our `insertSocietyLog` method (**Step 9**). Finally, we add code to handle the `No` button being clicked (**Step 10**). When this happens, we will throw an exception message.

How it works...

We want to be able to confirm that the user wants to insert a record into a table when they have clicked on the **Call DB Pkg** button. To do this, we have created a dialog message where we define the buttons and capture the response from the user. Now, we can run the page from the `EmpSocietiesPG` page again and click on the **Call DB Pkg** button, as shown in the following screenshot:

Now, we will be shown a dialog message with the **Yes** and **No** buttons.

If we click on **Yes**, the SQL statement will be executed as before, but if we click on **No**, we will be returned to the following **Create Society** page without executing the SQL.

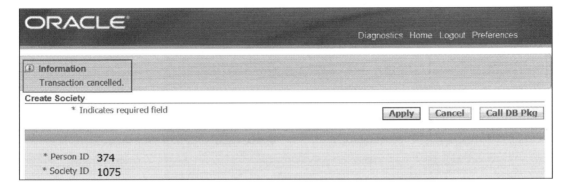

Partial Page Rendering

In **Partial Page Rendering** (**PPR**), a portion of the page refreshes some user actions for which PARTIAL PAGE ACTION is enabled. This means other items on the page will retain their values. When we add PPR to a page, the item on which we perform the action will be the result of the PPR code that the developer has written.

So, PPR is based on a user action on an item on our page, on which PARTIAL FIRE ACTION is enabled. This will be an item, or set of items, which are affected by that partial action. Meanwhile, the other items on the page will remain unaffected.

When PPR occurs, the entire page is refreshed. The PPR action takes place only on the affected item(s).

Developers can implement PPR to perform the following tasks:

- ▶ Configuring the selection of a pop list (drop down), which will in turn cause other fields to render, be updateable, be required, and so on
- ▶ Configuring the change in value of a text field to cause other fields to render, be updateable, be required, and so on
- ▶ Configuring the selection of a master's table record to automatically query and display child rows in a detail table.

The properties that are commonly modified by implementing PPR are as follows:

- ▶ Rendered
- ▶ Read Only
- ▶ Disabled
- ▶ Required

The name notation for PPR is coded using an **Application Properties View Object (PVO)**. A PVO always has one row and its columns are all transient attributes. Transient attributes are VO columns, which are not a part of the VO select query.

These columns are as follows:

- ▶ ROWKEY (NUMBER): Key attribute
- ▶ XXXXXX (BOOLEAN): This Boolean value is used to control other fields when it is set

A PVO always has only one row with `rowkey` set to 1.

So, on a page which has PPR to deal with, in `processRequest` of the page's controller, we have to write code to initialize the PVO. There is a standard code that we can just cut-copy-paste whenever we wish to initialize the PVO.

We can declaratively enable PPR on the following item types:

- ▶ `link`
- ▶ `messageCheckBox`
- ▶ `messageChoice`
- ▶ `button`
- ▶ `radioButton`
- ▶ `submitButton`
- ▶ `messageTextInput`

Finally, we must set the **FND: Disable Partial Page Rendering** profile option to **No** (if PPR is to happen).

Viewing a page from EBS

We are now going to see how we can run a standard OA Framework page in JDeveloper. We would want to do this to look at the structure of a page and to examine the logic of any code. We would also do this when we want to extend a page. We will also see how we can generate a .java file from an executable with a utility called **JAD**.

How to do it...

First of all, we will log on to EBS to look at the page we will load in JDeveloper. To do this, perform the following:

1. Log in to EBS and navigate to **Workflow Administrator Web (New)**.

> If you do not have the **Workflow Administrator Web (New)** responsibility, add the responsibility to your user by going to the **System Administrator** responsibility and adding it to your user.

2. Click on the **Home** link as shown in the following screenshot:

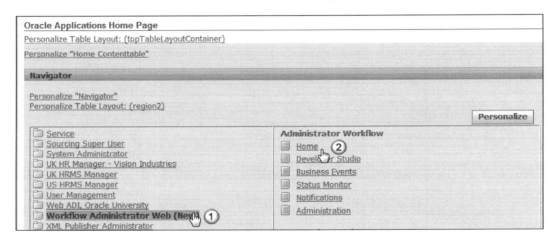

3. When the **Administrator Workflow** home page opens, click on the **About this Page** link, as shown in the following screenshot:

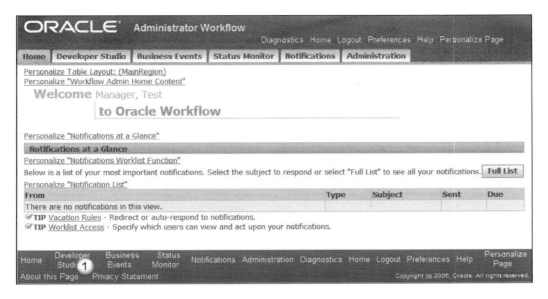

4. Make a note of the page location. We can see that the workflow home page is located at `/oracle/apps/fnd/wf/uihome/webui/AdminHomePG`, as shown in the following screenshot:

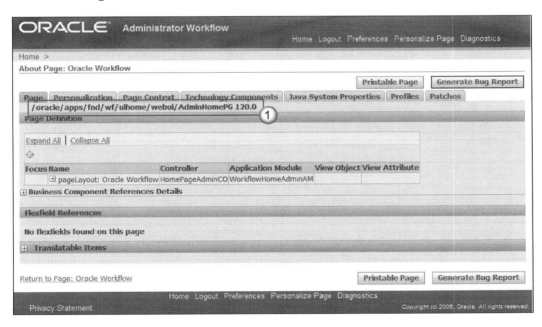

5. Click on the **Return to Page: Oracle Workflow** link.

How it works...

We have made a note of the location of the page we want to extract by making a note of the directory from the **About this Page** link. We need this location so that we know where to look for the required files on the application server.

Transferring the files

We are now going to locate the directory on the application server and transfer the files onto our local computer. We need to transfer the page and we will also need to transfer the java class files associated with the page.

How to do it...

To transfer the files, do the following:

1. Open a new PuTTY session and log on to the application server.

2. Navigate to the location for all of the FND java objects by typing in $JAVA_TOP/ oracle/apps/fnd on the command line.

3. Type pwd to view the full path, as shown in the following screenshot:

```
applsys@VisionR12:/oracle/apps/r12/visr12/apps/apps_st/comn/java/classes/oracle/apps/fnd
[APPS Tier] > cd $JAVA_TOP/oracle/apps/fnd
[APPS Tier] > pwd
/oracle/apps/r12/visr12/apps/apps_st/comn/java/classes/oracle/apps/fnd
[APPS Tier] >
```

4. Make a note of the full path:

   /oracle/apps/r12/visr12/apps/apps_st/comn/java/classes/oracle/ apps/fnd

Now, we are going to transfer the files from this directory to our local computer.

1. Open your preferred FTP client (we are using WinSCP in this book).

2. Transfer the whole fnd directory from the Apps server to the myclasses directory in your JDeveloper home, C:\oaf\jdevhome\jdev\myclasses\oracle\apps\fnd

   The following screenshot shows the transfer from the application server to the local PC:

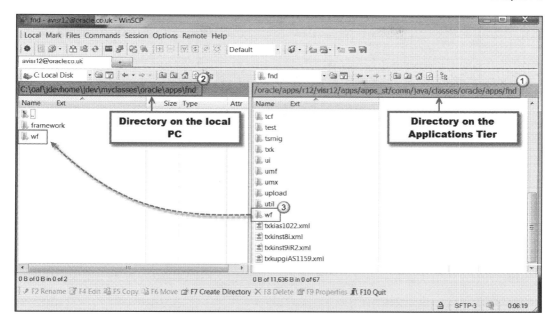

It may take a few minutes to transfer all of the files. Next, we will transfer all the page definitions from the application server. To do this perform the following:

3. Open a new PuTTY session and log on to the applications server. Navigate to the mds directory by typing the following command:

   cd $FND_TOP/mds

4. Now, type in pwd to get the path of the mds directory, as shown in the following screenshot:

```
applsys@VisionR12:/oracle/apps/r12/visr12/apps/apps_st/appl/fnd/12.0.0/mds
[APPS Tier] > cd $FND_TOP/mds
[APPS Tier] > pwd
/oracle/apps/r12/visr12/apps/apps_st/appl/fnd/12.0.0/mds
[APPS Tier] >
```

5. Transfer the `mds` directory of `FND` from the application server to the `myprojects\oracle\apps\fnd folder` on the local PC.

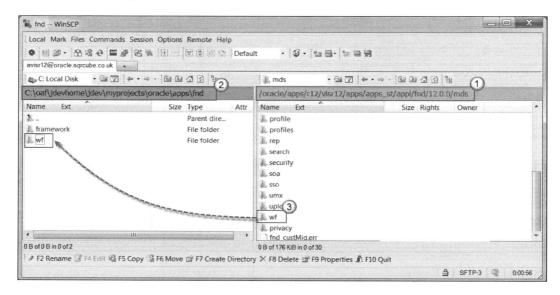

Now we are going to view the page in JDeveloper. To do this perform the following:

1. Open JDeveloper.

2. In **Applications Navigator**, right-click on the **Applications** node and select **New OA Workspace...** from the pop-up menu as follows:

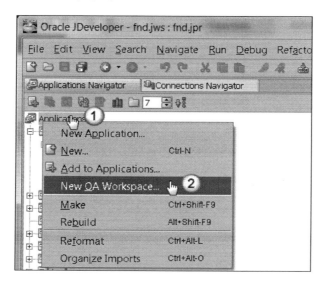

3. Set the **File Name:** field of the OA Workspace to `fnd.jws`, as shown in the following screenshot:

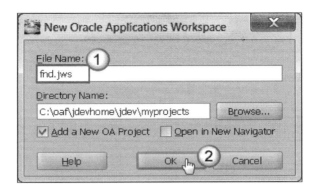

4. Set the project details as shown in the following screenshot:

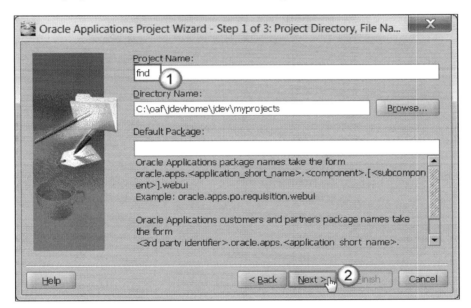

5. Click on **Next**.
6. Click on **Finish**.

Now, we are going to set the project settings so that we only view the `fnd\wf` directory on our `fnd` project. Perform the following steps to restrict the packages we see in the `fnd` project:

1. In **Applications Navigator**, double-click on the `fnd` project.

2. Set the directory in the **Included** tab as follows:

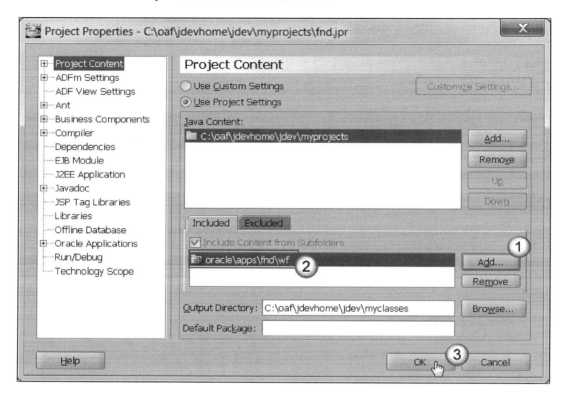

3. Click on **OK**.

   Now, we can navigate to **AdminHomePG.xml**, and to run it select **Run** from the pop-up menu as follows:

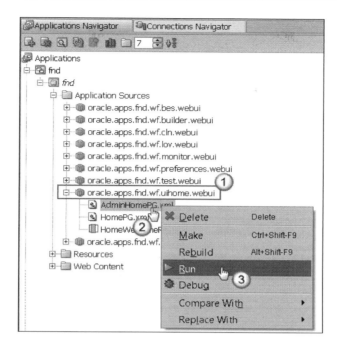

The page will now run on your local PC as shown in the following screenshot:

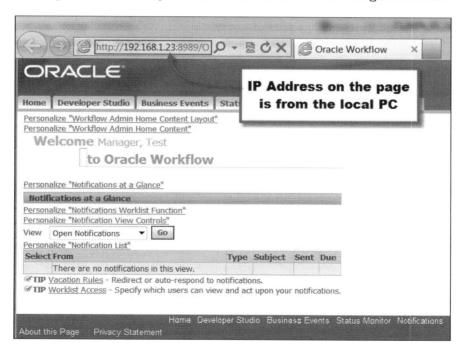

How it works...

We transfer the files to our local PC so that we can view them in JDeveloper. We may want to understand the properties that a page or components of a page has, or we may want to extend a component of the page.

There's more...

We may also wish to view the code from a page. The problem is that we cannot view the .class files as they are executable files. Therefore, to be able to view the code we need to decompile the .class file so that we can read it. To do this we need a decompiler and a common one that is used quite often if called JAD. We can download JAD from the internet. In your web browser search for JAD, and there will be a number of mirror sites where the decompiler can be downloaded from. One that I have used in the past is http://www.varaneckas.com/jad/.

Once you have downloaded the file, extract it into a directory on your local PC. (It often comes in a ZIP file and if so unzip it). In Windows Explorer navigate to C:\oaf\jdevhome\jdev\myclasses\oracle\apps\fnd\wf\uihome\webui and we can see the class files that we transferred from the application server as shown in the screenshot:

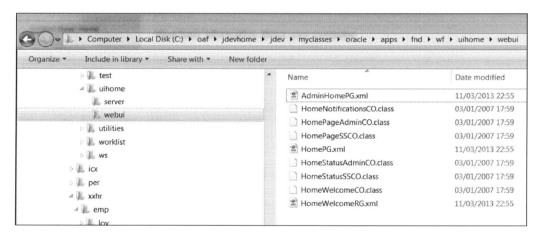

Now, if we open a command prompt and run JAD we can generate the java files. To do this perform the following:

1. Open a command prompt.
2. Navigate to the directory where our .class files are by entering the following command:

```
cd C:\oaf\jdevhome\jdev\myclasses\oracle\apps\fnd\wf\uihome\webui
```

3. Issue the following command to decompile the class files:

```
C:\jad\jad -sjava *.class
```

This will decompile all the class files in the directory as follows:

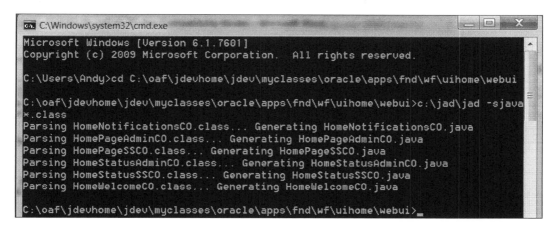

We can now open the java files in JDeveloper and view the code as follows:

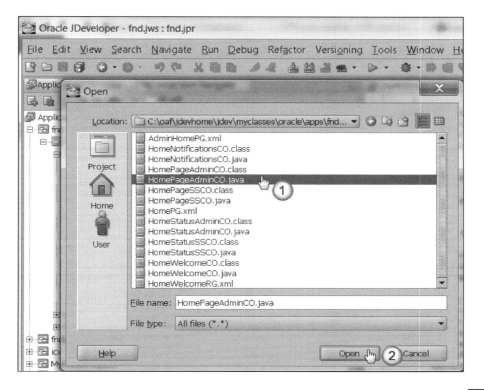

6

BI Publisher

In this chapter, we will cover the following recipes:

- ▶ Generating XML output using a concurrent program
- ▶ Making a concurrent program available to a user
- ▶ Using Oracle BI Publisher Desktop software to create a rich text format (RTF) template
- ▶ Creating a Data Definition
- ▶ Defining a template
- ▶ Running a BI Publisher report
- ▶ Generating PDF and Excel output using an RTF template
- ▶ Implementing BI Publisher Bursting (e-mail)
- ▶ Implementing BI Publisher Bursting (filesystem)

Introduction

In this chapter, we will be taking a look at BI Publisher. Previously known as XML Publisher, **Oracle BI** (**Business Intelligence**) Publisher is an enterprise reporting solution for authoring, managing, and delivering highly-formatted documents. The flexibility of BI Publisher is a result of the separation of the presentation of the report from its data structure. At runtime, BI Publisher merges returned data into pre-designed template files to create a variety of outputs to meet a wide range of business needs.

In this chapter, we will work through a number of recipes, which will explore the mechanisms for delivering XML-formatted data suitable for use against template files, the creation of template files, and the distribution of populated templates to designated locations and/or recipients.

The following diagram shows the basic processing when generating a report:

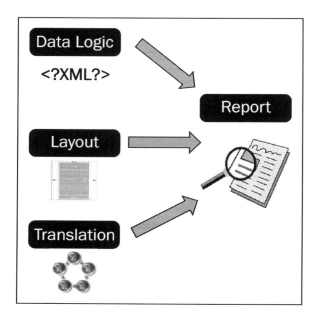

Generating XML output using a concurrent program

To generate XML output using a concurrent program, we simply need to write valid XML content to the concurrent program's output file. This can be done in a variety of ways, for example, PL/SQL procedure, SQL Query, and so on. We are going to explore the PL/SQL method.

The first step is to create a database package containing a single procedure that uses multiple calls of `FND_FILE.put_line` to write text to the Output File. Once that's done, we will define a concurrent program that calls our PL/SQL procedure and in turn delivers the desired output.

Getting ready

Firstly, what is XML? **Extensible Markup Language** (**XML**) is a markup language that defines a set of rules for encoding documents in a format that is both human-readable and machine-readable. XML documents normally begin by declaring some information about themselves, as follows:

```
<?xml version="1.0" encoding="UTF-8" ?>
```

This is also known as the prologue. It contains the XML declaration, the document type definition, and any processing instructions, which are optional.

Beyond this initial line, an XML file is made up of textual information that is described as markup and content.

Markup includes the following:

> ► **Elements**: An element is the basic building block of XML. It is a name given to describe the data that it contains. Elements start with < and end with >.
>
>   Markups conform to three tag types:
>
>   ❑ start-tags, for example, `<section>`
>
>   ❑ end-tags, for example, `</section>`
>
>   ❑ empty-element tags, for example, `<line-break />`
>
>   A root element is the first element in a document and will contain any other elements. An XML document must always contain a root element.
>
> ► **Attributes**: Attributes have a name and a value combination. An attribute will be defined in the start-tag of an element and any values are defined within double quotes.
>
> ► **Entities**: These are representations of text that is interpreted for reserved characters, for example, & would need to be represented as `&amp;`.

An example of a non-empty markup is as follows:

```
<FieldOne>Field One content</FieldOne>
```

Data grouping is achieved through nested XML fields, which are repeated for each group, for example:

```
<GroupOne>
  <FieldOne>G1 Field One content</FieldOne>
  <FieldTwo>G1 Field Two content</FieldTwo>
</GroupOne>
<GroupTwo>
  <FieldOne>G2 Field One content</FieldOne>
  <FieldTwo>G2 Field Two content</FieldTwo>
</GroupTwo>
```

Group field names must be kept unique, while the repeating data fields can be reused in more than one group. Code indenting is not mandatory, but it does assist in understanding your data better, when viewing XML file content.

In our first recipe, we are going to create an executable and then define a concurrent program that launches the executable. The executable in this example is a PL/SQL package that will generate an XML file. To configure a concurrent program, we need to perform the following tasks:

- Create and compile a database package
- Configure and run an executable
- Configure a concurrent program

Create and compile a database package

We are going to create a database package that will generate an XML file we will use in our recipe. The package will be executed via a concurrent program within E-Business Suite. We are going to create the database package specification and body. Create a database package with a single procedure as follows (remember to include the two mandatory parameters required to base a concurrent program on a PL/SQL procedure):

How to do it...

To create the database package, perform the following:

1. Open SQL Developer (or SQL*Plus) and connect as the `apps` user. (You will need to know the apps' user password.)

2. Create the following package specification as shown in the following screenshot:

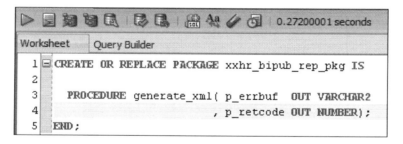

3. Now create the following package body (this is provided in the download bundle):

```
XXHR_BIPUB_REP_PKG.pkb
 1   CREATE OR REPLACE PACKAGE BODY APPS.xxhr_bipub_rep_pkg IS
 2
 3      PROCEDURE generate_xml( p_errbuf  OUT VARCHAR2
 4                            , p_retcode OUT NUMBER) IS
 5      BEGIN
 6          FND_FILE.put_line(fnd_file.output, '<?xml version="1.0" encoding="UTF-8"?>');
 7          FND_FILE.put_line(fnd_file.output, '<Roster>');
 8          FND_FILE.put_line(fnd_file.output, ' <Week>');
 9          FND_FILE.put_line(fnd_file.output, '  <WeekNo>1</WeekNo>');
10          FND_FILE.put_line(fnd_file.output, '  <Monday>Thomas</Monday>');
11          FND_FILE.put_line(fnd_file.output, '  <Tuesday>Emily</Tuesday>');
12          FND_FILE.put_line(fnd_file.output, '  <Wednesday>Annie</Wednesday>');
13          FND_FILE.put_line(fnd_file.output, '  <Thursday>James</Thursday>');
14          FND_FILE.put_line(fnd_file.output, '  <Friday>Gordon</Friday>');
15          FND_FILE.put_line(fnd_file.output, '  <Saturday>Rosie</Saturday>');
16          FND_FILE.put_line(fnd_file.output, '  <Sunday>Henry</Sunday>');
17          FND_FILE.put_line(fnd_file.output, ' </Week>');
18          FND_FILE.put_line(fnd_file.output, ' <Week>');
19          FND_FILE.put_line(fnd_file.output, '  <WeekNo>2</WeekNo>');
20          FND_FILE.put_line(fnd_file.output, '  <Monday>Bertie</Monday>');
21          FND_FILE.put_line(fnd_file.output, '  <Tuesday>Harold</Tuesday>');
22          FND_FILE.put_line(fnd_file.output, '  <Wednesday>Toby</Wednesday>');
23          FND_FILE.put_line(fnd_file.output, '  <Thursday>Clarabel</Thursday>');
24          FND_FILE.put_line(fnd_file.output, '  <Friday>Percy</Friday>');
25          FND_FILE.put_line(fnd_file.output, '  <Saturday>Edward</Saturday>');
26          FND_FILE.put_line(fnd_file.output, '  <Sunday>Trevor</Sunday>');
27          FND_FILE.put_line(fnd_file.output, ' </Week>');
28          FND_FILE.put_line(fnd_file.output, '</Roster>');
29      end generate_xml;
30   END xxhr_bipub_rep_pkg;
31   /
```

How to do it...

We have created a package that will be called from a concurrent program within E-Business Suite. It will generate an XML message we will use later in the chapter to mail merge data with a BI Publisher template.

Create and run an executable

We are now going to create a concurrent program with an associated executable based on the package we've just created. The responsibility we need to configure the concurrent program is **Application Developer**.

How to do it...

1. Log in to Oracle E-Business Suite with a user that can access the **Application Developer** responsibility.

2. Navigate to **Concurrent | Executable** and the **Concurrent Program Executable** window will open.

3. Enter data as shown in the following table:

Item name	Item value
Executable	XXHR_BIP_ROSTER
Short Name	XXHR_BIP_ROSTER
Application	XXHR Custom Application
Description	XXHR BI Publisher Roster Example
Execution Method	PL/SQL Stored Procedure
Execution File Name	xxhr_bipub_rep_pkg.generate_xml

 Please note that any fields that are not specified in this table should be left as their default value.

The screen should now look like the following:

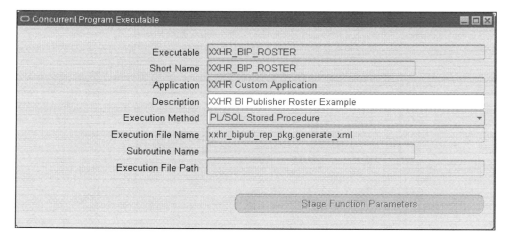

4. Click on the **Save** button in the toolbar (or *Ctrl + S*) to save the record.
5. Exit the form.

How it works...

We have defined an executable that will be launched by the concurrent program we are going to configure next. This has to be created before we can configure the concurrent program. This executable is calling the database package we created in the *Create and run an executable* recipe.

Configure a concurrent program

In the following recipe, we will configure a concurrent program to run our database procedure we created earlier. It will run the executable that we have just defined.

How to do it...

To configure the concurrent program, perform the following:

1. Log in to Oracle and select the **Application Developer** responsibility.

2. Navigate to **Concurrent | Program** and the **Concurrent Programs** window will open.

3. Enter data as shown in the following table:

Item name	Item value
Program	XXHR BI Publisher Roster Example
Short Name	XXHR_BIP_ROSTER
Application	XXHR Custom Application
Description	XXHR BI Publisher Roster Example
Name (in **Executable**)	XXHR_BIP_ROSTER

 Please note that any fields that are not defined in this table should be left as their default value.

The screen should now look like the following:

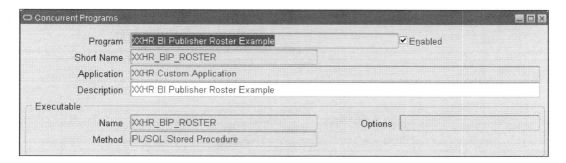

4. Click on the **Save** button in the toolbar (or *Ctrl + S*) to save the record.

5. Exit the form.

How it works...

So now we have configured the executable and also defined the concurrent program that launches the executable. These are the basic steps required to configure a concurrent program. As you will see there are a number of other regions on the screen and some buttons, and we will be looking at some of these later in the chapter. The next step is to run the concurrent program.

Making a concurrent program available to a user

We have now created the concurrent program, but now we want to run it. To be able to run it, we need to do some configuration. The concurrent program needs to be assigned to a request group and the request group needs to be assigned to a responsibility. The responsibility is assigned a menu that calls the concurrent request functions. So we are going to perform the following tasks:

- ▶ Configure a menu
- ▶ Create a new request group
- ▶ Create a new responsibility
- ▶ Assign the responsibility to a user
- ▶ Run the concurrent program
- ▶ View the request

Configure a menu

The following recipe will configure a menu, which will be attached to our new responsibility we are going to create. This will determine the concurrent programs and forms we will be able to access.

How to do it...

To create a menu, perform the following steps:

1. Log in to Oracle E-Business Suite with the **Application Developer** responsibility.
2. Navigate to **Application | Menu**, and the **Menus** window will open.
3. Enter data as shown in the following table for the master record:

Item name	Item value
Menu	XXHR_TEST_MENU
User Menu Name	Test Menu
Menu Type	Standard
Description	Test Menu

4. Enter data as shown in the following table for the detail records:

Seq	Prompt	Submenu	Function	Description	Grant
10	View Requests		View All Concurrent Requests		Select this
20	Submit Requests		Requests: Submit		Select this

The screen should now look like the following:

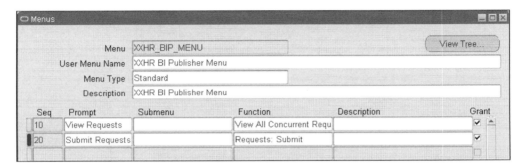

5. Click on the **Save** button in the toolbar (or *Ctrl* + S) to save the record.
6. Exit the form.

How it works...

We have created a menu that has the standard concurrent request functions added to it, so that we can run and view our concurrent program. The menu will be added to a responsibility to make the menu items available to that responsibility. The responsibility can then be assigned to users, giving them access to the menu functions.

Create a new request group

When we define a responsibility, we can also assign a request group to it. This is a list of concurrent programs or request sets that the responsibility will see, when they run a concurrent request. We need to add a request group that will have our concurrent program in it.

How to do it...

To create a request group, perform the following:

1. Log in to Oracle E-Business Suite with the **System Administrator** responsibility.
2. Navigate to **Security | Responsibility | Request** and the **Request Groups** window will open.

3. Enter data as shown in the following table for the master record:

Item name	Item value
Group	XXHR BIP Request Group
Application	XXHR Custom Application
Code	XXHR_REQUEST_GROUP
Description	XXHR Request Group

4. Now, we are going to add the concurrent program we created in the *Defining a concurrent program* recipe. Navigate to the **Requests** region and enter data as shown in the following table for the detail record:

Type	Name	Application
Program	XXHR First Concurrent Program	XXHR Custom Application

The screen will now look like the following:

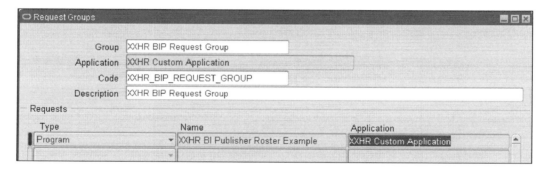

5. Click on the **Save** button in the toolbar (or *Ctrl + S*) to save the record.
6. Exit the form.

How it works...

We have now created a request group that contains our concurrent program. When we assign it to our responsibility, we will have access to programs in the request set assigned to it.

Create a new responsibility

Now, we will create our new responsibility that will run the concurrent program.

How to do it...

Perform the following steps to create a new responsibility called XXHR BI Publisher:

1. Log in to Oracle with the **System Administrator** responsibility.

2. Navigate to **Security | Responsibility | Define** and the **Responsibilities** window will open.

3. Enter data as shown in the following table for the master record:

Item name	Item value
Responsibility Name	XXHR BI Publisher
Application	XXHR Custom Application
Responsibility Key	XXHRBIP
Description	XXHR BI Publisher
Name (in **Data Group**)	Standard
Application (in **Data Group**)	XXHR Custom Application
Menu	XXHR BI Publisher Menu
Name (in **Request Group**)	XXHR BIP Request Group

The screen will now look like the following:

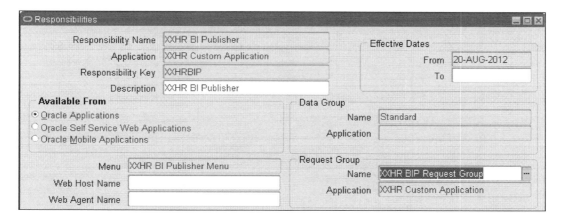

4. Click on the **Save** button in the toolbar (or *Ctrl* + *S*) to save the record.

5. Exit the form.

How it works...

We have now created a responsibility that has the menu we created earlier and our request group assigned to it.

Assign the responsibility to a user

Now, we are going to assign the responsibility to our user.

How to do it...

To add the responsibility to your user, perform the following steps:

1. Log in to Oracle with the **System Administrator** responsibility.
2. Navigate to **Security | User | Define** and the **Users** window will open.
3. Add the **XXHR BI Publisher** responsibility to your user.

How it works...

We have now added the responsibility to your user. This will allow you to access the menu functions we created and assigned to the **XXHR BI Publisher** responsibility.

Run the concurrent program

Now, we can run the concurrent program we have created.

How to do it...

To run the concurrent program, perform the following:

1. Log in to Oracle E-Business Suite with your user ID, and then select the **XXHR BI Publisher** responsibility.
2. Navigate to **Submit Requests | Submit**.
3. Select **Single Request** and click on the **OK** button.
4. When the **Submit Request** screen will open, click on the **Name** field and select **XXHR BI Publisher Roster** from the list of values.
5. Click on the **Submit** button.
6. Click on the **No** button if requested to submit another request.
7. Exit the form.

How it works...

The request has now been submitted. The next time the concurrent manager runs in the background it will execute the request. We now want to view the request to see if it has completed successfully. If the concurrent program completes with an **Inactive No Manager** message, the concurrent background engine is not running. Contact your DBA to start up the concurrent manager background processes.

View the request

We want to see the outcome of the concurrent request and we can do this from the menu.

How to do it...

To view the request, perform the following:

1. Navigate to **View | Requests**.
2. The **Find Requests** window will appear.
3. Click on the **Find** button in the bottom-right hand side corner.
4. The **Requests** window will appear and you will see the concurrent program that was run.
5. You can see that the concurrent program has been completed successfully.

> The **Requests** screen does not automatically refresh, so you will need to click on the **Refresh Data** button to refresh the screen, until the **Phase** has changed to **Completed**.

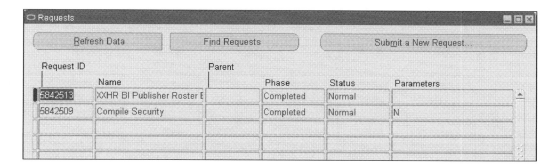

How it works...

We have now run the request we created, executed the concurrent program, and can see that the process has completed successfully. We've written a piece of code that outputs an XML message, and we then created a concurrent program to execute the code. Upon successful execution of the concurrent program, we are able to view the XML output by clicking the **View Output** button. The output file is fairly simple, yet perfectly-formed XML containing two repeating groups of data that define consecutive weeks of a duty roster, with each weekday field indicating the name of a person on duty for a given day.

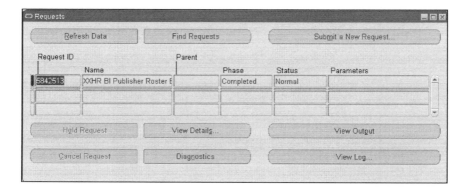

Click on **View Output** to see the output the concurrent program has created.

```xml
<?xml version="1.0" encoding="UTF-8"?>
<Roster>
  <Week>
      <WeekNo>1</WeekNo>
      <Monday>Thomas</Monday>
      <Tuesday>Emily</Tuesday>
      <Wednesday>Annie</Wednesday>
      <Thursday>James</Thursday>
      <Friday>Gordon</Friday>
      <Saturday>Rosie</Saturday>
      <Sunday>Henry</Sunday>
  </Week>
  <Week>
      <WeekNo>2</WeekNo>
      <Monday>Bertie</Monday>
      <Tuesday>Harold</Tuesday>
      <Wednesday>Toby</Wednesday>
      <Thursday>Clarabel</Thursday>
      <Friday>Percy</Friday>
      <Saturday>Edward</Saturday>
      <Sunday>Trevor</Sunday>
  </Week>
</Roster>
```

We will be using this XML code as a part of the next section, so save (**File | Save As**) the output file locally as `xxhr_roster.xml`.

Using Oracle BI Publisher Desktop software to create a rich text format (RTF) template

As mentioned in the introduction of the chapter, Oracle BI Publisher applies XML data against pre-prepared template files. Oracle has provided client side tools to aid in the building and testing of these required templates. These consist of plugins to MS Word and MS Excel for the building of RTF and Excel templates. The BI Publisher Desktop tools are not specifically required to develop BI Publisher templates, but they do make the creation of templates a lot easier through the use of wizards. This reduces the requirement to understand **Visual Basic for Applications** (**VBA**) code to design more complex templates.

The Desktop tools also provide a useful template preview feature, which essentially delivers your report using sample XML merged into your template. We will now perform the following tasks to download the software and generate a template:

  ▸ Download and install Oracle BI Publisher Desktop software
  ▸ Create an RTF template
  ▸ Remove XDO field codes
  ▸ Save the template as an RTF document
  ▸ Preview the RTF template

Download and install Oracle BI Publisher Desktop software

First, we need to download the BI Publisher Desktop software from Oracle.

How to do it...

To download and install BI Publisher desktop, perform the following:

1. Open your web browser and go to the following link: `http://www.oracle.com/technetwork/middleware/bi-publisher/downloads/index.html`

2. Download and install the correct version to match your operating system.

Oracle BI Publisher 11g Enterprise
BI Publisher 11g Enterprise is intended for production deployments. It is installed using the Oracle Business Intelligence 11g Installer. All Business Intelligence components are installed. To configure only BI Publisher, select only Business Intelligence Publisher on the Configure Components screen of the installation. Before installing BI Publisher you must run the Repository Creation Utility.

☐ Oracle Business Intelligence 11.1.1.6.0
  Release Notes | Documentation Library | Certification Information

☐ Oracle BI Publisher Desktop 11.1.1.6.0 for 32 bit Office on Windows (245 MB)
☐ Oracle BI Publisher Desktop 11.1.1.6.0 for 64 bit Office on Windows (245 MB)
  Choose the BI Publisher Desktop based on your version of Microsoft Office 32 bit or 64 bit

To download the file, you will need to have a free Oracle Web account and also accept the license agreement.

To find the version of office you have installed, open Microsoft Word and navigate to **File** | **Help** as shown in the following screenshot:

Once installed, you will notice that a BI Publisher menu tab will become available from within MS Word and Excel, as shown in the following screenshot:

The tab will also be available in other MS Office programs such as Excel, as shown in the following screenshot:

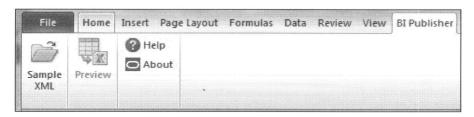

How it works...

We have downloaded and installed the Oracle BI Publisher Desktop plugin. Once installed, we can see a BI Publisher menu tab within MS Word and MS Excel.

Create an RTF template

We will now go through an example of creating a simple, tabulated template within MS Word, which is based on our generated XML data. We will then save the template as an RTF document.

How to do it...

To create an RTF template, perform the following:

1. Open a new, blank MS Word document.
2. Select the **BI Publisher** tab.

3. Click the **Sample XML** button, and open the saved `xxhr_roster.xml` file, which will make the XML data available to MS Word.

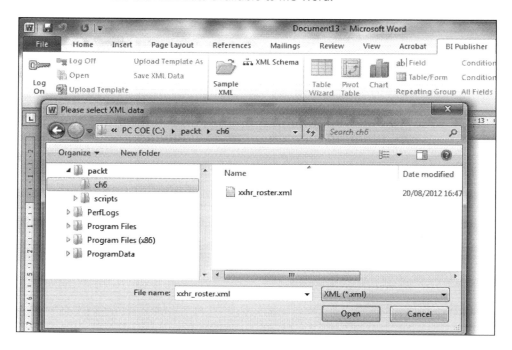

You will notice that once the XML data has been loaded, more options become available on the **BI Publisher** tab.

4. Click on **Table Wizard**.

5. For the report format, select **Table** and click on **Next**.

6. For the grouping field to report on, select **/Roster/Week** and click on **Next** as shown in the following screenshot:

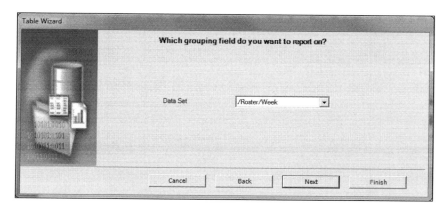

7. For the fields displayed on the report, click on the **>>** button and click Finish as shown in the following screenshot:

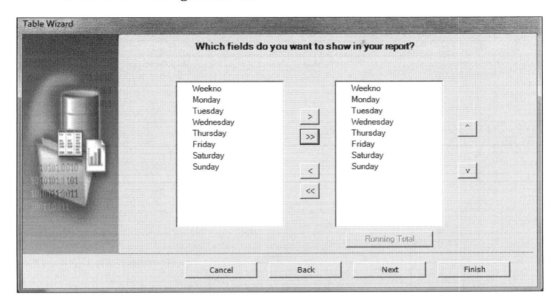

The result of the **Table Wizard** window should produce a table in your document as follows:

Weekno	Monday	Tuesday	Wednesday	Thursday	Friday	Saturday	Sunday
F WeekNo	Monday	Tuesday	Wednesday	Thursday	Friday	Saturday	Sunday E

Most of what you see in the resulting document should be self-explanatory. The F and E tags in the first and last cells define the beginning and end of a for-each row loop.

With a bit of tidying up we're able to make the template look a bit more meaningful. At this stage, you can add images, color, and additional static text as required. Our example receives a simple report heading and a renaming of the Week Number column heading:

1. Add a header called Duty Roster.
2. Rename the **WeekNo** header to Week Number.
3. Expand the column **Wednesday** to fit the heading on the top line.

4. After the changes the template will look like the following:

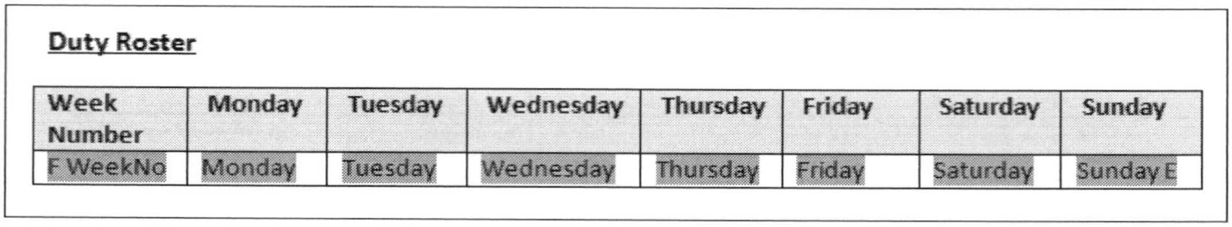

Duty Roster

Week Number	Monday	Tuesday	Wednesday	Thursday	Friday	Saturday	Sunday
F WeekNo	Monday	Tuesday	Wednesday	Thursday	Friday	Saturday	Sunday E

How it works...

We've used the BI Publisher Desktop software within MS Word to create a simple table based on our previously-generated XML data. We notice that the software has inserted various fields into our table.

Remove XDO field codes

Next, we need to tidy up a BI Publisher Desktop bug; when the wizard builds the table, it automatically inserts relevant fields and associated field codes into the document. The software automatically creates **Help Text** for each inserted field, but it unfortunately generates an XDO field code against each field and not our expected XML field codes. The BI Publisher Post Processor does not recognize these XDO field codes.

Our fix for the bug will be to replace the XDO tags with their correct XML tag equivalents.

How to do it...

To replace the XDO tags, perform the following:

1. Right-click the **F** field in the first table cell.

2. In the pop-up menu, navigate to **BI Publisher | Properties**. This will open up a **BI Publisher Properties** dialog box for that field.

3. Click on the **Advanced** tab to view the associated field code as shown in the following screenshot:

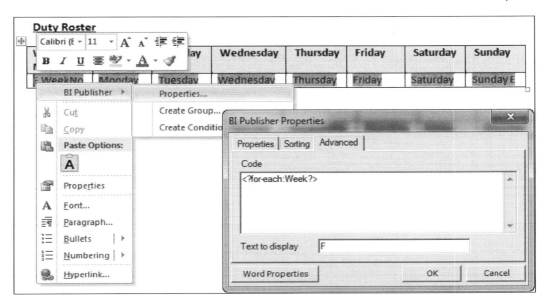

4. Copy the tag in the **Code** field (in this case `<?for-each:Week?>`).

5. Click on the **Cancel** button.

6. Right-click the `F` field in the first table cell.

7. Select **Properties** from the pop-up menu.

8. Click on the **Add Help Text** button.

    You will see that the Type your own field displays a tag in a similar format to the following screenshot:

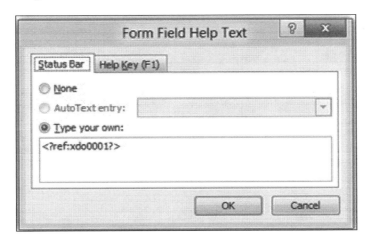

9. Replace the text in the **Type your own:** field with the tag copied from the associated field code we have just copied (in this case `<?for-each:Week?>`).

The automatically-created XDO field code is what causes all the problems. We will now replace this tag with the BI Publisher XML equivalent, which we copied from the BI Publisher dialog box a few steps back.

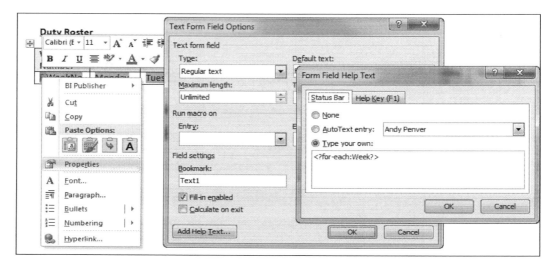

10. Click on **OK**.

These steps need to be repeated for each XML field in your template. Do not forget about the final E field in the final table cell!

How it works...

We've inspected the properties of each generated field and then replaced the automatically-inserted XDO help text field codes with the correct XML equivalents, which BI Publisher recognizes. By doing this, we circumvent a known Oracle BI Publisher Desktop bug.

Save the template as an RTF document

Our eventual goal is to produce a BI Publisher report based on an RTF template, which will allow us to specify the final output format of the report, for example, PDF, Excel, PowerPoint, and so on.

How to do it...

To save the file as an RTF document, perform the following:

1. In Word select **File | Save As** from the menu.
2. Select **Rich Text Format (RTF)** from the file type list.
3. Give our template a name of `XXHR Duty Roster`.
4. Click on **Save**.

How it works...

In this case, we have saved the template as an RTF document. Once we have saved the document, we will be able to see the following file on our local file system, saved to the location we specified: `XXHR Duty Roster.rtf`.

Preview the RTF template

Now that we have a completed template, we are in a position to preview it against our XML code. You will remember that we loaded the XML code into the document at the beginning of the template creation process, and as long as you haven't closed and reopened the template file, the data should still be loaded. If you have already closed the template file, reopen it and reload the XML data by navigating to the **BI Publisher** tab and clicking the **Sample XML** button as previously explained.

The **Preview** section of the **BI Publisher** tab provides a number of options. The advantage of using an RTF template is that it can easily be represented in a number of different formats, that is, PDF, HTML, Excel, PowerPoint, and so on.

How to do it...

To preview the report as a PDF document, perform the following:

1. Navigate to the **BI Publisher** tab and click on the **PDF** option as shown in the following screenshot:

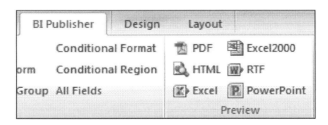

2. Clicking on the PDF option in the **Preview** section will deliver a PDF representation of your data formatted as per your template as shown in the following screenshot:

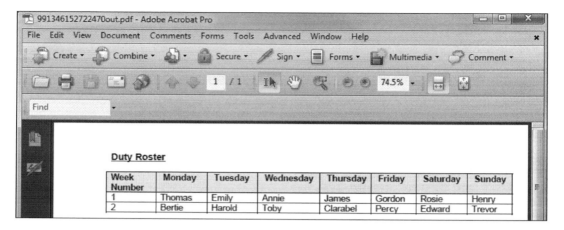

The data mirrors the XML output.

Likewise, clicking on the **Excel** option will deliver an Excel presentation of your data as shown in the following screenshot:

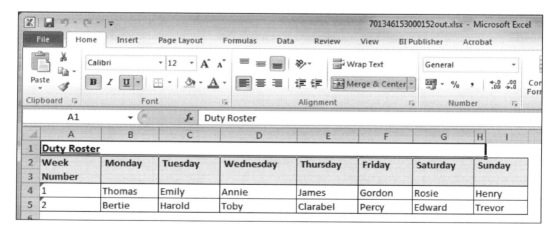

How it works...

Once a template has been created, we are able to use the built-in previewer to understand what our eventual BI Publisher report will look like in a number of output formats.

We are now ready to create an Oracle BI Publisher report based on our template.

Creating a Data Definition

A BI Publisher Data Definition is the required link between the mechanism that generates XML data and the template into which we wish to merge the XML data. We can create a Data Definition in a few simple steps:

- ▶ Log on to Oracle Applications
- ▶ Select the **XML Publisher Administrator** responsibility
- ▶ Select the Data Definitions menu option

How to do it...

To create a data definition, perform the following:

1. Log in to Oracle with the **XML Publisher Administrator** responsibility.

2. Click on the **Data Definitions** link as shown in the following screenshot:

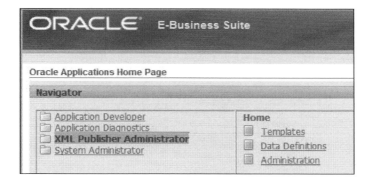

3. Navigate to the **Data Definitions** tab and click the **Create Data Definition** button as shown in the following screenshot:

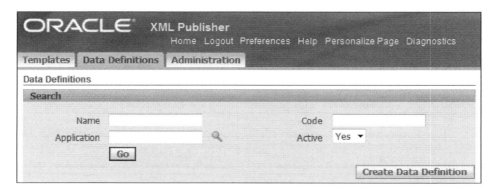

4. Enter data as shown in the following table:

Item name	Item value
Name	XXHR Duty Roster
Code	XXHR_BIP_ROSTER
Application	XXHR Custom Application
Start Date	01-Jan-1951
End Date	

 Please note that any fields that are not defined in this table should be left as their default value.

The screen should now look like the following:

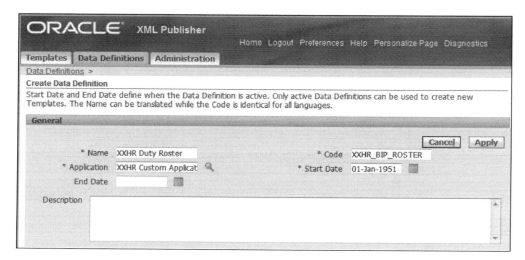

 The Data Definition Code (XXHR_BIP_ROSTER) *must* be identical to the concurrent program short name.

5. Click on the **Apply** button.

How it works...

We have now created a Data Definition to provide the link between our generated XML data and the RTF template, created in the *Create an RTF template* recipe. The Data Definition will link our concurrent program with the data definition. Next, we will take a look at defining our template within Oracle EBS and then creating a BI Publisher report.

Defining a template

A BI Publisher Template is a container of data that allows us to represent our chosen data in a meaningful way, depending on requirements. We create a Template definition in Oracle EBS in order to specify which data source (that is, Data Definition) is associated with a specific template file.

Similar to our Data Definition, we create a Template Definition in a few simple steps:

- ▶ Log on to Oracle Applications
- ▶ Select the **XML Publisher Administrator** responsibility
- ▶ Select the Templates menu option

How to do it...

To create a template, perform the following:

1. Log in to Oracle with the **XML Publisher Administrator** responsibility.
2. Click on the **Templates** link as shown in the next screenshot (if you are already in the **XML Publisher Administrator** screen, just click on the **Templates** tab).
3. Click on the **Create Template** button.
4. Define the template as follows:

Item name	Item value
Name	XXHR Duty Roster
Code	XXHR_BIP_ROSTER
Application	XXHR Custom Application
Data Definition	XXHR Duty Roster
Type	RTF
Start Date	01-Jan-1951
End Date	
Subtemplate	
Default Output Type	
File	C:\.....\XXXHR Duty Roster.rtf

This is where we link our template to the Data Definition created in the previous recipe. This is also the point where we need to upload our previously-prepared template file (XXHR Duty Roster.rtf)—browse to and select the file as saved on your local file system.

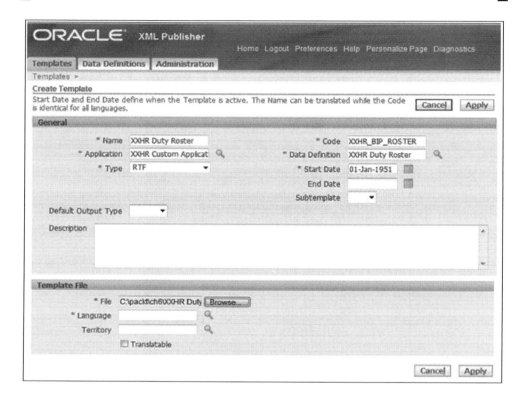

5. Click on the **Apply** button.

How it works...

We have now created a Template to link our data source with our data container. To do this, we logged into Oracle EBS and created a Template Definition, which we linked back to our Data Definition and RTF template file.

Running a BI Publisher report

We now have all the necessary building blocks in place to actually run a BI Publisher report based on our XML data and RTF template.

How to do it...

To run our BI Publisher report, we need to run our XXHR BI Publisher Roster Example concurrent program once again:

1. Log in to Oracle Applications with the **XXHR BI Publisher** responsibility.
2. Navigate to **Submit Requests**.
3. Select **Single Request** and click on **OK**.

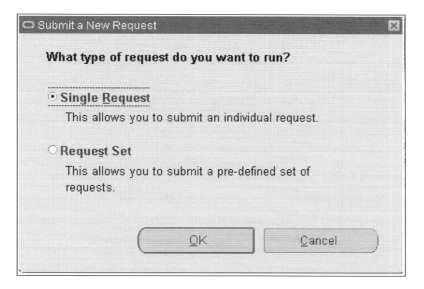

Notice that our Template is automatically specified as the **Layout** for this concurrent program within the **Upon Completion...** section of the **Submit Request** form. This is due to the Data Definition having the same code as our concurrent program short name and the Data Definition in turn being linked to our Template.

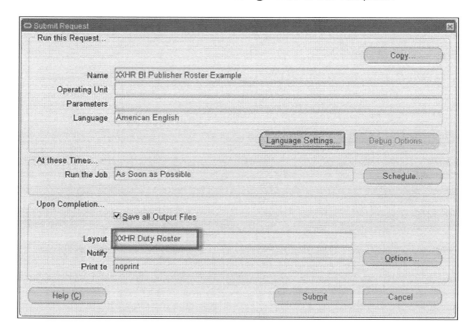

4. Click on the **Submit** button and wait for the process to execute till completion.

5. Click on the **View Output** button, and either save or open the resulting output file.

   The output file returned is not the usual unformatted text-based document we're used to, but rather a richly-formatted document based on the template we created in the *Defining a template* recipe, as shown in the following screenshot:

XXHR Duty Roster

Week Number	Monday	Tuesday	Wednesday	Thursday	Friday	Saturday	Sunday
1	Thomas	Emily	Annie	James	Gordon	Rosie	Henry
2	Bertie	Harold	Toby	Clarabel	Percy	Edward	Trevor

You will notice that the output is an RTF document, which is opened in MS Word. Next, we will take a look at how we get the output to display as a PDF and Excel document instead.

How it works...

We ran our concurrent program once again, and noticed that a Layout was applied to the process before it was executed. This was due to us defining a Data Definition against the concurrent program and with a template linked to the Data Definition. Once our concurrent program completed execution, the resulting output file was our RTF template with our XML data merged into it. We have just successfully created and run a BI Publisher report!

Generating PDF and Excel output using an RTF template

When we created our report template, we saved it as an RTF document, which lends itself to conversion to a number of different output formats. Within our Template Definition, we are able to specify a default output for the Template and we originally left this property undefined, which has delivered the native RTF format of the document as report output.

We will now revisit the Template Definition, and choose a different default output format to deliver PDF and Excel-based BI Publisher reports based on our RTF template.

How to do it...

We need to carry out the following steps to modify our Template Definition:

1. Log in to Oracle EBS and with the **XML Publisher Administrator** responsibility.
2. Select the **Templates** menu option.
3. In the **Search** region in **Templates**, enter XXHR Duty Roster in the **Name** field and click on the **Go** button.

4. Click the **XXHR Duty Roster** link in the returned search results as shown in the following screenshot:

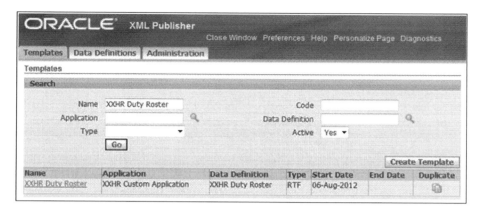

5. Click on the **Update** button in the **General** section as shown in the following screenshot:

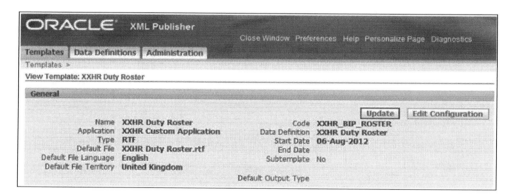

6. Change the **Default Output Type** selection to **PDF**.

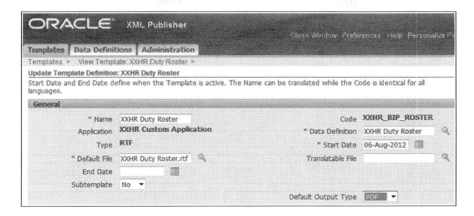

7. Rerun the **XXHR BI Publisher Roster Example** concurrent program and save the output file upon completion, which should look similar to the following screenshot when opened:

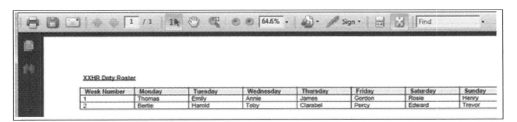

8. Similarly, go back to the Template Definition and change the **Default Output Type** selection to **Excel**.

9. Rerun the **XXHR BI Publisher Roster Example** concurrent program and save the output file upon completion, which should look similar to the following screenshot when opened:

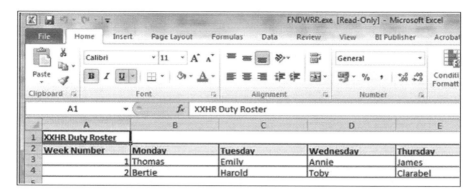

How it works...

Specifying a Default Output Type against our RTF Template, results in the BI Publisher report output adopting that output type, for example, PDF and Excel.

Implementing BI Publisher Bursting (e-mail)

Bursting is one of the most widely implemented features of BI Publisher. Bursting a report is essentially a process that accepts a data stream and splits it based on multiple criteria, generates output based on a template, then delivers the individual documents through the delivery channel of choice.

We will investigate an example where we burst our XXHR Duty Roster report into two individual reports, one for each week of our roster, and deliver the reports to a chosen e-mail address.

Creating the bursting file

In creating our XXHR Duty Roster report, we have already done all the hard work; the only missing piece of the puzzle with respect to bursting, is a Bursting Control file that needs to be linked to our Data Definition.

How to do it...

A sample Bursting Control file can be obtained from Oracle (search online or refer to a relevant BI Publisher guide). The following is the XML code for the Bursting Control file that we are going to use in our example (XXHR Duty Roster BC.xml)—explanations on key sections of the code will follow:

```
XXHR Duty Roster BC.xml *
<?xml version="1.0"?>
<xapi:requestset xmlns:xapi="http://xmlns.oracle.com/oxp/xapi">
<xapi:request select="/ROSTER/WEEK"> 1
<xapi:delivery>
<xapi:email server="192.168.1.2" port="25" from="noreply@yourdomain.com" reply-to="">
<xapi:message id="123"
      to="emailaddress@domain.com"
      cc="" attachment="true"
      content-type="text/html"
      subject="XXHR Duty Roster - Week${WeekNo}">
<![CDATA[ <html>
<style type="text/css">
.style01 {font-family: Calibri;
      font-size: 12pt;
      color: #000000;}  2
</style>
<body>
<div class="style01">
<b>THIS IS AN AUTOMATED EMAIL.</b>
<br><br>
Please find the attached Duty Roster for Week${WeekNo}.
<br><br>
</body>
</html> ]]>
</xapi:message>
</xapi:email>
</xapi:delivery>
<xapi:document output="Duty Roster Week${WeekNo}.pdf" output-type="pdf" delivery="123">
<xapi:template type="rtf"
   location="xdo://XXHR.XXHR_BIP_ROSTER.en.GB/?getSource=true"  3
   filter=""></xapi:template>
</xapi:document>
</xapi:request>
</xapi:requestset>
```

Open the above file in a text editor rather than your browser. The Bursting Control file is an XML file that holds relevant data that instructs the BI Publisher Bursting Engine how to split our report and where to deliver the resulting files.

1. The first thing we need to specify is how we want to split our data. This is done within the following tag and we make reference to our XML data file:

    ```
    <xapi:request select="/ROSTER/WEEK">
    ```

    In our example, we are going to split our data into individual weeks, hence the /ROSTER/WEEK reference.

2. Next, we need to specify how we intend on delivering the files. In our example we are going to e-mail the individual files to ourselves. The following lines of the Bursting Control file specify this.

 The highlighted fields (enclosed in square brackets) must be replaced with values relevant to yourself and your Oracle environment.

```
1   <xapi:delivery>
2   <xapi:email server="[YourServer]" port="25" from="[EmailAccount@YourDomain.com]"  reply-to="">
3    <xapi:message id="123" to="[YourEmailAddress]" cc="" attachment="true" content-type="text/html"
4   subject="XXHR Duty Roster - Week${WeekNo}">
5   <![CDATA[ <html>
6   <style type="text/css">
7   .style01 {font-family: Calibri;
8        font-size: 12pt;
9        color: #000000;}
10  </style>
11  <body>
12  <div class="style01">
13  <b>THIS IS AN AUTOMATED EMAIL.</b>
14  <br><br>
15  Please find the attached Duty Roster for Week${WeekNo}.
16  <br><br>
17  </body>
18  </html> ]]>
19  </xapi:message>
20  </xapi:email>
21  </xapi:delivery>
```

The `<xapi:message>` component is the actual body of the e-mail that we will be sending, and this can be specified as plain text or HTML.

3. Lastly, we need to specify the template that we are using to apply our data against, and `//XXHR.XXHR_BIP_ROSTER.en.GB` is the internal naming convention of our template.

   Once our Bursting Control file has been configured, we need to upload it against our Data Definition.

4. Log in to Oracle EBS and choose the **XML Publisher Administrator** responsibility.

5. Select the **Data Definitions** menu option.

6. On the **Data Definitions Search** screen, enter XXHR Duty Roster in the **Name** field and click on the **Go** button.

7. Click on the **XXHR Duty Roster** link in the returned search results.

8. Click the **Bursting Control File | Add File button**.

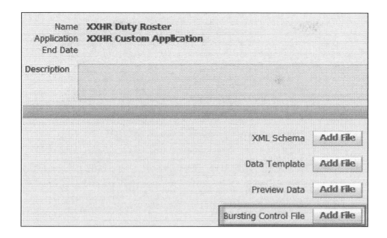

9. Browse to and select the saved Bursting Control file (`XXHR Duty Roster BC.xml`), and click on **Apply**.

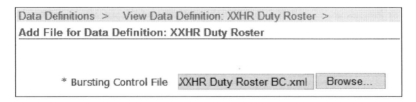

The Bursting Control filename should now be displayed as shown in the following screenshot:

How it works...

We have now created our Bursting file and added it to our Data Definition. This holds the relevant data to instruct the BI Publisher Bursting Engine about how to split our report and where to deliver the resulting files.

Running the Bursting concurrent program

Now, we need to rerun the **XXHR BI Publisher Roster Example** concurrent program. When the process has completed, we will run the seeded XML Publisher Report Bursting Program concurrent program, specifying the **Request ID** of the completed XXHR BI Publisher Roster Example report as a process parameter. Firstly, we will add the seeded concurrent program to our request group.

How to do it...

To add the XML Publisher Report Bursting Program concurrent program to our request group, perform the following:

1. Log in to Oracle E-Business Suite with the **System Administrator** responsibility.
2. Navigate to **Security | Responsibility | Request** to open the **Request Groups** window.
3. Add XML Publisher Report Bursting Program and save the changes as shown in the following screenshot:

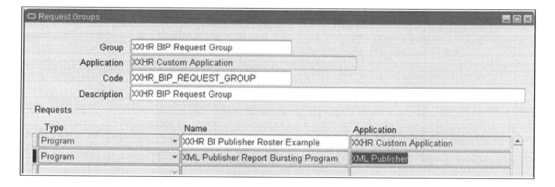

In reality, we would probably launch the bursting concurrent program from our packaged procedure, so that it will automatically produce the output files. In this instance, we will run it manually so that we can see the process working step-by-step.

4. Now switch to the **XXHR BI Publisher** responsibility.

5. Double-click on **Submit Requests** to open the **Submit Request** window.

6. Select **Single Request** and click on **OK**.

7. Select the **XXHR BI Publisher Roster Example** concurrent program and make a note of the **Request ID** as shown in the following screenshot (this will be different in your environment):

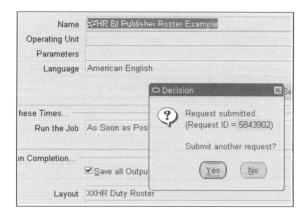

8. After the request has completed, submit a new request.

9. Select the XXHR BI Publisher Report Bursting Program concurrent program.

10. For the **Request ID** parameter, select the **XXHR BI Publisher Roster Example** concurrent program from the list as shown in the following screenshot (this will be the program with the **Request ID** we have just made a note of, but will probably be the program that is first in the list):

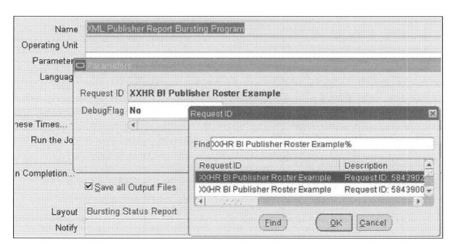

Upon completion, we can view the output file for a summary of the Bursting process. After a few minutes, the two expected e-mails should arrive in the inbox of the e-mail address we specified in the Bursting Control file.

How it works...

We used our BI Publisher report as a starting point, and defined a Bursting Control file to specify how we wish to split our data, and how and where we would like to deliver the resulting files.

Implementing BI Publisher Bursting (file system)

We are going to work through an example, where we burst our XXHR Duty Roster report into two individual reports, one for each week of our roster, and deliver the reports to a chosen location on the file system (that is, on the Oracle server).

How to do it...

A sample Bursting Control file can be obtained from Oracle (search online or refer to a relevant BI Publisher guide). The following is the XML code for the Bursting Control file that we are going to use in our example (XXHR Duty Roster BC fs.xml). This file is available in the code download bundle. Explanations on key sections of the code will follow.

```xml
<?xml version="1.0"?>
<xapi:requestset xmlns:xapi="http://xmlns.oracle.com/oxp/xapi">
<xapi:request select="/Roster/Week">
<xapi:delivery />
<xapi:document output="/usr/tmp/bip_out/XXHR Duty Roster - Week${WeekNo}" output-type="pdf">
<xapi:template type="rtf" location="xdo://XXHR.XXHR_BIP_ROSTER.en.GB/?getSource=true" filter="" />
</xapi:document>
</xapi:request>
</xapi:requestset>
```

1. The first thing we need to specify is how we want to split our data. This is done within the following tag and we make reference to our XML data file:

   ```
   <xapi:request select="/Roster/Week">
   ```

   In our example, we are going to split our data into individual weeks, hence the /Roster/Week level reference.

2. Next, we need to specify how we intend on delivering the files. In our example, we are going to write the files to a specified location on the file system, so all we need to ensure is that the specified directory location exists!. The following lines of the Bursting Control file specify this:

```
1  <xapi:document output="/usr/tmp/bip_out/XXHR Duty Roster - Week${WeekNo}" output-type="pdf">
2    <xapi:template type="rtf" location="xdo://XXHR.XXHR_BIP_ROSTER.en.GB/?getSource=true" filter="" />
3  </xapi:document>
```

> Visit the `http://docs.oracle.com/cd/E10091_01/doc/bip.1013/b40017/T421739T479695.htm` website for more information about the API's for BI Publisher.

Once our Bursting Control file has been configured, we need to upload it against our Data Definition as we did before:

3. Log in to Oracle EBS with the **XML Publisher Administrator** responsibility.

4. Select the **Data Definitions** menu option.

5. On the **Data Definitions Search** screen, enter `XXHR Duty Roster` in the **Name** field, and click on the **Go** button.

6. Click on **XXHR Duty Roster** in the returned search results.

7. Click on the **Add File** button in **Bursting Control File** as we did in the previous example.

8. Browse to and select the saved Busting Control file (`XXHR Duty Roster BC fs.xml`) and click on **Apply**.

   Now we need to rerun the XXHR BI Publisher Roster Example concurrent program. When the process has completed, we will run the seeded XXHR BI Publisher Roster Example concurrent program, specifying the Request ID of the completed XXHR BI Publisher Roster Example report as a process parameter:

9. Submit the process.

10. Upon completion, we can view the output file for a summary of the Bursting process.

Bursting Status Report

Date: 2012-08-30 11:08:10
Page 1 Of 1

Request ID	5843904
Parent Request ID	5843902
Report Name	XXHR BI Publisher Roster Example
Output File	/oracle/apps/r12/visr12/inst/apps/visr12_focusthreadr12/logs/appl/concout/o5843904.zip

Key	Output Type	Delivery	Output	Status
	pdf	FILESYSTEM	/usr/tmp/bip_out/XXHR Duty Roster - Week1.pdf	success
	pdf	FILESYSTEM	/usr/tmp/bip_out/XXHR Duty Roster - Week2.pdf	success

11. Next, we can use WinSCP (or your preferred file transfer application) to navigate to the specified directory location on the UNIX server, to see the results of the output file for a summary of the Bursting process.

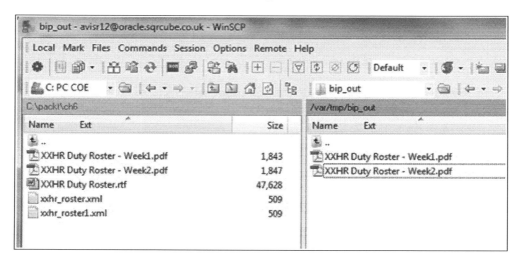

How it works...

We used our BI Publisher report as a starting point, and defined a Bursting Control file to specify how we wish to split our data, and how and where we would like to deliver the resulting files.

We chose to implement Bursting to the file system and once we had uploaded the Bursting Control file to the Data Definition, we ran our report, followed by XML Publisher Report Bursting Program.

Once the processes had completed, we were able to navigate to the specified location on the file system to view the files created by the Bursting process.

7

Desktop Integration

In this chapter, we will cover the following recipes:

- ▶ Installing the database objects
- ▶ Getting started with desktop integration
- ▶ Configuring the browser and MS office settings
- ▶ Registering a table and its columns with Oracle E-Business Suite
- ▶ Creating a custom integrator
- ▶ Creating a function for an integrator
- ▶ Adding an integrator to a menu
- ▶ Adding advanced features to an integrator
- ▶ Defining an importer

Introduction

Web ADI allows us to integrate Oracle E-Business Suite data with common MS Office desktop applications such as MS Word, Excel, and Project. It enables us to extract data from E-Business suite into a spreadsheet, where familiar data entry functionality can be utilized in these tools to complete end to end Oracle E-Business suite processes. We can download, view, edit, and create Oracle E-Business suite data into these applications and then utilize the full functionality of these applications.

We can also use Web ADIs called integrators to upload data to Oracle EBS. We can call procedures to perform validating data before uploading it to the Oracle E-Business suite using public Oracle APIs. When validation fails, we can pass messages from the message dictionary to the spreadsheet to inform users of erroneous data.

Before we get going, we will install the database objects that we will use in this chapter. Please note that this chapter requires Version 12.1.3 of Oracle E-Business Suite as a minimum requirement. In this version, Oracle has introduced a new user interface for us to be able to add integrators.

Installing the database objects

Create the database objects for this chapter before you start, by using a script provided. The code comes with the `Readme_7_1.Txt` readme file.

How to do it...

We are going to create a number of objects that we will use throughout the chapter. For all the database objects, there is a script provided called `7126_07_01.sh`. The following steps explain of how to run the script:

1. Create a local directory `C:\Packt\Scripts\Ch7`, where the scripts are downloaded to.

2. Open PuTTY and connect to the Application Tier user.

3. Create a new directory on the Application Tier under `$XXHR_TOP/Install` with the following commands:

   ```
   cd $XXHR_TOP/Install
   mkdir Ch7
   ```

4. Navigate to the new directory with the following command:

   ```
   cd Ch7
   ```

5. Open WinSCP and transfer (ftp) the files from `C:\Packt\Scripts\Ch7` to `$XXHR_TOP/Install/Ch7`.

6. In Unix, change the permissions of the script with the following command:

   ```
   chmod 775 7126_07_01.sh
   ```

7. Run the following command to create all of the database object commands:

   ```
   ./7126_07_01.sh apps/apps
   ```

8. The script checks that all of the files are present in your `$XXHR_TOP/Install/Ch7` directory and will prompt you to continue if they are all there, so type `Y` and press **Return**.

9. After the script has completed, check the `XXHR_7126_07_01.log` file for errors. (It will be created in the same directory, that is, `$XXHR_TOP/Install/Ch7`.)

10. Run the following query to check that all of the objects have been created successfully:

```
SELECT OWNER, OBJECT_NAME, OBJECT_TYPE, STATUS
FROM ALL_OBJECTS
WHERE (OBJECT_NAME LIKE 'XXHR%ABS%'
OR OBJECT_NAME LIKE 'XXHR%XML%')
ORDER BY 1, 2
```

Getting started with desktop integration

We are now going to create a menu, request group, and responsibility that will be used for the integrators, which we will create in this chapter. To do this, we will perform the following:

▸ Configure a menu

▸ Create a new request group

▸ Create a new responsibility

▸ Assign the desktop integration responsibility to a user

Configure a menu

The following recipe will configure a menu, which will be attached to our new responsibility we are going to create. This will determine the concurrent programs and forms we will be able to access.

How to do it...

To create a menu, perform the following steps:

1. Log in to Oracle with the **Application Developer** responsibility.

2. Navigate to **Application | Menu**, and the **Menus** window will open.

3. Enter data as shown in the following table for the master record:

Item Name	Item Value
Menu	XXHR_DI_MENU
User Menu Name	Test Desktop Integration Menu
Menu Type	Standard
Description	Test Desktop Integration Menu

4. Enter data as shown in the following table for the detail records:

Seq	Prompt	Submenu	Function	Description	Grant
10	View Requests		View All Concurrent Requests		Select this
20	Submit Requests		Requests: Submit		Select this

The screen should now look like the following:

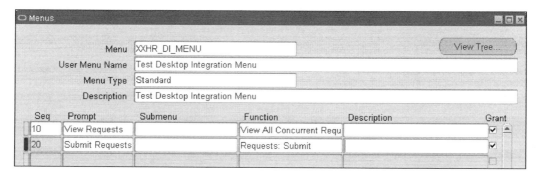

5. Click on the **Save** button in the toolbar (or *Ctrl + S*) to save the record.
6. Exit the form.

How it works...

We have created a menu that has the standard concurrent request functions added to it, so that we can run and view our concurrent program. The menu is assigned to a responsibility, and this is what a user will see when they switch to the responsibility associated with the menu. We have assigned the View Requests and Submit Requests functions to this menu, as we want to allow users to run concurrent programs from this menu.

Create a new request group

When we define a responsibility, we can also assign a request group to it. This is a list of concurrent programs or request sets that the responsibility will see, when they run a concurrent request through the Standard Request Submission (SRS) form. We need to add a request group that will have our concurrent program in it.

How to do it...

To create a request group, perform the following:

1. Log in to oracle with the System Administrator responsibility.

2. Navigate to **Security | Responsibility | Request** to open the **Request Groups** window.

3. Enter data as shown in the following table for the master record:

Item Name	Item Value
Group	XXHR DI Request Group
Application	XXHR Custom Application
Code	XXHR_REQUEST_GROUP
Description	XXHR DI Group

The following screenshot shows the form with the request group data entered:

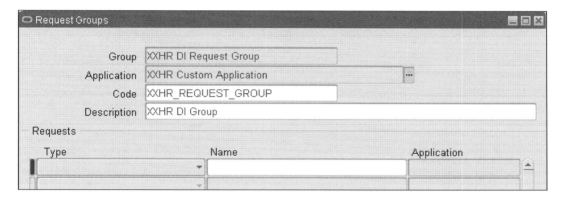

4. Click on the **Save** button in the toolbar (or *Ctrl + S*) to save the record.

5. Exit the form.

How it works...

The request group will contain the concurrent programs that we want the user to be permitted to run. We need to assign the request group to a responsibility, and this will allow that responsibility to access the concurrent programs associated with the request group.

Create a new responsibility

Now, we will create a new responsibility that we can associate the menu we have just created to.

How to do it...

Perform the following steps to create a new responsibility called XXHR Desktop Integration.

1. Log in to oracle with the **System Administrator** responsibility.

2. Navigate to **Security | Responsibility | Define**, and the **Responsibilities** window will open.

3. Enter data as shown in the following table for the master record:

Item Name	Item Value
Responsibility Name	XXHR Desktop Integration
Application	XXHR Custom Application
Responsibility Key	XXHRDINT
Description	
Name (in **Data Group**)	Standard
Application (in **Data Group**)	Service
Menu	Test Desktop Integration Menu
Name (in **Request Group**)	XXHR DI Group

The **Application** field in **Request Group** will inherit the **Application** from the **Request Group** we have previously created and will be populated automatically.

The screen will now look like the following:

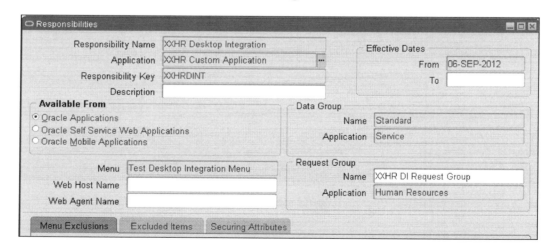

4. Click on the **Save** button in the toolbar (or *Ctrl* + *S*) to save the record.

5. Exit the form.

How it works...

The responsibility we have just created can now be added to a user to provide access to the menu and request groups that we have created.

Assign the desktop integration responsibilities to a user

Now we are going to assign the responsibility to our user.

How to do it...

To create a new user, perform the following steps:

1. Log in to oracle with the System Administrator responsibility.
2. Navigate to **Security | User | Define**, and the **Users** window will open.
3. Query back and add the following responsibilities to your user:

   ❑ Desktop Integration
   ❑ Desktop Integration Manager
   ❑ Desktop Integrator
   ❑ XXHR Desktop Integration
   ❑ System Administrator
   ❑ Application Developer

   The screen should look similar to the following:

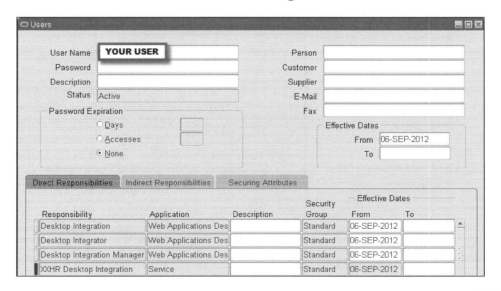

How it works...

Assigning these responsibilities to your user will mean that they will be displayed when you log in to the system. Each responsibility will have a menu, which will give users access to different functionalities of the system. In this case, we have provided access to the **Desktop Integrator** functions that will allow us to create and administer a new integrator. Notice that in release 12.1.3 of EBS, the login screen now has a different menu structure. It is more like a folder structure, which is much easier to navigate with.

The following screenshot is what we will see when we log in to Oracle EBS:

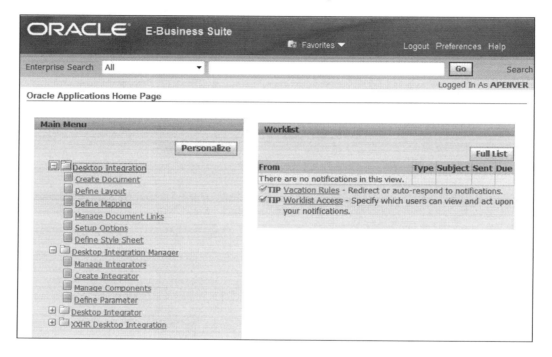

Configuring the browser and MS Office settings

When we create an integrator, the generation is performed through a browser. To allow this to happen, we must ensure that the browser allows certain functionality to be switched on. In this case, we must enable a security setting if using an Internet Explorer browser. In this recipe, we will perform the following:

- ▸ Configure the browser
- ▸ Configure MS office security settings

Configure the browser

In this recipe, we will set the Internet Explorer browser settings.

How to do it...

To set the browser settings, perform the following:

1. Open an Internet Explorer browser window.
2. Click on **Internet Options**.
3. Click on the **Security** tab.
4. In the security page, click on the **Internet** zone as shown in the following screenshot:

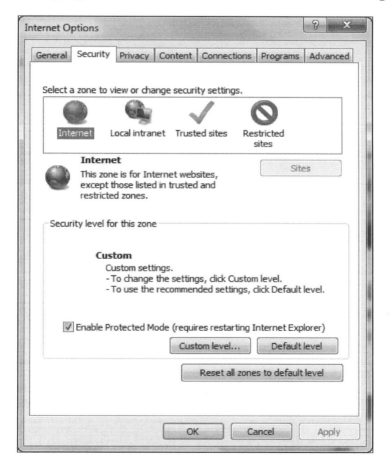

5. Now, click on the **Custom level...** button.

6. Scroll down **Security Settings** until you get to **Scripting**.

7. Set the **Allow status bar updates via script** radio button to **Enable** as shown in the following screenshot:

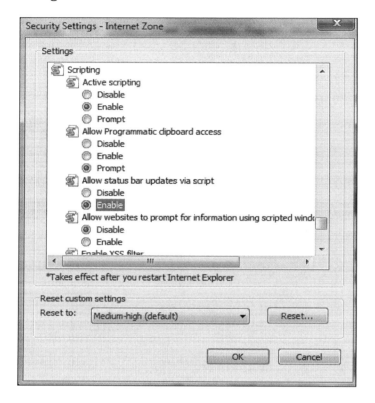

8. Click on **OK**.

9. Click on **Yes** when prompted with the **Are you sure you want to change the settings for this zone** warning message.

10. Finally, click on **OK** to close the **Internet Options** dialog box.

11. Restart the browser, so that the new settings can take effect.

How it works...

We must change some browser settings to allow integrators to be created, as the integrator creation user interface is browser based.

Configure MS Office security settings

When an integrator is created by Oracle, it uses VBA code in the background. By default, the security settings in Microsoft Office does not allow VBA code to be run. Therefore, we must change the security settings to allow the VBA code to be run.

How to do it...

To configure the MS Office settings, perform the following:

1. Open Microsoft Excel (Office 2010).

2. Click on the **File** tab and select **Options** from the menu.

3. Select **Trust Center** and then click on **Trust Center Settings...**.

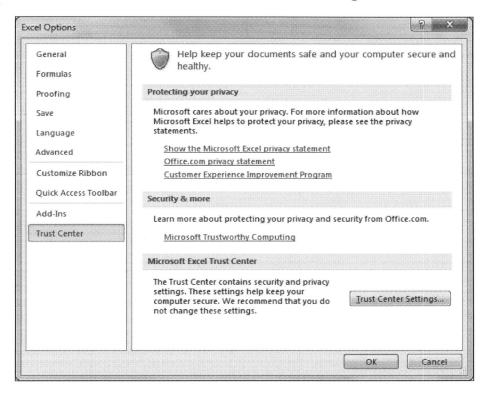

4. Click on **Macro Settings** and check the **Trust access to the VBA project object model** checkbox as shown in the following screenshot:

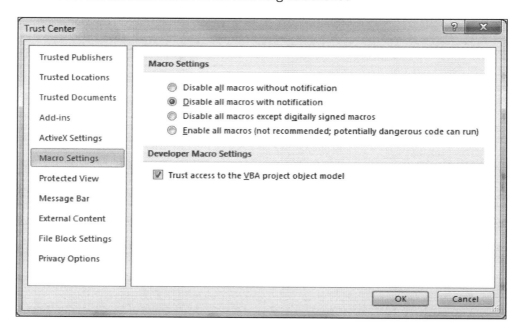

How it works...

When we create integrators, there are a number of macros that Oracle uses, which run in the background. If we do not set the **Macro Settings**, the integrator will not be created.

Registering a table and its columns within Oracle E-Business Suite

We need to register our table that we are going to load data into within EBS. This is required when we create the integrator, so that we can see the table definition in the user interface. We will run the script to register the XXHR_PARTY_UPLOAD table and all of its columns.

How to do it...

To run the script to register the XXHR_PARTY_UPLOAD table, perform the following:

1. Start SQL Developer and open the XXHR_PARTY_UPLOAD_REG.sql file available from the download bundle.

2. Click the run script icon from the toolbar as shown in the following screenshot.

   You can run the script in SQL*Plus or another development tool such as TOAD if you prefer.

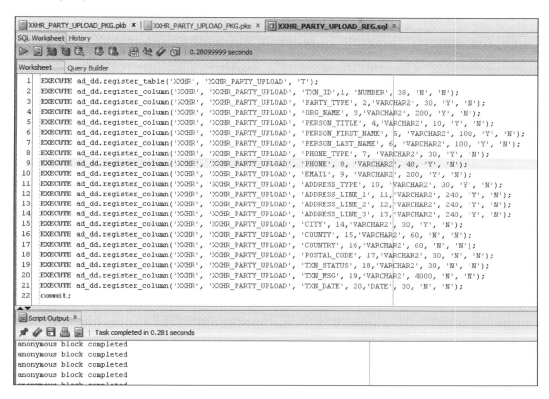

Now we have run the script to register the table, we can check that it has been successfully registered in EBS.

How it works...

To register the table, we must use the AD_DD package that is provided by Oracle, as the form does not allow users to enter records. The script has been provided and this has been run to register the database table. Let's have a look at the syntax; an example of the code is shown as follows:

```
EXECUTE AD_DD.REGISTER_TABLE('XXHR', 'XXHR_PARTY_UPLOAD', 'T');
```

The parameters are as follows:

Parameter	Meaning
P_APPL_SHORT_NAME	The application short name of the table. This is our custom application XXHR.
P_TAB_NAME	Table name (this needs to be in uppercase).
P_TAB_TYPE	Type of table. We will nearly always use T.

Likewise, we have added each item and we did this by calling the AD_DD.REGISTER_COLUMN procedure for each column.

An example would be as follows:

```
EXECUTE AD_DD.REGISTER_COLUMN('XXHR', 'XXHR_PARTY_UPLOAD', 'TXN_ID',1,
'NUMBER', 38, 'N', 'N');
```

The parameters are as follows:

Parameter	Meaning
P_APPL_SHORT_NAME	The application short name of the table. This is our custom application XXHR.
P_TAB_NAME	Table name (this needs to be in uppercase).
P_COL_NAME	Type of table. we will nearly always use T.
P_COL_SEQ	This is a unique number of the columns.
P_COL_TYPE	This parameter is the type of column,for example, NUMBER or DATE etc.
P_COL_WIDTH	This parameter specifies the width of the column.
P_NULLABLE	This parameter is a Y/N parameter to determine if NULL values are allowed.
P_TRANSLATE	This parameter is a Y/N parameter to determine if the values will be translated by Oracle.

Checking the table has been registered in Oracle

We have run the script to register our table in EBS. Now we will log in to Oracle to check that the table has been registered successfully.

How to do it...

To check that the table has been registered in EBS, perform the following:

1. Log in to Oracle with the Application Developer responsibility.

2. Navigate to **Application | Database | Table**, and the **Tables** window will open.

3. Press *F11* to enter a query.

4. Enter XXHR_PARTY_UPLOAD in the table name field and press *Ctrl + F11* to execute the query.

How it works...

We can see that the table has been registered correctly using the script that we ran. This will mean that the table will be available to the integrator UI, when we come to create one in the next recipe. The following screenshot shows the table we have registered in EBS, which means the scripts we ran have been completed successfully:

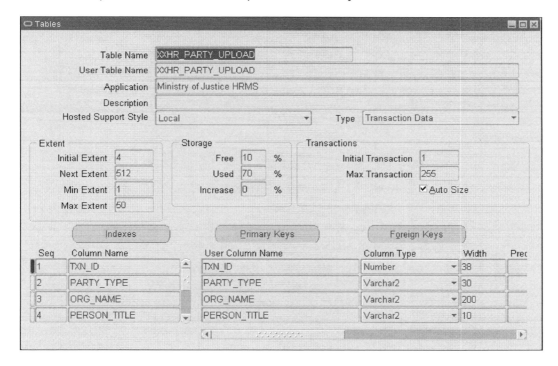

Creating a custom integrator

We are now going to create a custom integrator. To this we are to perform a number of actions. We will first need to define the integrator before, and then define the interface. We will then create a layout for the integrator will then show how to generate it. Once we have done this, we can then look at the editing attributes, amending titles, and adding things, like lists of values. In this recipe, we will therefore perform the following tasks:

- ▸ Configure the integrator
- ▸ Configure the interface
- ▸ Create a layout for the integrator
- ▸ Generate the integrator
- ▸ Edit the attributes
- ▸ Add the lists of values

Configure the integrator

We are now going to configure the integrator. There are different objects that an integrator can be based upon. In this example, we are going to base the integrator upon the table we created and registered in EBS.

How to do it...

To create a custom integrator, perform the following:

1. Log in to Oracle with the **Desktop Integration Manager** responsibility.
2. Select **Create Integrator** from the menu.
3. In **Step 1 of 5**, in the **Integrator Information** region, enter the following details:
   - ❑ **Integrator Name**: Party Upload
   - ❑ **Internal Name**: XXHR_PARTY_UPLOAD
   - ❑ **Application**: XXHR Custom Application
   - ❑ **Reporting Only**: Unchecked
   - ❑ **Enabled**: Yes
   - ❑ **Display in create document page**: Checked
4. When completed click the Next button.

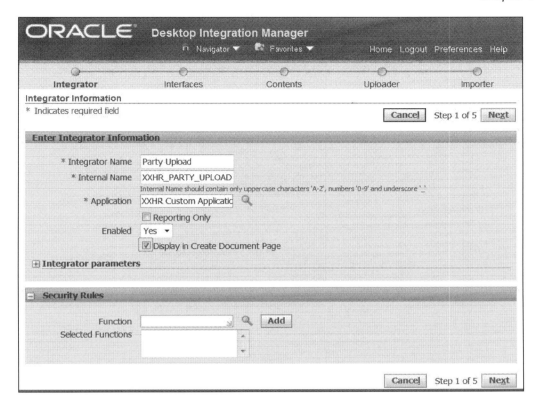

Configure the interface

When we configure the interface, we will be defining a name for the interface and the type of the interface. For example, the type of the interface could be a PL/SQL procedure or based upon a database table that we can upload data to. We can also define the return values from the interface, such as an error message.

How to do it...

To create the interface, perform the following:

1. In **Step 2 of 5**, in the **Integrator Information** region, enter the following details:

    -   **Interface Name**: Party Upload
    -   **Interface Type**: Table
    -   **Table Name**: XXHR_PARTY_UPLOAD

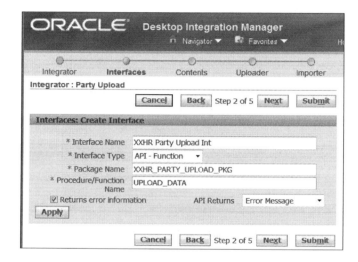

2. Click on **Apply**.

    The screen will then display a message to say that the interface has been created successfully, as shown in the following screenshot:

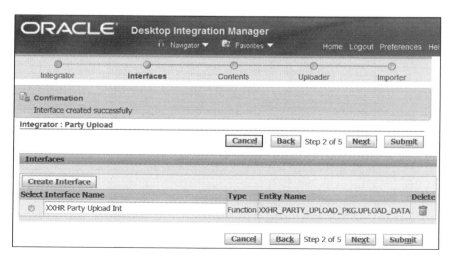

3. If you now click on the radio button for the **Party Upload** interface, you will see that the attributes are imported from the table definition. The screen will refresh automatically and the attributes will be displayed in the **Interfaces** screenshot as follows:

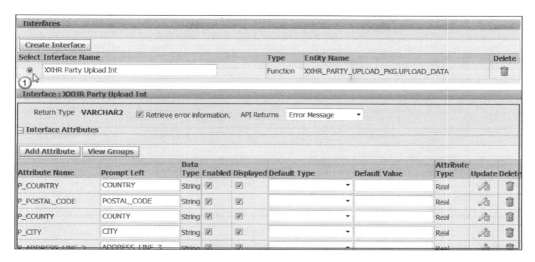

4. At this point, click on the **Submit** button and the integrator will be saved. When defining the integrator it is better to save it regularly as the screen quite often crashes. That's not to say that it will in your environment, as you may have a later version of the page. After the **Submit** button is clicked, the screen will return to the manage integrators page as shown in the following screenshot:

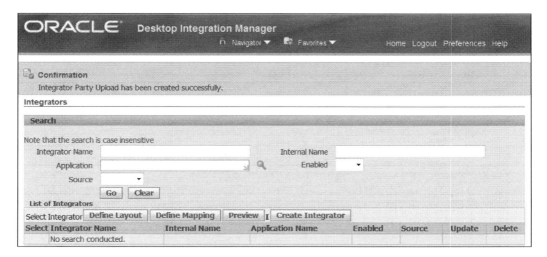

This screen can be opened at any time by navigating to **Desktop Integration Manager | Manage Integrators**.

At this point, we have done all we need to do to create our integrator. We will add some more advanced features later, but let's now generate the integrator in its basic form. However, before we can do this, we need to create a layout for the integrator.

Create a layout for the integrator

We are now going to define the layout for the integrator. Before we can preview our integrator, we must create a layout. Here, we can define whether the attributes are formatted horizontally or vertically. We can also define the width of the fields for the headings.

How to do it...

To create a layout for the integrator, perform the following:

1. Log in to oracle with the **Desktop Integrator** responsibility.

2. Select **Define Layout** from the menu.

3. In the **Select Integrator** screen, select the **Party Upload** integrator from the list of values, and click on the **Go** button as follows:

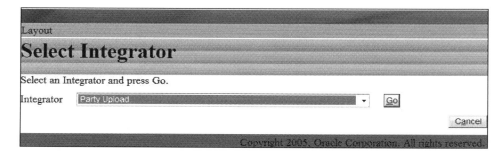

4. In the next screen, click on the **Create** button.

5. In the **Layout Name** field, type in Party Upload Layout and click on **Next** as follows.

   Leave **Number of Headers** as **1**.

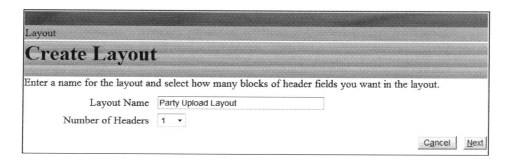

6. Check the following records to be displayed in the integrator and leave the **Placement** field to **Line** for each of the checked attributes.

In the next page, we can set some attributes about how the way the page behaves. We can choose to protect the sheet, change the stylesheet, or choose to apply filters for the page. We can also define how many rows are created for the integrator by setting a number for the data entry rows field. We can also define the order in which the fields are displayed to the user.

Set the values as shown below:

- **Protect Sheet**: Yes
- **Style Sheet**: Default
- **Apply Filters**: Yes
- **Data Entry Rows**: 10

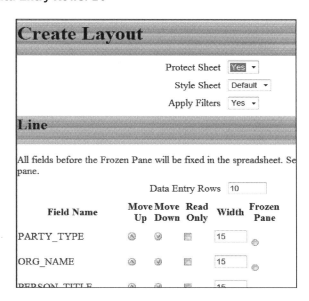

7. Click on **Apply**.

How it works...

This screen allows us to create a layout for our integrator. We can change the order of attributes and set properties here as well.

Generate an integrator

We will now generate the integrator that will allow us to upload data into our table.

How to do it...

To create the interface, perform the following:

1. Log in to Oracle with the **Desktop Integration Manager** responsibility.

2. Select **Manage Integrator** from the menu.

3. Type `Party%` in the **Integrator Name** field and click on the **Go** button.

4. Select the **Party Upload** integrator and click on the **Preview** button as follows:

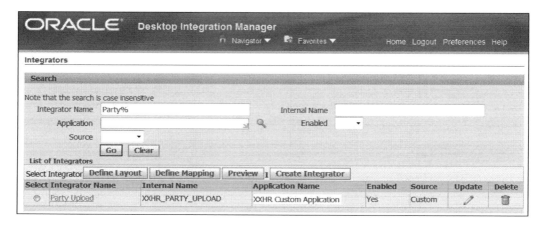

5. In the **Select Viewer** screen, choose the version of Microsoft Excel from the list of values, and then click on the **Next** button.

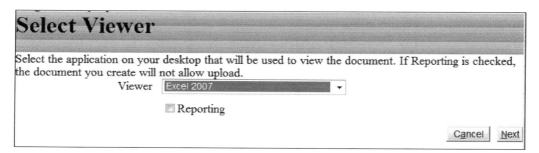

6. In the **Document Creation Review** window, check the summary of the values you have entered, and then click the **Create Document** button.

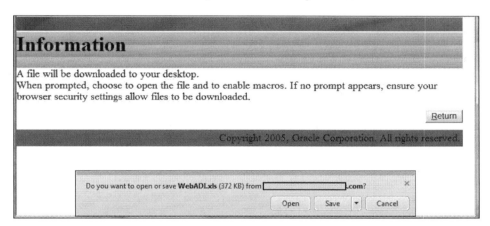

Document Creation Review

The following parameters will be used to create your document. The Viewer will automatically launch when you press the Create Document button. Press the Back button to make changes. Press the Save button to save these selections to a Create Document Shortcut.

Integrator	Party Upload
Viewer	Excel 2007
Reporting	No
Layout	Party Upload Layout
Content	NONE

Cancel | Back | Save | Create Document

7. The file will now be downloaded to your desktop. You will be prompted to download the file called the WebADI.xls, so click on the **Open** button.

Information

A file will be downloaded to your desktop.
When prompted, choose to open the file and to enable macros. If no prompt appears, ensure your browser security settings allow files to be downloaded.

Return

Copyright 2005, Oracle Corporation. All rights reserved.

Do you want to open or save **WebADI.xls** (372 KB) from [   ].com?   ✕

Open | Save ▾ | Cancel

8. Once Microsoft Excel has opened, you may be prompted to **Enable Editing**. If so, click the **Enable Editing** button as follows:

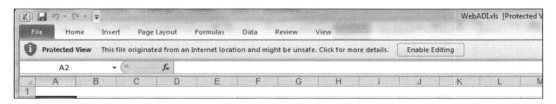

9. You may also be prompted with a **Security Warning**. If so, click the **Enable Content** button as follows:

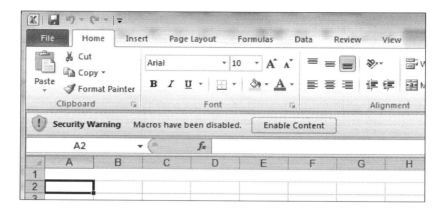

After a short while, you'll be prompted that the document has been created as shown in the following screenshot:

Once the process is finished, you will see that the Microsoft Excel spreadsheet has created the integrator. We can see that the headings are displayed as we defined them in the layout for the integrator. Later, we will go back and edit the headings so that they are more meaningful for the user.

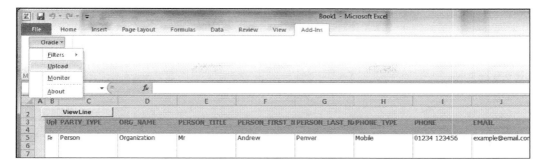

We are now going to test the integrator, enter some dummy data into columns, and upload the data to ensure that the data is inserted into the database table. At present, we have not put any validation on the fields, so we can enter any data to test the upload process.

10. Enter some data into each of the columns (just enter some data relevant to the field as shown in the next screenshot).

11. Now click on the **Oracle** button to bring up a submenu.

12. Now select the **Upload** item from the submenu.

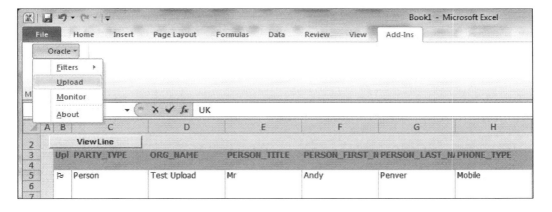

13. When the **Upload to Oracle Applications** dialogue screen is displayed, click on the **Upload** button as shown in the following screenshot:

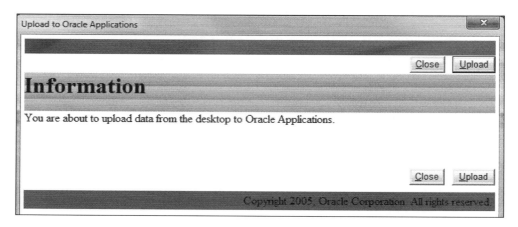

After a short period, **Confirmation** will be displayed as shown in the next screenshot. Dismiss the **Confirmation** screen by clicking the **Close** button as shown in the next screenshot. We can see that the **Confirmation** screen shows that the one row has been successfully uploaded. Later, we will go and check that the record has been inserted into the database table.

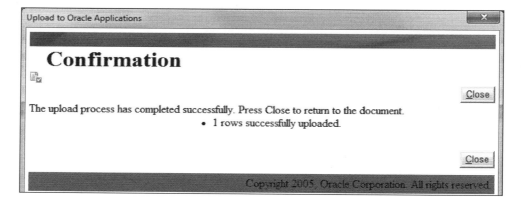

14. Open **SQL Developer**, perform the following query to check that the row we uploaded using the integrator has been inserted into the database table:

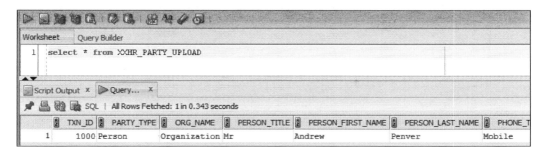

How it works...

The integrator can be used to insert some data into a database table. At present, it is fairly basic, but later, we'll add some more advanced features to the integrator, such as lists of values and validation to some of the fields. We can even create our own custom upload screen, which will also be discussed later.

Edit the attributes

Now, we are going to edit the attributes in the integrator to have more meaningful headings and to use lists of values.

How to do it...

To edit the attributes for integrator, perform the following:

1. Log in to Oracle with the **Desktop Integration Manager** responsibility.

2. Select Manage Integrator from the menu.

3. Type `Party%` in the **Integrator Name** field, and click on the **Go** button.

4. Select the **Party Upload** integrator and click the Edit icon as shown in the following screenshot:

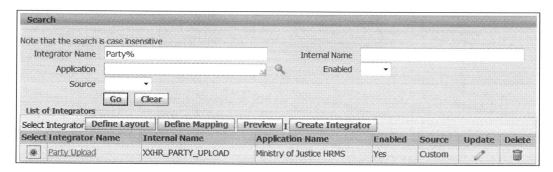

5. In **Step 1 of 5**, click on **Next**.

6. In **Step 2 of 5**, click on the **XXHR Party Upload Int** interface and wait for a short while for the attributes to be displayed.

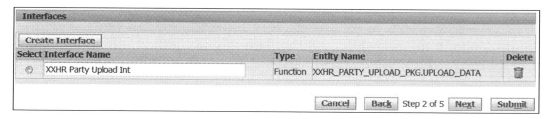

Once the attributes are displayed as shown in the following screenshot, we will edit the attributes by clicking on the update icon. We will do this to edit the headings of each of the attributes for our integrator.

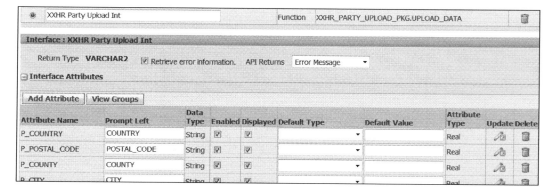

We can see that the value for **Prompt Left** is already set to COUNTRY. If our integrator had our attributes displayed vertically, we would edit this column to make the prompt more suitable for the user. However, we have to find our layout to display our attributes horizontally in the Excel spreadsheet. Therefore, we have to define the attribute heading by clicking the update icon and editing the **Prompt Above** field.

7. For the COUNTRY attribute, click on the update icon.

8. Scroll down the **Interface Attribute Definition** window until the **Prompt Above** field is displayed.

9. Set the **Prompt Above** field to Country as shown in the following screenshot:

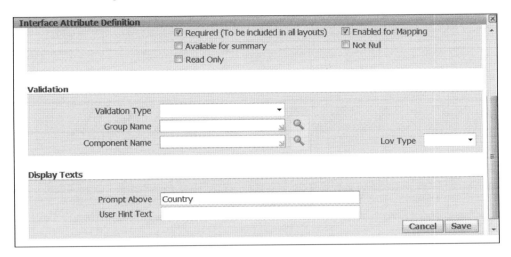

10. When completed, click on the **Save** button.

Now, repeat this process and add meaningful headings for all of the other attributes. For example, go to the P_PHONE attribute and change the **Prompt Above** field to Phone. We can also add text to be displayed to show the user formatting required, or indeed any other help text we feel may be required.

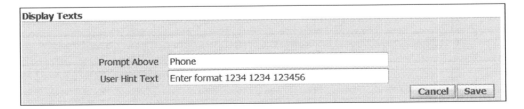

How it works...

We should now have meaningful headings for all of the attributes. This process should be done after we have tested that the integrator works properly. Also, it is advisable to update a few headings at a time and then save the integrator, as the interface occasionally does crash. If you are updating a large number of attributes, this can be rather annoying, as you have to start all over again.

Add the lists of values

In this recipe, will be editing the attributes to add a list of values. We want to do this where we want the users to enter structured data based upon a list of values. Therefore, a user can only input data that we want them to. This means that validation for valid values is automatically done for the user and we prevent the users entering erroneous data.

How to do it...

To add lists of values, perform the following:

1. Log in as **Desktop Integration Manager** as we have done previously and query back the **Party Upload** integrator.

2. In **Step 1 of 5**, click on **Next**.

3. In **Step 2 of 5**, click on the **XXHR Party Upload Int** interface and wait for a short while for the attributes to be displayed, as we did in the previous receipe.

   The first list of values we are going to add will be a list of countries for the country attribute.

4. Click on the update icon for the COUNTRY attribute.

5. To add a list of values, enter the following details:

   - **Validation Type: Table**
   - **ID Column**: TERRITORY_CODE
   - **Meaning Column**: TERRITORY_SHORT_NAME
   - **Desc Column**: TERRITORY_SHORT_NAME
   - **Validation Entity**: FND_TERRITORIES_VL
   - **Where Clause**: 1=1 (Note: Where clause cannot be null that's why we put 1=1)
   - **Lov Type: Pop List**

   The following screenshot shows the **Lov** configuration as we have just defined it:

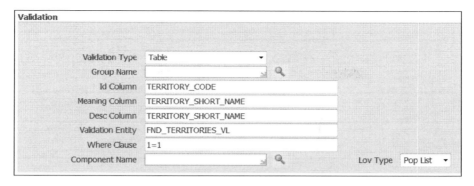

6. Click on **Save**.

Now, we are going to create another list of values for the PHONE_TYPE attribute.

7. Click on the update icon for the **PHONE_TYPE** attribute.

8. Set the following field values:

   ❑ **Validation Type: Table**

   ❑ **ID Column**: LOOKUP_CODE

   ❑ **Meaning Column**: MEANING

   ❑ **Desc Column**: DESCRIPTION

   ❑ **Validation Entity**: FND_LOOKUP_VALUES

   ❑ **Where Clause**: lookup_type = 'PHONE_LINE_TYPE' AND enabled_flag = 'Y'

   ❑ **Lov Type: Pop List**

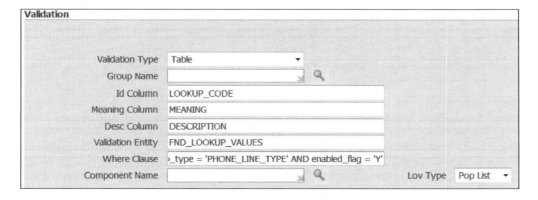

We have now created a list of values for the PHONE_LINE_TYPE attribute. Now we are going to create another list of values for the salutation attribute. This attribute is called Title.

9. Click on the update icon for the `Title` attribute.

10. Set the following field values:

   ❑ **Validation Type**: **Table**

   ❑ **ID Column**: LOOKUP_CODE

   ❑ **Meaning Column**: MEANING

   ❑ **Desc Column**: DESCRIPTION

   ❑ **Validation Entity**: AR_LOOKUPS

   ❑ **Where Clause**: `lookup_type(+) = 'CONTACT_TITLE' and enabled_flag = 'Y'`

   ❑ **Lov Type**: **Pop List**

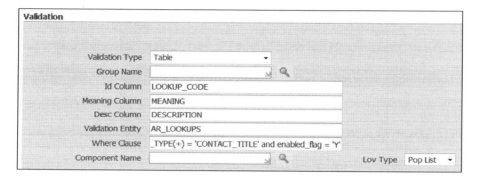

11. Click on **Save**.

How it works...

We use lists of values to minimize user data entry errors. We can preview the integrator to see the changes we have made. As we have done previously, log in to the Manage Desktop Integrator responsibility and query back the party upload integrator. Click on the **Preview** button and generate the integrator as we have done before. Once the `WebADI.xls` integrator has been created, we can see the titles we have edited. If we click on the title field, we can see that there is now a list of values that we can select from, as shown in the following screenshot:

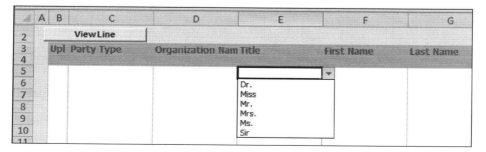

Let's now create a new test record and upload that to the database. Add some dummy data to the first line of integrator using the lists of values which we created, and enter free text for the other fields. Click on **Oracle upload** to upload the data into the database table.

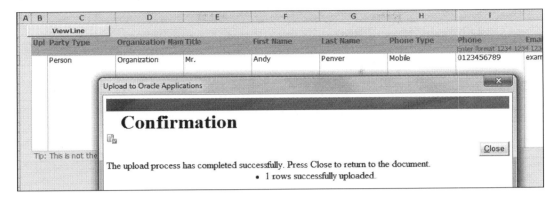

Now, switch to SQL Developer and perform the same query as we did previously. We can now see that there are two records in the database table. If we examine the second record closely, we can see that the PERSON_TITLE field has been formatted by the list of values. We can see the PHONE_TYPE field also has a formatted value returned from the list of values associated with the attribute in the integrator, as show in the following screenshot:

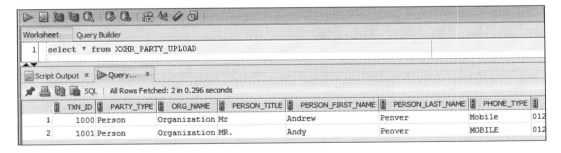

Now that we are happy with our integrator, we can save it to a desktop just as we would save any other Excel spreadsheet by navigating to **File | Save As**. Please note that we need to save the file as a type, Excel macro enabled template as shown in the following screenshot:

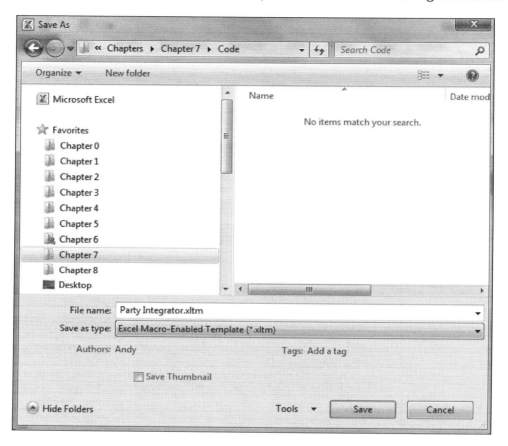

Creating a function for an integrator

Now we need to create a function that we can add it to a menu, so that our integrator will be displayed in a menu for a given responsibility. Desktop integrator will create a function for us automatically, when we run the integrator as follows.

How to do it...

To generate a function for our integrator, perform the following:

1. Switch to the **Desktop Integration Manager** responsibility.

2. Query back the **Party Upload** integrator.

3. Select the integrator and click on the **Preview** button.

4. Select **Excel 2010**, and click on **Next**.

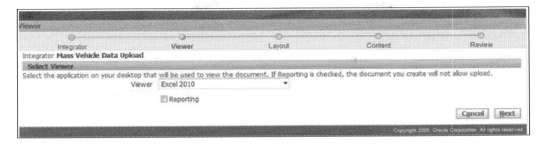

5. Click on the **Save** button.

6. In the **Shortcut Name** field, type a name for the integrator, for example, XXHR
   Party Integrator.

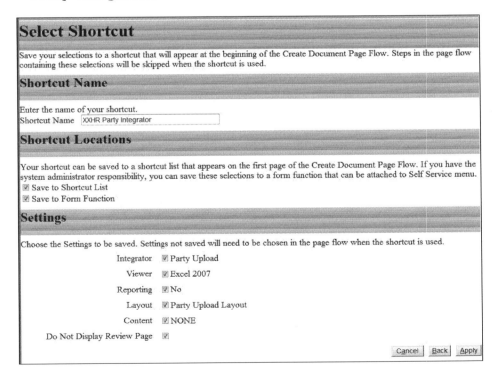

7. Check the **Save to Shortcut List** and **Save to Form Function** checkboxes, then
   click on **Apply**.

How it works...

When we check the **Save to Shortcut List** checkbox and then click on **Apply**, a form function will be automatically generated. The function will be created with a prefix of BNE_. We can find the function that has been created, as it will have the same **User Function Name** as the shortcut name we have created.

Adding an integrator to a menu

Now that we have created a form function, we can bring this back in the form function for screen. In this recipe, we will be querying back the form function and looking at the attributes it has been created with. Then we will add the function to a menu, so that other users can access the integrator.

Adding form functions to menu

First of all, let's query the form function that has been automatically created by the integrator.

How to do it...

To query back the function for the integrator, perform the following:

1. Navigate to **System Administrator Responsibility | Form Functions**.

2. Query back the form function name (XXHR Party Integrator).

   We can see that the form function name is **BNE_XXHR_PARTY_INT**. The user function name is the same name that we gave to the shortcut of the integrator. We can add a description to the function as shown in the following screenshot:

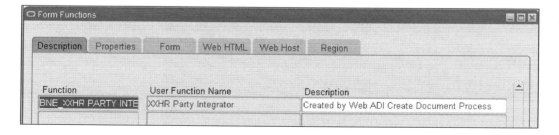

If we navigate to the other tabs, we can see the values of the other attributes for the function. In particular, take note of the **Parameters** field and the entry that has automatically been created, so that a user can access the integrator. We do not need to configure this, as it has been generated for us automatically when the function was created in the *Creating a function for an integrator* recipe. The **Parameters** field has the following entry: **Bne:Page=BneCreateDoc&Bne:Viewer=BNE:EXCEL2007& Bne:Reporting=N&Bne:Integrator=XXHR:XXHR_PARTY_UPLOAD_XINTG&Bne:La yout=XXHR:PARTYUPLOADLAYOUT&Bne:Content=XXHR:XXHR_PARTY_UPLOAD_ CNT1&Bne:Noreview=Y**.

The following screenshot shows the **Form** tab and the generated **Parameters** field as just described:

3. Using the System Administrator responsibility, navigate to the **Menus** screen.

4. Query back the menu for the responsibility we created earlier in this chapter. Reminder, the menu name is XXHR_DI_MENU.

5. Now add a new menu entry for the **Party Integrator** as follows:

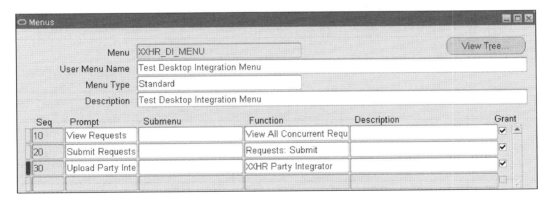

6. Save the record.

How it works...

The function is added to a menu, so that a user can access the integrator we have created. This can then be accessed by users who have the XXHR_DI_MENU associated with a responsibility they have assigned to their user.

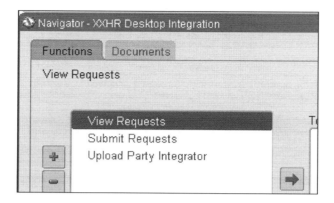

Adding advanced features to an integrator

As discussed earlier, we can also perform more advanced techniques when configuring an integrator. We can customize the upload screen for the integrator to give a user more options, before their upload is performed. We can also associate other activities to be performed synchronously or asynchronously to the integrator upload. For example, triggering a concurrent program or PL/SQL procedure.

How to do it...

To edit the standard upload screen, perform the following:

1. Log in to Oracle with the **Desktop Integration Manager** responsibility.
2. Select **Manage Integrator** from the menu.
3. Type Party% in the **Integrator Name** field and click on the **Go** button.
4. Now click on the update icon for the **Party Upload** integrator that is returned from the query.
5. Click on **Next** until we reach **Step 4 of 5**.

   This step is used to define the upload screen for an integrator. It will supersede the standard upload screen that we had seen previously while uploading the integrator. It is not necessary to configure this, unless we wish to change standard behaviour. You can try creating an upload screen of your own if desired. The following screenshot summarizes an example of an integrator **Uploader**:

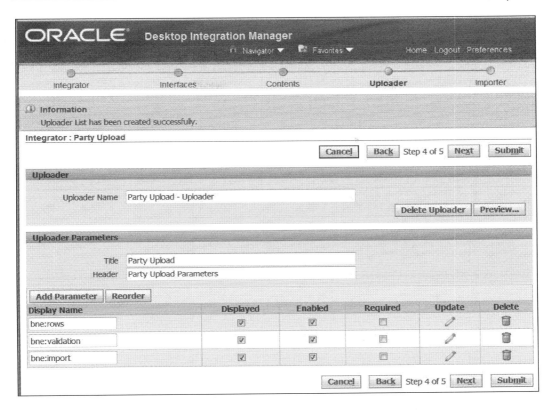

Now if we were to preview the integrator again and upload some data, we will see the upload that we have now defined.

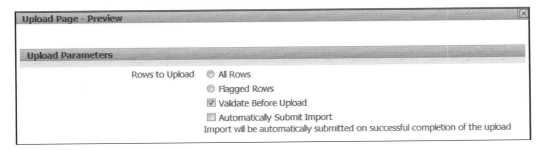

How it works...

We can use the **Uploader** and **Importer** screens to perform specific actions, when the importer is run. We do not need to configure anything on these screens, as the importer is generated with basic functionality. However, we can refine how we want the **Uploader** screen to perform by explicitly configuring the screen.

Defining the importer

We can also define the behavior of the importer and trigger additional processes that can be performed when the integrator is uploaded. We can do this by doing a query about the importer and moving to **Step 5** of the **Integrator** wizard. In this recipe, we will override the standard functionality of the integrator, by triggering a concurrent program automatically when the integrator is executed. In this particular example, it means that data will be uploaded to the table by the integrator, and then a concurrent program will automatically be triggered to process the data that we uploaded. The following assumes that we have created a concurrent program to process the rows in the upload table. We have not gone through the creation of the concurrent program in this recipe. See if you can do that and add the concurrent program using the following instructions.

How to do it...

To override the standard integrator functionality and trigger a concurrent program when our integrator is run, perform the following:

1. In **Step 5 of 5**, set the following:

   □ **Importer Type**: Asynchronous concurrent request

   □ **Importer Name**: Party Upload Importer

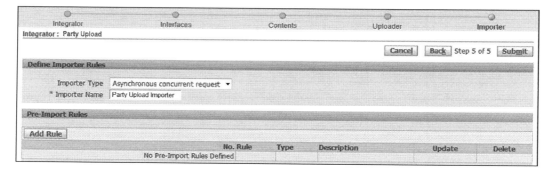

2. Click on the **Add Rule** button.
3. Click on the green plus button and then add all of the integrator attributes.

4. Now, click on the green plus button to add the concurrent program as follows:

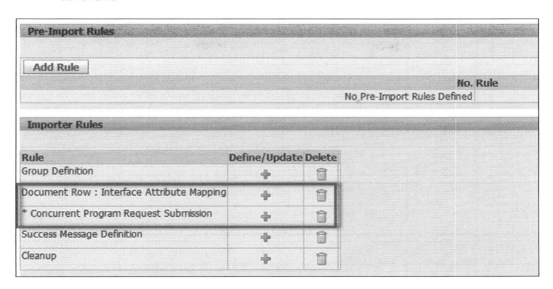

5. Click on **Submit** to save the changes.

How it works...

This screen is used to override the standard behavior of an integrator. We can spawn other processes, such as launching a concurrent program that we want to launch automatically, when the integrator is run.

8
Utilities

In this chapter, we will cover the following recipes:

- ▶ Setting the environment variables
- ▶ Starting and stopping an environment
- ▶ Creating a custom schema
- ▶ Using a script for migrating objects

Introduction

In this chapter, we are going to look at some utilities that Oracle provides, which will assist you as a developer to migrate code from one environment to another. We will also look at how to create a custom schema for the environment you will be working on. This would normally be done by a DBA, but we will need a custom schema for the work that we will be doing in this book. We will also look at using scripts to help with packaging scripts, and running just a single script to load multiple objects.

Setting the environment variables

Environment variables are named variables that are defined when we log on to an operating system. Throughout the book, you will see references to $APPL_TOP or $XXHR_TOP. These are like shortcuts, and are set usually when we log on to the application server with the application tier OS user. On the application and database servers, the environment variables are used to navigate directly to specific directories. The variables are normally set when we log on the application server or database server. There is a file that is used to set all of the environment variables. It is a consolidated environment file called APPS_<CONTEXT_NAME>.env, which sets up both the Oracle E-Business Suite and Oracle technology stack environments.

In this recipe, we will show how to perform the following tasks:

> ▸ Setting the environment variables on the application server
>
> ▸ Setting the environment variables on the database server

Setting the environment on the application server

When Oracle E-Business Suite is installed, Rapid Install creates the environment file in the `APPL_TOP` directory. We may well not log in with a user that does not execute the environment file when we log in. If this is the case, we will need to source the environment file and execute it manually. The environment file on the application server is in the `APPL_TOP` directory.

How to do it...

To set the environment on the application server, perform the following:

1. Open PuTTY and log on to the application server with the Applications Tier OS user.

 PuTTY is a free Telnet and SSH software for Windows and Unix platforms, along with an xterm terminal emulator. It is not provided by Oracle and can be downloaded from `http://www.putty.org/`.

2. Assuming the `APPL_TOP` directory is `/oracle/apps/r12/visr12/apps/apps_st/appl`, type the following in the command prompt:

   `/oracle/apps/r12/visr12/apps/apps_st/appl/APPS<CONTEXT_NAME>.env`

 On Windows, the equivalent consolidated environment file is called `%APPL_TOP%\envshell<CONTEXT_NAME>.cmd`. Running it creates a command window with the required environment settings for Oracle E-Business Suite.

How it works

The environment file is normally called from the `.profile` of a UNIX user's login. However, if it is not, it must be set manually. This is important when running any oracle script, as they all nearly refer to environment variables and not implicit directory structures.

Setting the environment on the database server

If we need to set the environment on the database server, we can perform the same action from Database Tier owner OS user. The environment file is in the RDBMS_ORACLE_HOME directory.

How to do it...

To set the environment on the database server, perform the following:

1. Open PuTTY and log on to the application server with the Database Tier user.

2. Assuming the RDBMS_ORACLE_HOME directory is /oracle/apps/r12/visr12/db/tech_st/11.1.0, type the following in the command prompt:

   /oracle/apps/r12/visr12/db/tech_st/11.1.0/<CONTEXT_NAME>.env

How it works

We must run the environment file, because we use the variables to navigate to specific directories. This allows us to go directly to directories that we would commonly access. It is also important to set the environment, as Oracle scripts refer to the variables when executing commands and not implicit directories.

Starting and stopping an environment

Normally, we would develop on an environment provided by an organization that employs a full time DBA. Their role is to manage the environment and ensure that it is up and running. However, sometimes we may have to manage our own environment for training purposes or there is a small development team. Therefore, the next recipe will cover the following tasks:

- Starting an environment
- Stopping an environment

Starting an environment

The following steps will start an idle environment. The install has completed and the environment is idle.

How to do it...

To start an environment, perform the following:

1. Open PuTTY and log on to the database server with the database OS owner.
2. Set the environment (if not already set).
3. Connect to SQL*Plus as `sysdba` with the following command:
   ```
   DB Tier> sqlplus "/as sysdba"
   ```

4. When connected to SQL*Plus, type the following command to start the database:
   ```
   SQL>startup
   ```

5. Exit SQL*Plus by typing `exit`.
6. When back in the **UNIX** prompt, start the listener by typing the following:
   ```
   DB Tier> lsnrctl start visr12
   ```

7. Open PuTTY and log on to the applications server with the applications OS owner.
8. Set the environment (if not already set).
9. Navigate to the `$ADMIN_SCRIPTS_HOME` directory by typing the following command in the **APPS** tier prompt:
   ```
   APPS Tier> cd $ADMIN_SCRIPTS_HOME
   ```

10. Test the connection to the database by connecting to SQL*Plus as the `apps` user.
    ```
    sqlplus apps/<apps password> (This step is to check that
    application tier can connect to Database).
    ```

11. Exit SQL*Plus and start the apps processes by running the following script:
    ```
    APPS Tier>./adstrtal.sh apps/apps
    ```

Now we can check that the environment has started, by opening the home page in our browser as shown in the following screenshot. Note that it may take a minute or two.

If the browser is Internet Explorer 8, you get an error as shown in the following screenshot:

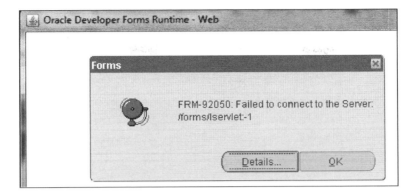

XSS filter in **Security Settings** needs to be disabled as follows:

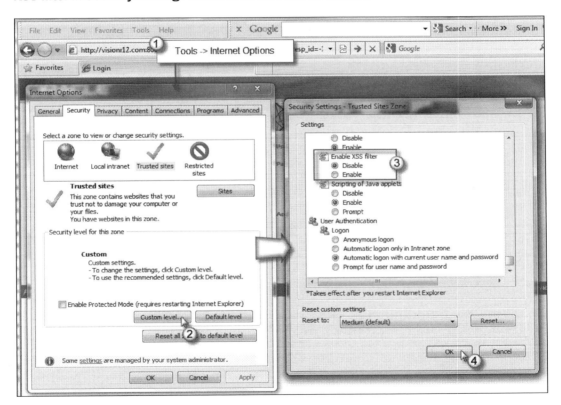

How it works

The environment has now been started and we can log on with our applications user. If we have not set up our user yet, we can log on as the system administrator and create a new user. The **System Administrator** user name is SYSADMIN and the password is SYSADMIN by default, although this will most certainly be changed after install.

Stopping an environment

The following steps will stop an idle environment. The steps have to be completed in reverse order to starting the environment. The applications service must always be stopped before shutting down the database.

How to do it...

To stop an environment that is running, perform the following:

1. Open PuTTY and log on to the applications server with the applications OS owner.

2. Set the environment (if not already set).

3. Navigate to the $ADMIN_SCRIPTS_HOME directory by typing the following command in the APPS tier prompt:

   ```
   APPS Tier> cd $ADMIN_SCRIPTS_HOME
   ```

4. Test the connection to the database by connecting to SQL*Plus as the apps user.

   ```
   sqlplus apps/apps (This step is to check that application tier can
   connect to Database).
   ```

5. Exit SQL*Plus and start the apps processes by running the following script:

   ```
   APPS Tier> ./adstpall.sh apps/apps
   ```

6. Open PuTTY and log on to the database server with the database OS owner.

7. Set the environment (if not already set).

8. In the **UNIX** prompt, stop the listener by typing the following:

   ```
   DB Tier> lsnrctl stop visr12
   ```

9. Connect to SQL*Plus as sysdba with the following command:

   ```
   DB Tier> sqlplus "/as sysdba"
   ```

10. When connected to SQL*Plus type the following command to start the database:

    ```
    SQL> shutdown immediate
    ```

11. Exit SQL*Plus by typing exit.

How it works

The environment has now been stopped. We have performed the start-up process in reverse. Always shut down the services on the application server before shutting down the database.

Creating a custom schema

When we create custom objects, we need to put them in a custom schema. Oracle **E-Business Suite (EBS)** has its own schemas for each of its modules, such as HR or AP. The schema is linked to the application defined in EBS. For each standard schema we extend, we would create a custom schema. A custom schema will begin with **XX**, so that we can identify any extensions that have been applied to an environment, and avoid any objects being impacted by any patches that are applied. So, for example, we are extending HR, so we will create a custom schema called **XXHR**.

We are going to create a schema with the following details:

SCHEMA Name	XXHR
TOP Name	XXHR_TOP
Application	XXHR Custom Application
Data Group	**Standard**
Request Group	XXHR Request Group
Menu	XXHR_CUSTOM_MENU
Responsibility	XXHR Custom
APPL_TOP	/oracle/apps/r12/visr12/apps/apps_st/appl
Instance Name	VISR12
Server Name	oraclevisionr12

There are several tasks that need to be completed, which are as follows:

- ▸ Making a new environment parameter
- ▸ Running AutoConfig (adautocfg.sh)
- ▸ Creating a CUSTOM schema directory structure
- ▸ Adding the custom schema to the environment
- ▸ Creating a new tablespace
- ▸ Creating a database user
- ▸ Registering an Oracle schema
- ▸ Registering an Oracle user

Making a new environment parameter

We are now going to create a new environment parameter for our custom application. This is the only supported way to modify parameters that AutoConfig maintains. Do not edit any context files manually, as they will be overwritten the next time AutoConfig is run.

How to do it...

To create a new environment parameter, perform the following:

1. Log in to Oracle with the System Administrator responsibility.

2. Navigate to **Oracle Applications Manager | Autoconfig**, and the **Applications Manager** window will open.

3. Click on the **Manage Custom Paramaters** link as follows:

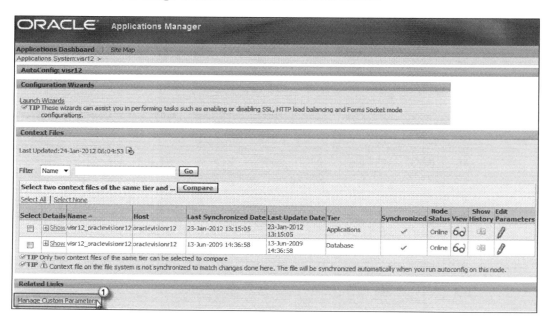

4. Click on the **Add** button to add a new custom parameter to the context file as follows:

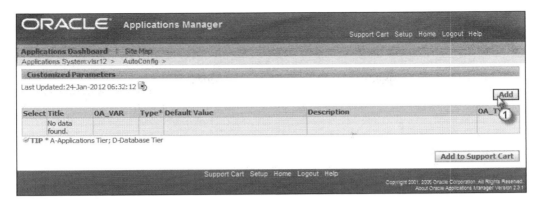

5. Select the **Applications Tier** radio button, and click on **Next** as shown in the following screenshot:

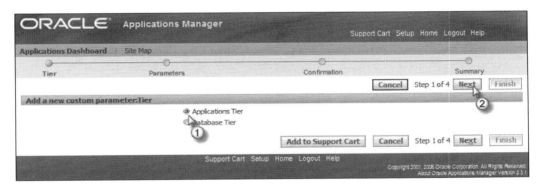

6. Enter the parameters as shown in the following table and click on the **Next** button:

Attribute	Value	Description
OA_VAR	c_xxhr_top	Naming convention in lower caps with no spaces, and a "c_" prefix to indicate a non-standard parameter.
Default Value	%s_at%/xxhr/12.0.0	Refer to the standard context-variable s_at for $APPL_TOP.
Title	XXHR_TOP	Name of the TOP.
Description	Custom top for HR	Description of the TOP.
OA_TYPE	Select **PROD_TOP**	Defines that it is a PRODUCT TOP.

The following screenshot shows the data that we have entered:

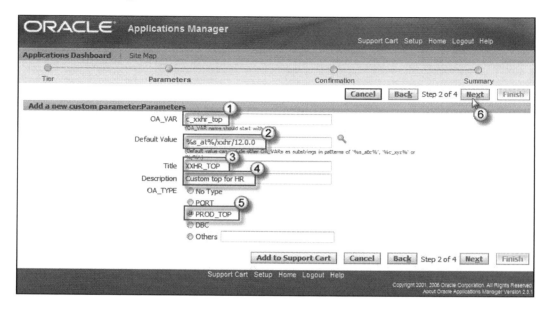

7. Click on **Next** as shown in the following screenshot to confirm the details:

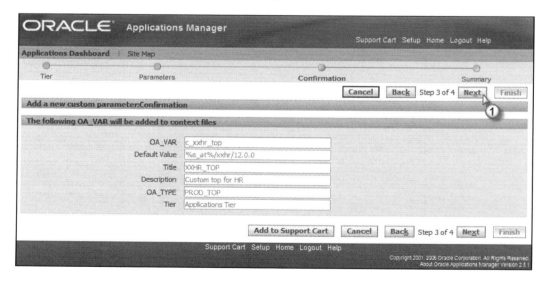

8. Click on **Finish**.

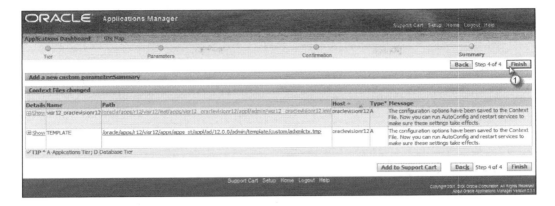

The parameter has now been created as shown in the following screenshot:

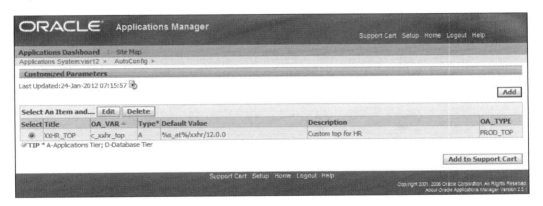

Running AutoConfig (adautocfg.sh)

AutoConfig is a utility provided by Oracle. It is run to configure the environment. It can be run both on the Applications Tier and the Database Tier, and it is run by executing a script called `adautocfg.sh`. We are only going to run it on the Applications Tier to pick up the environment parameter we have just created.

How to do it...

To run AutoConfig, perform the following:

1. Open PuTTY and connect to the application server with the OS user that owns the application tier.

2. Navigate to $INST_TOP/admin/scripts.

3. In the command prompt, type the following command to run AutoConfig:

    ./adautocfg.sh

4. The script will prompt for the APPS password; so, enter it and press **RETURN** as shown in the following screenshot:

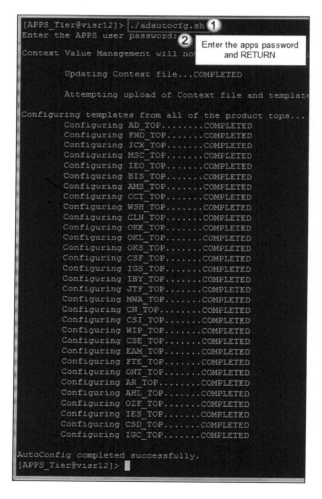

5. Wait for the script to complete before closing down PuTTY.

How it works

We have now run AutoConfig, which will update the configuration files

There's more

Further information on configuring the environment can be found with note *387859.1 Using AutoConfig to Manage System Configurations in Oracle E-Business Suite Release 12*

Creating a CUSTOM schema directory structure

Now that we have run AutoConfig, we need to create the directory structure for our custom application files. The directories are created on the application server under the $APPL_TOP directory. Each product then has its own directory structure under a short name acronym. This is known as the PRODUCT TOP. Oracle assumes that objects are stored in specific directories. This is why we need to be specific about the directory structure we create. We will log on to the application tier and create the directories with the Applications Tier user.

How to do it...

To create the CUSTOM TOP directory structure, perform the following:

1. Open PuTTY and log on to the application server with the Applications Tier user.

> We must log out of PuTTY or reset the environment after we have run AutoConfig to pick up the new environment variable for XXHR_TOP.

2. Set the environment (if not already set).

```
[avisr12@oraclevisionr12]$ . /oracle/apps/r12/visr12/apps/apps_st/appl/APPSvisr12_oraclevision.env
```

3. Navigate to the XXHR_TOP directory using the following command:

    ```
    cd $XXHR_TOP
    ```

4. Create a directory structure using the following commands:

    ```
    mkdir $XXHR_TOP/admin
    mkdir $XXHR_TOP/admin/sql
    mkdir $XXHR_TOP/admin/odf
    mkdir $XXHR_TOP/sql
    mkdir $XXHR_TOP/bin
    mkdir $XXHR_TOP/reports
    mkdir $XXHR_TOP/reports/US
    ```

```
mkdir $XXHR_TOP/forms
mkdir $XXHR_TOP/forms/US
mkdir $XXHR_TOP/lib
mkdir $XXHR_TOP/install
mkdir $XXHR_TOP/install/ch1
mkdir $XXHR_TOP/install/ch2
mkdir $XXHR_TOP/install/ch3
mkdir $XXHR_TOP/install/ch4
mkdir $XXHR_TOP/install/ch5
mkdir $XXHR_TOP/install/ch6
```

 Unix is case sensitive and therefore, directory names must be created exactly as shown. You will notice that some of the directories have already been created (log, out and, mesg).

After the directories have been created the structure should resemble the following hierarchy:

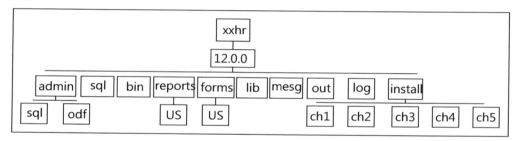

How it works

The custom schema has been added to the context file by the configuration we did in the *Running AutoConfig (adautocfg.sh)* recipe. The environment context file is an XML file that is on the application server. When we register the custom schema later, we will define the CUSTOM TOP called XXHR_TOP within the application. The applications context file is a repository for environment-specific details used by AutoConfig to configure the application tier. AutoConfig is a utility provided by Oracle that gets the information from the context file (and other files) and automatically generates Oracle E-Business Suite configuration files and updates relevant database profiles.

Creating a new tablespace

We now need to create a physical file to store data of our custom objects.

How to do it...

To create a tablespace, perform the following:

1. Log on to SQL*Plus as the `applsys` user.

2. Run the following command:

```
SQL>create tablespace XXHR datafile '/oracle/apps/r12/visr12/db/
apps_st/data/XXHR01.dbf' size 500M
```

 The directory in the above SQL statement is for the environment that is used for writing the book. The DBF files need to be created in the DATA_TOP of the environment you are using.

3. Exit SQL*Plus.

How it works

We have created a data file that will store all of our custom data of any database objects we create in our custom schema.

Creating a database user

We also need to create a database user, where we will create all of our database objects.

How to do it...

To create a database user, perform the following:

1. Log on to SQL*Plus as the `applsys` user.

2. Run the following command:

```
SQL>create user XXHR identified by XXHR
default tablespace apps_ts_tx_data
temporary tablespace temp
quota unlimited on apps_ts_tx_idx;
```

3. Exit SQL*Plus.

How it works

We have now created a database user with the password `xxhr`. When we create custom objects that store any data, they will be owned by the custom user. The custom user uses the tablespace we created earlier.

Registering an Oracle schema

We must register the new XXHR schema in Oracle E-Business Suite. We need to create the application, so that Oracle knows where to look on the file system for custom objects. We defined our environment variable in an earlier recipe that translates our application base path. We create a custom application, so that we can isolate any customizations we make.

 If you have already created the application in *Chapter 1, Personalizing OA Framework Pages*, you will not need to do it again.

How to do it...

To register an Oracle schema, perform the following:

1. Log in to Oracle with the System Administrator responsibility.
2. Navigate to **Application | Register**, and the **Applications** window will open.
3. Enter the application details as per the following table:

Application	XXHR Custom Application
Short Name	XXHR
Basepath	XXHR_TOP
Description	XXHR Custom Application

The screen should now look like the following:

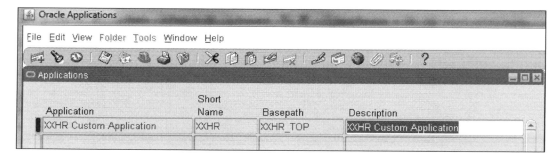

4. Save the record.

How it works

We have now registered the custom schema in Oracle. This corresponds to the environment variable that is assigned to the custom schema we have created (for example, $XXHR).

Registering an Oracle user

We will now register the Oracle user. We have already created the database user, and here we are registering that user within the Oracle Application Library. We only need to register an Oracle user when we create a custom application.

How to do it...

1. Log in to Oracle with the System Administrator responsibility.
2. Navigate to **Security | ORACLE | Register**.
3. Enter the application details as per the following table:

Database User Name	XXHR
Password	xxhr
Privilege	Enabled
Install Group	0
Description	XXHR Application User

The screen should now look like the following:

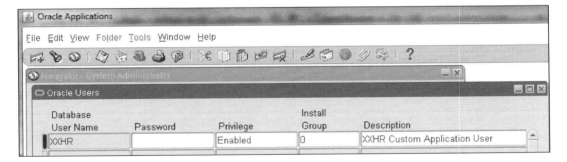

How it works

The database user is the user that owns the schemas database objects. We can log in with this user to view/create/edit the schemas database objects.

> Registering the user also enables this schema in the "gather schema statistics" standard concurrent program and the schema can then be analyzed.

Index

S

setForwardURL method 234, 246
Simplest Possible Expression Language. *See* SPEL
SPEL
about 60
used, for triggering personalizations 60
SPEL statement
adding 60, 62
function, adding to menu 63
function, creating 62
standard OA Framework files
EO 73
UIX and CO 73
VO and AM 73

T

tool tips
adding, to page 35, 36
long message tip type, adding 40, 41
messages, creating 37, 38
short tip type, adding 38-40

U

updateSociety method 248
user interface XML (UIX)
about 14, 72, 163
User interface XML (UIX)
user-level personalization
creating 30-34
user, personalizations
creating 17, 18
utilities
about 359
custom schema, creating 365
environment, starting 361-364
environment, stopping 364, 365
environment variables, setting 359

V

validation
adding, to page 249-252
view 14
view layer, for query page

creating 106, 107
default region (PG, renaming 108, 110
item properties, setting 114, 115
page (PG), adding 107, 108
page (PG), testing 115, 116
query region (RG), adding 110, 111
results region (RG), adding 111-114
view object (VO) 14, 72, 163
Visual Basic for Applications (VBA) code 289

W

Web ADI 317

X

XDO tags
replacing 294-296
XML 276
XML file
markup and content 277
XML markup
attributes 277
elements 277
entities 277
XML output
generating, concurrent program used 276, 278
XML Publisher 275
XX 365
XXHR 365
XXHR BI Publisher Roster Example 315
XXHR Duty Roster report
bursting 314
XXHR_PARTY_UPLOAD table
registeration, checking 330, 331
registering 328-330
XXUSER 171

Thank you for buying
Oracle E-Business Suite R12 Integration and
OA Framework Development and Extension Cookbook

About Packt Publishing

Packt, pronounced 'packed', published its first book "*Mastering phpMyAdmin for Effective MySQL Management*" in April 2004 and subsequently continued to specialize in publishing highly focused books on specific technologies and solutions.

Our books and publications share the experiences of your fellow IT professionals in adapting and customizing today's systems, applications, and frameworks. Our solution-based books give you the knowledge and power to customize the software and technologies you're using to get the job done. Packt books are more specific and less general than the IT books you have seen in the past. Our unique business model allows us to bring you more focused information, giving you more of what you need to know, and less of what you don't.

Packt is a modern, yet unique publishing company, which focuses on producing quality, cutting-edge books for communities of developers, administrators, and newbies alike. For more information, please visit our website: www.PacktPub.com.

About Packt Enterprise

In 2010, Packt launched two new brands, Packt Enterprise and Packt Open Source, in order to continue its focus on specialization. This book is part of the Packt Enterprise brand, home to books published on enterprise software – software created by major vendors, including (but not limited to) IBM, Microsoft and Oracle, often for use in other corporations. Its titles will offer information relevant to a range of users of this software, including administrators, developers, architects, and end users.

Writing for Packt

We welcome all inquiries from people who are interested in authoring. Book proposals should be sent to author@packtpub.com. If your book idea is still at an early stage and you would like to discuss it first before writing a formal book proposal, contact us; one of our commissioning editors will get in touch with you.

We're not just looking for published authors; if you have strong technical skills but no writing experience, our experienced editors can help you develop a writing career, or simply get some additional reward for your expertise.

Oracle E-Business Suite R12 Core Development and Extension Cookbook

Over 60 recipes to develop core extensions in Oracle E-Business Suite R12

Oracle E-Business Suite R12 Core Development and Extension Cookbook

ISBN: 978-1-849684-84-2   Paperback: 480 pages

Over 60 recipes to develop core extensions in Oracle E-Business Suite R12

1. Gain key skills to extend Oracle E-Business Suite Release 12.

2. Build forms with advanced features and deploy them in the application

3. Create personalizations and understand how to modify functionality through them

Oracle Enterprise Manager Cloud Control 12c: Managing Data Center Chaos

Get to grips with the latest innovative techniques for managing data center chaos including performance tuning, security compliance, patching, and more

Oracle Enterprise Manager Cloud Control 12c: Managing Data Center Chaos

ISBN: 978-1-849684-78-1   Paperback: 394 pages

Get to grips with the latest innovative techniques for managing data center chaos including performance tuning, security compliance, patching, and more

1. Learn about the tremendous capabilities of the latest powerhouse version of Oracle Enterprise Manager 12c Cloud Control

2. Take a deep dive into crucial topics including Provisioning and Patch Automation, Performance Management and Exadata Database Machine Management

3. Take advantage of the author's experience as an Oracle Certified Master in this real world guide including enterprise examples and case studies

Please check **www.PacktPub.com** for information on our titles

Oracle SOA Infrastructure Implementation Certification Handbook (1Z0-451)

ISBN: 978-1-849683-40-1   Paperback: 372 pages

Successfully ace the 1Z0-451 Oracle SOA Foundation Practitioner exam with this hands on certification guide

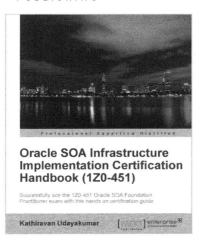

1. Successfully clear the first stepping stone towards becoming an Oracle Service Oriented Architecture Infrastructure Implementation Certified Expert

2. The only book available to guide you through the prescribed syllabus for the 1Z0-451 Oracle SOA Foundation Practitioner exam

3. Learn from a range of self-test questions to fully equip you with the knowledge to pass this exam

Oracle WebCenter 11*g* PS3 Administration Cookbook

ISBN: 978-1-849682-28-2   Paperback: 348 pages

Over 100 advanced recipes to secure, support, manage, and administer Oracle WebCenter

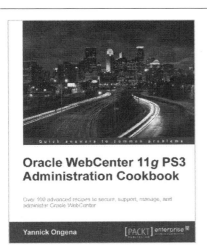

1. The only book and eBook in the market that focuses on administration tasks using the new features of WebCenter 11*g* PS3

2. Understand the use of Wiki and Discussion services to build collaborative portals

3. Full of illustrations, diagrams, and tips with clear step-by-step instructions and real-world examples

4. Learn how to build rich enterprise 2.0 portals with WebCenter 11g

Please check **www.PacktPub.com** for information on our titles

30362166R00224

Made in the USA
Lexington, KY
05 March 2014